The European Science Foundation (ESF) is the European association of 78 national research organisations in 30 countries devoted to scientific research.

The ESF provides a common platform for its Member Organisations in order to:

■ Advance European Research;

■ Explore new directions for research at the European level.

Through its activities, the ESF serves the needs of the European research community in a global context.

THE PROFESSIONALISATION OF POLITICAL COMMUNICATION

CHANGING MEDIA, CHANGING EUROPE

VOLUME 3

EDITED BY R. NEGRINE, P. MANCINI, C. HOLTZ-BACHA AND
S. PAPATHANASSOPOULOS

intellect Bristol, UK / Chicago, USA

First published in the UK in 2007 by
Intellect Books, PO Box 862, Bristol BS99 1DE, UK

First published in the USA in 2007 by
Intellect Books, The University of Chicago Press, 1427 E. 60th Street, Chicago,
IL 60637, USA

A catalogue record for this book is available from the British Library

Cover Design: Gabriel Solomons
Copy Editor: Heather Owen
Typesetting: Mac Style, Nafferton, E. Yorkshire

ISBN 978-1-84150-159-8
ISSN 1742-9439

Printed and bound in Great Britain by The Cromwell Press

Foreword

This volume is the product of a major programme under the title Changing Media – Changing Europe supported by the European Science Foundation (ESF). The ESF is the European association of national organisations responsible for the support of scientific research. Established in 1974, the Foundation currently has seventy-six Member Organisations (research councils, academies and other national scientific institutions) from twenty-nine countries. This programme is the first to be sponsored by both the Social Sciences and the Humanities Standing Committees of the ESF, and this unique cross-disciplinary organization reflects the very broad and central concerns which have shaped the Programme's work. As co-chairpersons of the Programme it has been our great delight to bring together many of the very best scholars from across the continent, but also across the disciplinary divides which so often fragment our work, to enable stimulating, innovative, and profoundly important debates addressed to understanding some of the most fundamental and critical aspects of contemporary social and cultural life.

The study of the media in Europe forces us to try to understand the major institutions which foster understanding and participation in modern societies. At the same time we have to recognize that these societies themselves are undergoing vital changes, as political associations and alliances, demographic structures, the worlds of work, leisure, domestic life, mobility, education, politics and communications themselves are all undergoing important transformations. Part of that understanding, of course, requires us not to be too readily seduced by the magnitude and brilliance of technological changes into assuming that social changes must comprehensively follow. A study of the changing media in Europe, therefore, is indeed a study of changing Europe. Research on media is closely linked to questions of economic and technological growth and expansion, but also to questions of public policy and the state, and more broadly to social, economic and cultural issues.

To investigate these very large debates the Programme is organised around four key questions. The first deals with the tension between citizenship and consumerism, that is the relation between media, the public sphere and the market; the challenges facing the media, cultural policy and the public service media in Europe. The second area of work focuses on the dichotomy and relation between culture and commerce, and the conflict in media policy caught between cultural aspirations and commercial imperatives. The third question deals with the problems of convergence and fragmentation in relation to the development of media technology on a global and European level. This leads to questions about the concepts of the information society, the network society etc., and to a focus on new media such as the internet and multimedia, and the impact of these new media on society, culture, and our work, education and everyday life. The fourth field of inquiry is concerned with media and cultural identities and the relationship between processes of homogenization and diversity. This explores the role of media in everyday life, questions of gender, ethnicity, lifestyle, social differences, and cultural identities in relation to both media audiences and media content.

In each of the books arising from this exciting Programme we expect readers to learn something new, but above all to be provoked into fresh thinking, understanding and inquiry, about how the media and Europe are both changing in novel, profound, and far reaching ways that bring us to the heart of research and discussion about society and culture in the twenty-first century.

Ib Bondebjerg
Peter Golding

Contents

1

POLITICAL COMMUNICATION IN THE ERA OF PROFESSIONALISATION

Papathanassopoulos, Negrine, Mancini and Holtz-Bacha

INTRODUCTION

The central argument in this book is that contemporary practices in the content and conduct of political communication can be best understood when looked at in both an historical and comparative context. Rather than focus on, or become excited by, the most recent development in the conduct of political communication, be it new techniques of polling, 'spin doctoring', targeting or marketing, we need to develop a broader understanding of what each of these developments – singly and collectively – signifies. Furthermore, we need to do this in such a way as to begin to outline some of the common themes that permit us to understand changes in the conduct of political communication that pull together what has been, at least in the past, a fairly loose set of ideas, subjects and areas of interest.

One way in which this could be done, and we would argue should be done, is to provide a common point of focus, a common way in which we can begin to explore similarities as well as differences. That way is through the elaboration of the idea of the professionalisation of political communication.

As an idea, professionalisation – and we are fully aware of the contested nature of this word, as well as of its variants of profession, professionalisation, professionalism, and professional – allows us to identify and link up many things that should really be linked together. For example, the use of polls, the use of political consultants, practices of news management, the creation of a 'war room', or the use of focus groups, are probably best understood as part and parcel of the modern election campaign, as part of the 'professionalised Paradigm'. As Holtz-Bacha argues in this book.

> professionalisation of political communication is a process of adaptation to, and as such a necessary consequence of, changes in the political system on the one side and the media system on the other and in the relationship of the two systems. These changes follow from the modernisation of society, which is a development that is still going on and will take place in similar political systems sooner or later. Professionalisation in this sense is a general and not culture-bound concept. Its actual appearance and the degree of professionalisation in a given country are however dependent on a country's specific social and political structures and processes.

More generally, professionalisation can also be treated as an idea that permits us to examine issues that go beyond the immediate concern with political communication during elections. It can, for instance, provide a prism through which one can begin to explore the centralisation of governmental communication, the communication strategies of governments and interest groups (Davies, 2002; Schlesinger & Tumber, 1994) and the developing relationship between all political actors, including political parties, candidates and social movements and the media. Nevertheless, the main focus in this book is on political parties, candidates for political office, and governments.

Professionalisation, as understood in this book, thus refers to a process of change, in the field of politics and communication as elsewhere, that, either explicitly or implicitly, brings about a better and more efficient – and more studied – organisation of resources and skills in order to achieve desired objectives, whatever they might be. In effect, the idea of the professionalisation of political communication suggests a number of things:

■ It suggests the creation of a more 'rational' and more streamlined organisational structure or a more 'appropriate' set of practices.[1] This could be taking place in relation to the operation of communication facilities (a more skilful use of television, for example), campaigning techniques (better use of polling data or better targeting of voters, for example), the re-organisation of political parties themselves (as in centralisation), the re-organisation of government communication systems (as in the creation of a centralised communication directorate to co-ordinate publicity) and even in respect of media-politics relations (as in news management techniques). This use of the word parallels the idea, proposed by Leon Mayhew, that what we are currently experiencing is a 'rationalisation of persuasion' and that the intent behind this process is to find and utilise 'effective means of persuasion based on research on audiences and the organisation of systematic campaigns' (1997, p. 190).
■ It suggests that the process of professionalisation is ongoing and takes place within societies that are themselves undergoing a process of modernisation. The word

The Professionalisation of Political Communication

modernisation may have many different meanings: here we are referring essentially to the processes of differentiation and secularisation taking place within contemporary societies. At the same time, we wish to emphasise the growth of a plurality of sources of information that make individuals less dependent on a single source of information and/or persuasion. This would apply to many different fields, including the field of religion, politics, culture, etc.

■ It suggests that there are many reasons as to why it unfolds (see Chapter 2). In the case of political parties, the reasons might include the need to confront a changing electorate with no particular allegiances, as well as the need to find ways to persuade and mobilise them. In the case of governments and interest groups the reasons might include the need to find better ways to get media attention and to place items on the public's agenda. There are other such reasons which locate the process of professionalisation within what Wernick has called 'the logic of electoralism' (1994, p. 142), namely, the process whereby political parties, amongst others, employ a range of skills to meet their objectives of gaining and sustaining power. Sometimes, the development of professional skills is linked to technological change, as in the use of television or internet technologies, but, at other times, it could also be linked to developments in the scientific field more generally. Mayhew, for example, observes how the use of polling was predicated on improvements in the understanding and use of sampling methods (1997, p. 191).

■ It suggests that the process of professionalisation of political communication is inextricably bound up with developments in the media, in the past and in the present. In this respect, the media are not simply channels of communication between the worlds of politics and the public. What they do and how they do it impacts on the conduct and practice of politics. Those in charge of politics and communication, more generally, are aware of the presence and 'logic' of the media and so anticipate the selection and processing of messages *by* the media. This is often referred to as the 'mediatisation of politics'. As Mazzoleni and Schulz have pointed out:

> To characterise politics as being *mediatised* goes beyond a mere description of system requirements. Mediatised politics is politics that has lost its autonomy, has become dependent in its central functions on mass media, and is continuously shaped by interactions with mass media. This statement of the mediatisation hypothesis is based on observations of how mass media produce political content and interfere with political processes. (1999, p. 250).

■ It suggests the development and growth of a set of specialisms and specialist skills that are used in the context of the persuasion and mobilisation of individuals as citizens, voters and consumers.

The professionalisation of political communication refers not only to a move away from traditional forms of election campaigning to more modern ways and means, but also to changes within the political system. These developments do not only reflect a changing media environment but also changes in the standing of the political parties within the political system as a whole. Professionalisation, in other words, focuses on the mutual developments and changes; it also reflects the convergences as well as interdependencies between the political and communication systems.

It would thus be a mistake to consider the process of professionalisation in the context of political communication only, or mainly, as above. Our argument is that processes of professionalisation take place in all walks of life as individuals and groups develop practices that are deemed better, or an improvement on, earlier practices and then apply them to particular contexts. Pollsters, for instance, constantly improve their skills for measuring public opinion; advertisers continually update practices; those in the business of communications – PR, marketing, etc. – constantly review and learn new skills, and so on. At each stage, individuals are improving their skills or, in common parlance, becoming more professional at what they are doing. Unlike the case of the traditional professions of medicine and law where one is either a professional or not, in the range of occupations surrounding the arts of communications – advertising, PR, marketing, etc. – there is a more continuous process of development and application in order to remain at the cutting edge of change.

In this much broader context, processes of professionalisation are not in evidence simply in relation to political communication, but are a feature of modernisation itself. Consequently, it is a process that is not related to particular eras or technologies but is part of a much longer historical process of change. The importance of this point becomes apparent, as Chapter 2 shows, when we begin to consider the points at which political parties begin to use professionals to help them achieve their objectives of election success.

Often, as we shall see, political parties have turned to outsiders to help them run their campaigns or organisations. These would have been individuals, usually politically sympathetic individuals, who turned their skills to party political use. Advertisers, polling experts, film experts form such a group: individuals brought in to improve the strategies and tactics of the political parties. Such outsiders form only one of many types of individuals that have been used and only one of many different ways in which the process of professionalisation has impacted on political communication.

Outsiders entering an organisation offer a simple example of a process of professionalisation, but sometimes the change takes place from within. Outsiders might act as volunteers or might be employed for a temporary period, but professionals (e.g. journalists, managers) may be employed permanently by a political party and then use their skills to modernise and professionalise the party from within. Similarly, professionals often advise politicians on how to improve their communication skills or demeanour, but politicians, in due course, internalise those skills and might employ them within other contexts and use them to advise others. This relates to a more general distinction between an era in which party bureaucrats mobilised and administered election campaigns and one in which a 'culture of marketing' has established itself at the centre of a party organisation and offers both executive and strategic support to the running of the election campaign.

In thinking about the professionalisation of political communication in respect of the individuals to which it refers, we therefore need to consider both the external dimension (e.g. who is being employed to do what?) but also the internal dimension (e.g. what is happening from within) alongside a more general question relating to the changing location of control (e.g. pollsters are being employed but who directs their work and who makes the final decision?). In other words, there is a complex interplay between outsiders and insiders and between those who exercise control (e.g. are they party employees, party leaders, outside professionals?) and those who simply act as experts or specialists fulfilling particular tasks. What we need to do is not simply ask questions about the professionalisation of political communication but about the insertion of the process of professionalisation in the development of political parties themselves that sees them adopting models of organisation that had proved themselves in other sectors. Forza Italia, for example, was modelled on a 'company model' that had presumably worked for Berlusconi (Calise, 2000; Diamanti, 1994); the Labour Party in 1997 adopted a campaign that was structured around the idea of a 'war-room' (Gould, 1998; Scammell, 1998). And the Labour Party's 'war-room' was the model for the German Social Democrats (SPD) when they established the 'Kampa' for their 1998 election campaign. In both cases, campaign specialists from within the party worked hand in hand with experts from market and media research or advertising agencies (von Webel, 1999). These developments can be taken to represent a process whereby political parties adapt by using 'models' or 'practices' that have been tried and tested elsewhere; just as they did when they absorbed the lessons from advertising and commerce (Kelly, 1956; Mayhew, 1997).

Nevertheless, the process of professionalisation is complex and uneven: different political arrangements, different usages of technologies, different stages of developments, and so on all create different conditions in which professionalisation can take place. This explains why not all countries display the same characteristics in the way that commerce has been injected into politics.

Framing the book's central theme in this way, it places the contributions at a distance from accounts that link contemporary developments to single causes – be they Americanisation, or developments in particular technologies. To understand the processes of professionalisation, we need to adopt a more holistic approach and one that connects change in different spheres – politics, commerce, communication, social change – and across time itself. Obviously not all spheres are equally significant or dominant but the interaction and interpenetration of influences produces the contemporary arrangements.

We need therefore to monitor the trends among different societies and to try to trace these trends where in some cases and countries they are apparent while in others are latent. This is the reason that this book follows both a comparative and country-by-country approach.

PROFESSIONALISATION, MODERNISATION AND AMERICANISATION

Professionalisation, as we use it here, cuts across other equally contested concepts such as modernisation, Americanisation, homogenisation, as it deals with a more general process of change taking place in contemporary societies. In this respect, professionalisation does touch on the idea of Americanisation (see, amongst others, Negrine & Papathanassopoulos, 1996) – in as much as it highlights the existence of practices in the US that are also used elsewhere – but it sees these developments not simply as a *transfer* of ideas or practices from one country to another but as essentially representing the desire that appears to be ever-present in nearly all contemporary societies to utilise the best ideas and practices available. So, for example, even in Hungary, a country that has only recently undergone a process of democratisation, the willingness to use modern methods, i.e. methods that are deemed to be the best ideas and practices currently available, is very much in evidence (see chapter 10).

The emphasis we place on the idea of professionalisation is of a process of continual self-improvement and change towards what is deemed to be a better way of doing things, be it winning an election, achieving consensus, gaining support for policies, ensuring successful governance, that is made possible by technological and communications innovations, as well as a more general process of skills specialisation. Though it obviously does matter where these ideas originated, it matters less than the apparent willingness to use them in different settings. The idea of professionalisation touches on that element of willingness to change, and the reasons underpinning that willingness.

What does the idea of professionalisation derive from the idea of modernisation which also addresses this sense of gradual change and improvement? Paolo Mancini and David Swanson suggest that in the modernisation process one finds an

> increasing functional differentiation within society (that) leads to growing numbers of subsystems of all kinds that develop to satisfy the specialised demands of particular groups and social actors. The rise of these subsystems undermines the traditional aggregative structures of socialisation, authority, community, and consensus, producing social fragmentation and exclusion (1996, p. 253).

Our view is that inherent in the idea of modernisation is not only the creation of differentiation in employment generally, but also the general trend towards claims to professionalisation amongst many old and newer occupations. These things go hand in hand with such things as rising educational levels, high levels of specialisation, the possibility of comparing practices and skills across frontiers and, generally, a greater desire to improve practices so that they attain what is deemed to be the best at any moment of time. Put differently, it is unlikely that any political groups would employ a political consultant unless he or she was versed in the latest available techniques.[2]

The idea of professionalisation takes from the idea of modernisation the knowledge that functional differentiation is part of the process of change but it does not see this as necessarily related to specific factors in contemporary political communication only. As some of the chapters illustrate, those with skills in aspects of campaigning and political communication – TV directors, organisers, PR experts – have been used at numerous points in the past and in a context when political parties were still strong and the mass media was anything but autonomous. One example of this would be from Britain with evidence of advertisers being used by the Conservative Party during the 1950s when political parties were still mass parties and television was very much in its infancy (see chapter 3). Germany offers us another example: the Social Democrats used experts from a group of advertisers affiliated to the party in the 1949 national election campaign. Their competitors, the German Christian Democrats (CDU), soon overtook the SPD in professionalising their strategies and in 1976 finally hired six advertising agencies to work on different campaign channels (see chapter 4).

The underlying theme of this book, then, is that we need to understand developments in political communication as part and parcel of a long and continuing process of adaptation and change whereby the skills of those outside politics are increasingly applied to the conduct of politics. But more than this, those who possess such skills – the 'professionals' for the sake of argument – and the practices they advocate, in turn come to influence those in politics. Politics then begins to change from the inside, as it were, as the lessons of the world of commerce become internalised: political parties become more professional in their activities, as do the politicians who are now much more aware of the needs of proper communication skills, dress and manner.

SIMILARITIES AND DIFFERENCES ACROSS COUNTRIES

In reviewing the chapters in this book, one becomes aware that all the authors have identified similar processes of changes in their societies and in the media system even if, at the same time, they stress differences not only between the US and Europe, but also amongst European countries themselves. This can be seen not only in the level and speed of modernisation of societies, media systems, and subsequently, political communication practices, but also in the different elements of professionalisation of political communication that have been analysed. Some chapters pay more attention to the professionalisation of campaigning (Italy, Greece, Germany), whilst others place more emphasis on professionalisation of particular governments' communications management infrastructure (the Netherlands, Sweden). But in both cases, we see those skilled in communications and marketing entering the field of politics. However, this does not mean that professionals from communications and marketing dominate the political communication field as in the US; or that there is a growth of a political consultancy employment sector in the same way as there has been in the US.

Despite differences, there are also similarities across European countries. Some of these, such as the growth in the level of mistrust of politicians and the general querying of the efficacy of governments to resolve contemporary problems probably (see Mazzoleni & Schulz 1999) extend to the US also, but many have a more European 'feel' to them. These include:

The decline of the mass party
As chapter 2 analyses, and most chapters note, there has been a process that political parties in Europe have witnessed a decline in their membership (see also Mair & Biezen 2001) and a changed relationship between voter and public. The most often referred-to trend is one of dealignment, whereby voters are no longer making political decisions on the basis of traditional allegiances (e.g. class, religion) and are more prepared to switch votes, and hence are more open to persuasion. This has major implications for the political process. In Italy, the political system underwent dramatic changes following the scandals and the judiciary inquiries that have caused the death of most of the traditional parties and the arrest of many important political leaders. The political subculture, in which Italy was divided between the social-communists and the Catholics, has progressively lost its importance and has almost disappeared. In Sweden, traditional political stability has to a certain extent been challenged by a more volatile public opinion. In the Netherlands, ideology and religion are less of a dominant factor in voter choices and party membership has fallen to one of the lowest in Europe. Moreover, as Kees Brants notes in his chapter, the number of floating voters has grown at every election and the number who have been 'turned-off' politics has also increased. Just as in Italy, the traditional pillars of Dutch society (the catholic, the protestant and the socialist ones) have almost disappeared. In Germany, where three parties dominated the political process for decades, the establishment of new parties, and of the Greens in particular, has changed the party landscape and brought about new competition. The high number of undecided voters prior to election day in Germany is probably a good indicator of the dissolution of formerly strong party ties. In Britain, first the Labour Party and more recently the Conservatives have restructured themselves in order to attract the electorate, while in Greece the leading political parties have faced considerable difficulties in getting their agendas placed before the public, since they are less able to differentiate themselves and Greek citizens have become less supportive of the political parties. In Hungary, although the political system has changed completely over the last dozen or so years, the new political parties are characterised by their lack of embeddedness in society, their lack of formal party structure and small party memberships.

Across Europe, then, political parties must worry about the way in which they can communicate with the public, how they can get their messages across, how they may persuade and mobilise voters, and so on. Furthermore, in a situation where citizens have become less supportive of political parties, less trusting of the political system and more likely to abstain, there is likely to be a greater incentive to employ those skilled in the arts of communication and marketing – the 'professional' consultants, communicators and organisers – to help the political parties to position themselves in the minds of the citizen/ voter.

The triumph of media logic
Although political parties have always sought to use new technologies and communication systems to improve their electoral chances, the decline of their traditional positions within the political process – e.g. voters are no longer 'aligned', they no longer have access to their 'own' media – has made them even more dependent on the media and communication practitioners that lie outside their immediate control. Therefore parties have been forced to become more centralised in order to take advantage of media opportunities, i.e. propagating agreed key messages, and not to be caught out by the media, e.g. allowing dissenting voices. Parties have, in effect, learned the importance of the media and the need to deal with, and confront, the 'media's logic'.

All chapters note that the media have come to play an increasingly central role in day-to-day politics. In Italy, Silvio Berlusconi, 'Sua Emittenza'[3] has become the prime-minister in Germany, Chancellor Gerhard Schröder became known as the 'media chancellor'; in the Netherlands, the late populist politician Pim Fortuyn, had increased his popularity by using the magnifying glass of television for his adversarial tone, style and culture. Politicians are constantly under pressure to adapt to new technologies in their attempt to improve their communication strategies. Similar examples regarding the impact of 'media logic' over politics can also be seen in most European countries.

It is not a coincidence that during every presidential campaign European media and campaign consultants, as well as political executives travel, to the US to see and study the Republican and Democratic strategies at close range, since 'media logic' has strongly influenced the behaviour of party politicians. In the same way, American political consultants are very often employed in European election contests: Stanley Greenberg was one of the major consultants for Rutelli, Berlusconi's challenger in 2001; Dick Morris has travelled across Europe offering advice; James Carville has also been involved in campaigning, as has Joe Napolitan, who offered advice to the Labour Party in 1997 (Gould, 1998), and so on. More recently, in 2004 the British Conservative Party turned to Australian experts to help it fight the British general election. More generally, the introduction of television from the 1950s onwards has transformed the nature of election campaigning and the relationship between politicians, political parties and publics. The reliance on the 'modern publicity campaign' (Blumler, 1990) has also altered the relationship between traditional party members and the political party apparatus, at the same time as transforming the 'traditional' campaigns into media campaigns (Mazzoleni & Schultz, 1999, p. 257). Furthermore, the increasingly sophisticated use of polling data and advertising techniques has led many to speculate on the extent to which campaigns are now engaged in a wholesale process of the marketing of political parties. (See Kavanagh, 1995; Lees-Marshment, 2001; Plasser, 2002; Mayhew, 1997)

One of the key themes developed in this book is that political parties and candidates have come to appreciate the need for robust means with which to communicate with their constituencies through, and in spite of, the media, and that those means have often been imported from the world of commerce and particularly advertising and public relations. At its most extreme, one could argue that politics has transformed itself into a branch of commerce (which partly explains the growth of interest in the subject area of political *marketing*).

Centralisation of communication activities

All the chapters have identified a process of centralisation, both within political parties but also in government, that has created a tight framework for the control and conduct of communication functions. In probably all cases, more care has been taken to deal with communication, and to reflect and alter the processes and content of communication to meet the challenges that have arisen from the changing nature of media, changing nature of government and the changing nature of the parties themselves.

There is also evidence of centralisation of political parties and their functions and an acceptance that much of the professionalisation takes place at the centre rather than at the periphery of each electoral system. In Italy, Berlusconi planned and followed a highly personalised campaign based on the model of his companies. 'Il Tavolo per l'Italia' (The Table for Italy) was the place where all important strategic decisions were taken, and it is not by chance that these meetings used to take place at the same location, and at the same time, that all the strategic decisions regarding Fininvest used to take place. In Germany, centralisation was demonstrated at its best by the SPD's 1998 campaign headquarters Kampa and the strategic use of an intranet for advising members and activists during the campaign. In Britain, the 1997 and 2001 national elections were run from the Labour Party's headquarters in Millbank. Similar examples are mentioned in most chapters in this book.

On the road to professionalisation?

There appears to be a general pattern to the involvement of skilled communicators and marketeers across political parties and governments. At the (centralised) headquarters of political parties, skilled and professional communication practices and practitioners are used but not usually on a permanent, full-time basis. In practice, their use is most common in the run-up to election campaigns and, as these tend to take place at intervals of four or five years in Europe, there is less of a tendency to employ such practitioners for anything but the duration of the campaign. Moreover, the employment of professionals is limited by the important role that political party machines still play in most European societies, and very often the party connections and political allegiances of skilled personnel are important considerations in the decision to employ such experts. The importance of political parties cannot therefore be underestimated and this may be one of the major differences between the conduct of electoral politics across Europe and in the US.

But the insertion of professionals into the political communication process at both party and governmental level leads to a complex set of conditions for both parties and governments. For governments, it raises the question of the extent to which managing the agenda is the same as managing and resolving the real problems that they have to tackle. As Holtz-Bacha points out in this book, there is a 'professionalisation at two speeds' in Germany: that is, 'when it comes to campaign communication, professionalisation has come far and progresses quickly, but the process is more restrained where routine political communication is concerned because the constraints are more effective where politics is made instead of only being represented.'

For political parties, professionalisation raises the spectre of parties with no members, or ideologies attempting to persuade the citizens/voters that they are, truly, the best managers. As Lars Nord notes though, professionalisation will neither kill existing parties nor give them unlimited success. 'Instead, it is reasonable to think that the professionalisation process poses considerable conflicts for the parties regarding their objectives. They can either become more professionalised and accept the new conditions for campaigning and opinion formation, or they can remain as a consolidating party organisation and balance internal interests within the party. In the first case, they risk party unity and coherence in politics. In the second case, voter support and political influence are in jeopardy'.

Issue of control and responsibility
This is a more general issue, namely, who is in charge of the professional communicators and practitioners, especially if they are imported from outside? Sometimes those employed or, perhaps more properly, used with those skills come from within the party itself. In Greece, for example, the people who are called political communication experts are usually party members or affiliates and do not come from outside the political system, they are, rather, part of it, as we have just noted. The difference is that their political marketing techniques have been adapted to the new communication landscape. Their knowledge on professional communication practices is not due to any special political communication training, and their relationship with journalists in the political communication subsystem is still very much characterised by cooperation for mutual benefit.

In other instances where 'outsiders' are employed, there is still a debate as to whether they determine the strategy, but under the full control of party leaders and employees, or whether they determine the strategy and consequently the nature and content of the campaign. Indeed, it is possible that there is a complex interaction whereby the influences work both ways: where, in other words, form influences content and *vice versa*.

Professionalisation in proportional/ majoritarian electoral vote

Do different electoral systems have an effect or impact on the nature of political communication and the levels of professionalisation? One could argue, for example, that in a proportional representation system, the centralisation of political communication is usually more advanced than in a majoritarian system. This might be because, in a proportional representation system, the most important consideration is the number of votes cast for each party at the national level. In circumstances such as this, the party undertakes all the communication functions and the individual candidate thus matters much less than the party as a whole.

This was the situation in Italy up to 1994 when the majoritarian system was introduced. Prior to this, for example, candidates from the Communist Party were not allowed to campaign for themselves. Since 1994, and under the (mainly) majoritarian system (as 25% of Parliament seats are still gained through the proportional system), what counts is the vote for the individual candidate. However, as parties are now relatively weak, they are not able to lend their support to all the candidates, who now increasingly come from outside the party structure. These candidates are therefore forced to employ their own personal professionalised communication teams. This process has advanced furthest in 'simple-majority' elections at governor and mayor levels, where the candidates come from outside the party and so have very little party support for their election activities. In such cases, the power of the party lies primarily in the selection of candidates and the placing of candidates in 'safe' seats or districts, but then the party is no longer able to provide candidates with their communication structure. It thus campaigns at the national level for the main leader (e.g. Berlusconi, Prodi) and for the general image of the party. It is at this level that the process of centralisation takes place, but at the local level, each candidate has to campaign through his or her own 'professionalised' team. In the 'German model', with its combination of a proportional system with a personalised element where the party vote is the decisive vote, the professionalisation process *has* impacted on the parties and their top candidates, but much less on the regional candidates (see Holtz-Bacha, 2004).

However, even under majoritarian electoral systems, many seats are often considered to be 'safe' seats – i.e. traditionally going for one or other of the major parties – and so unlikely to swing (except in 'landslide' elections as in Britain in 1997 where large numbers of seats did shift). Parties therefore have to make strategic decisions with respect to campaigning for elections. They will increasingly target those seats that are most likely to change political colour – because the majorities are slim – at the same time as pursuing a national campaigning strategy. But in targeting particular seats, the resources of a party are concentrated on electoral activities on behalf of the party and the candidate standing for the party. Tradition has it that the individual candidate *as an individual* standing in a constituency does not affect the vote, and often candidates see themselves as 'legal necessities' for the furtherance of the aims and objectives of the political parties. However, there is now more attention devoted to individual constituency campaigning in the belief that the greater the level of activity – the larger the turnout and, hence, the possibility of altering the pattern of votes cast. Individual candidates, as individuals, are nevertheless less important than the party as a whole unless, of course, they have a high profile, e.g. if they are television personalities or well-known and very established political figures.

In either case it seems to be an incremental process for individual candidates to use professional practices. For example, as in the case of Greece, the party announces the list of candidate MPs, but those who will be elected for a seat in the Parliament depend on the preferences of the voters. The voters put a cross on the candidates they prefer from the party list on Election Day. This forces candidates of the same party to seek individual votes from the voters who vote for their party. Consequently, they also have to use media professionals in order to raise their profile and to get media publicity in the national or local media. In this respect they have to spend money concerning their own individual campaign. Some spend money on preparing leaflets, media material, creating their own website and organising meetings, in order to have a presence in the media.

By and large, professionalisation gradually takes place both at the national and at the local levels, but in either case more often during the election campaign period. We can, therefore, identify three main trends of electoral systems that affect professionalisation:

In pure proportional systems we can identify a stronger centralisation of political parties that favours the professionalisation of the central party machine.

In majoritarian systems, one can see that the professionalisation of political communication develops at both the party headquarters that are responsible for the whole campaigning at a national level and at a constituency level, since local candidates have to compete against their counterparts in order to be elected, irrespective of the total numbers of votes cast for their party at the national level.

In some proportional systems, as in Greece, there is also competition between the candidates from within the same party. In this case the professionalisation of political communication could be identified at both the central as well as at the municipal levels. Other political systems have different features. The German electoral system, that is the 'German Model', has some unique characteristics: it is a proportional system with a personalised element. Voters have two votes. One goes to a party, the other to a regional candidate. The party vote, however, is the more important vote because the percentage of votes an individual party gets in the country as a whole decides the number of seats in the parliament. Regional candidates from different parties compete in each constituency and the candidate who gets the majority of votes is elected. The candidate who wins a constituency gets one of the seats gained by the party as a whole. Those seats that are not taken directly by the constituency winners are filled through party lists. Because the party vote is more important, all parties campaign for the party vote in the first place. This leads to party-centred campaigns with an emphasis on the parties' top candidates, who usually are placed on the first ranks of the party lists. The campaigns at the constituency level receive much less attention than the national campaign. Also, candidates in the constituencies have fewer opportunities to use the mass media for their campaign and instead put more emphasis on those means that allow direct address to the voters. (See Holtz-Bacha, 2004)

Media commercialisation and professionalisation
Many of the contributions to this book suggest that some of the major processes of change in political communication professionalisation have taken place as a consequence of the commercialisation of the mass media in the 1980s. Before then there had already been changes to the nature of political competition and in respect of government relations with the media (see in particular the case of Great Britain), but these changes have probably accelerated and deepened as the processes of commercialisation has gathered pace. In some countries, the move from an essentially public service broadcasting system towards commercial television has had dramatic impact on politics. In effect, the more commercial the media system, the more parties and governments have sought new and different ways to get their messages across to (usually a declining) audience for political content. In Germany, the move from an essentially public service broadcasting system towards a dual system, and sometimes fierce competition, has had a dramatic impact on politics. While this has meant more potential outlets for campaigners, they also had to adapt to the new commercial logic that came to prevail on the broadcasting market. This has also brought about new formats and new environments for politics that has also required new skills of the politicians. Or they have led to the emergence of new types of politicians: Berlusconi decided to enter the political arena in 1994, exactly at the end of the commercialisation process of the 80s. In Greece the modernisation of political campaigning and marketing has changed as a result of the arrival, the development and the dominance of private television in the communication landscape. In The Netherlands the progressive disappearing of the traditional social pillars has been accelerated by the new media environment.

Are there dangers in the professionalisation of political communication?
Are there risks in the trends towards greater professionalisation? Are there clangers to the democratic process to which we need to be alerted? One position, expressed particularly strongly by Leon Mayhew (1997), is that there are. In the course of the 'rationalisation of persuasion', the place for genuine discussion within the public sphere disappears. Specialists/professionals dictate the content of the communication, set out

the options and determine the strategies into which the public has to buy. Politics, and political communication, has become a top-down activity that presents voter-citizens with choices, just as consumers are presented with products. Hence professionalisation in politics – or the 'rationalisation of persuasion' in Mayhew's phrase – is geared towards the improved production of the product for consumption. And, if the product does not sell well, as in the case of a TV programme, we replace the leading actors (in this case politicians) or the programme itself (the party and the programme). The danger in these processes is that politics as an activity does not take root, it becomes 'skin-deep'. As Mayhew put it:

> When persuasion becomes entirely instrumental, its techniques *governed* by the criterion of effectiveness, the warrants of sincerity that allow audiences to extend credit to their persuaders are undermined. There is no longer a presumption that persuaders' tokens will be redeemed on demand. On the contrary, the strategies employed by the new breed of expert communicators are designed to avoid confrontations that would require serious elaboration of their claims. In consequence, influence becomes inflated in the sense that it lacks what I have called 'relational backing.' Influence comes to be based not on conversation but on token appeals to the general predispositions of the audience, which does not build commitment to common cause (1997, p. 190).

And as more and more skills and techniques already developed in the area of business and commerce (e.g. marketing techniques, news media management, advertising, etc.) *and* entertainment are progressively invading the area of politics, it makes sense to consider the continuous overlap between commerce and culture, commerce and politics.

But there are other concerns also: will greater professionalisation drive away the committed amateur? Would it lead to – and is it a cause of – heightened levels of distrust and disenchantment as the parties, led by professionals, fight it out? Will it speed up the transformations of the European political parties into American style leader-led, fund-raising campaign machines with no deep roots into communities? And how much will the electorate accept? As Johnson concludes part of his own study of political consultants in the US:

> the ultimate test is what the electorate will believe and what the electorate will bear. This is an era in which politics is an extension of entertainment, where the foibles of politicians provide the laugh lines. ... If we are not appalled by the corrosion of popular culture, where is the sustained anger and outrage that will rid our airwaves and mailboxes of the shocks of modern campaigning? What penalties do candidates or consultants pay for playing hardball – or gutter ball? (2001, p. 246)

In many ways, then, professionalisation seems to be an unavoidable consequence of a whole series of inter-connected changes. The German Greens offer a good example of this. They adapted their campaign strategies to the necessities of a mediatised environment even though, when they entered the political scene during the 1980s, their declared objective was to avoid any personalisation and to put the issues first. Over the years, however, the Greens had to come to terms with some of their politicians becoming more popular than others and taking a more central role in the media, and therefore they finally succumbed to the necessities of a personalised strategy. While the Greens started with some personalised elements in the 1998 campaign, they openly declared several of their leading politicians as their top candidates and concentrated much of their campaign on their star politician Joschka Fischer.

These, in brief, are the main themes of this book. It sets out to explore the professionalisation of political communication in particular countries in order to identify the processes which are now impacting on the conduct of politics in the 21st Century.

NOTES

1. One of the arguments developed in chapter 2 is that what is deemed 'rational' and 'appropriate' may be time bound, so that what is 'appropriate' for the 1950s may not be so for the 1990s. Hence, what is deemed to be 'appropriate' professional behaviour is never fixed.
2. This is a separate point from the reasons why such practices might take root. Swanson and Mancini argue that campaign innovations are more likely to develop when political parties are weak, and when the media emerge as independent forces in political communication. (1996, p. 254)
3. He has acquired this name because of the close similarity between the two Italian phrases: *sua eminenza* (his eminence), a phrase usually used to refer to cardinals , and *sua emittenza*, (his broadcaster)

REFERENCES

Blumler, J. (1990) 'Elections, the media and the modern publicity process', pp. 101–113 in M. Ferguson (ed) *Public Communication. The New Imperatives*. London: Sage.

Calise, M. (2000) *Il Partito Personale*. Bari: Laterza.

Diamanti, I. (1994) 'La politica come marketing', in *Micromega*, 2.

Gould, P. (1998) *The Unfinished Revolution*. London: Abacus.

Johnson, D. W. (2001) *No Place for Amateurs. How political consultants are reshaping American democracy*. London: Routledge.

Kavanagh, D. (1995) *Election Campaigning: The New Marketing of Politics*. Oxford: Blackwell.

Lees-Marshment, J. (2001) *Political marketing and British political parties: The party's just begun*. Manchester: MUP.

Mair, P. & I.van Biezen (2001) 'Party Membership in Twenty European Democracies 1980–2000', *Party Politics*, Vol. 7. 1, pp. 5–21

Mancini, Paolo & David L. Swanson (1996) 'Politics, media and modern democracy: introduction', pp. 1–26. In David L. Swanson, & Paolo Mancini (eds) *Politics, Media and Modern Democracy: An International Study of Innovations in Electoral Campaign and their Consequences*. New York: Praeger.

Mayhew, L. (1997) *The New Public*. Cambridge: CUP.

Mazzoleni, Gianpietro & Winfried Schulz (1999): 'Mediatisation of politics: a challenge for democracy?' *Political Communication*, 16 (3), pp. 247–62.

Negrine, Ralph & Stylianos Papathanassopoulos (1996) 'The "Americanisation" of Political Communication: A Critique'. *Press/Politics*, 1 (2), pp. 45–62.

Papathanassopoulos, Stylianos (2002) *European Television in the Digital Age; issues, realities and trends.* Cambridge: Polity.

Scammell, M. (1998) 'The Wisdom of the War Room: US Campaigning and Americanisation', *Media, Culture and Society*, 20:2, pp. 251–276.

Scammell, M. (1999) 'Political marketing: lessons for political science', *Political Studies*, 48, pp. 718–39.

Schlesinger, Philip & Howard Tumber (1994) *Reporting Crime. The Media Politics of Criminal Justice.* Oxford: Oxford University Press.

Webel, D. von (1999) 'Der Wahlkampf der SPD', pp. 13–39. In E. Noelle-Neumann, H. M. Kepplinger & W. Donsbach (1998) *Kampa. Meinungsklima und Medienwirkung im Bundestagswahlkampf .* Freiburg: Alber.

Wernick, Andrew (1994) *Promotional Culture.*

2

THE PROFESSIONALISATION OF POLITICAL COMMUNICATION IN EUROPE

Ralph Negrine

INTRODUCTION

How should one explore new developments in political communication and, perhaps more critically, in what ways can these developments be considered part and parcel of a process of professionalisation?

The key to answering both these questions probably lies in analyses of the changing nature of political parties. Over the last century more and more political parties have been transformed from parties with mass memberships to parties with small, and ever declining, memberships. At the same time, and in a not unrelated way, they have come to learn to utilise the newest communication technologies and campaigning and persuasion techniques available in order to persuade and mobilise voters. And as political parties continue to adapt to changing circumstances – declining memberships, new leaders, election defeats – or to incorporate new technologies of communication or new persuasion and communication practices, they become transformed, and they transform themselves, into vehicles geared up for electoral success. They become, in other words, more professional and more professional in their communication of politics. It is a point that one finds in Leon Mayhew's work on *The New Public* (1997). As he writes, the 'new public', a public 'that is subject to mass persuasion through systematic advertising, lobbying, and other forms of media manipulation' (1997, p. i) did not emerge full blown. It grew in increments as each component built upon and reshaped practices already in place to create the system of rationalised, specialised, and professionalised, public communication that defines and dominates the New Public (Mayhew, 1997, pp. 190–191).

The significance of these comments becomes very apparent when we consider recent, and future, studies of 'the media and elections'. Recent studies fall into a common pattern of outlining contextual backgrounds and they then usually make references to innovations in electioneering practices in political communication, such as the sophisticated use of opinion polls, the use of focus groups, the use of the web, and so on. But what precisely do these studies tell us? What different insights do they bring to the study of political communication? What new findings do they present?

It would be far too negative to suggest that such studies tell us nothing new. Each election study undoubtedly brings forward something that is new but one could argue that there is a danger that the focus on the contemporary has clouded our ability to place the new within a longer historical narrative of continual change. Furthermore, that in the era of globalisation, 'Americanisation' and modernisation, there are connections and overlaps that are better understood as a part of a more overarching whole, so that one needs to develop a deeper understanding of what each of these developments – singly and collectively – signifies, and also of how they fit with one another.

The fundamental task, then, is to develop a way of comprehending contemporary change as part and parcel of a longer term process in which political parties – and governments, corporations, and individuals – continually respond to change, and the need for change, in the ways in which they organise themselves and seek to communicate with their constituencies, be they voters or citizens. One of the ways in which we can begin to comprehend this process is by offering a common point of focus, a common theme, which can connect what are seemingly very different experiences in political communication. That theme is the professionalisation of political communication.

WHAT DO WE MEAN BY PROFESSIONALISATION?

We use the idea of professionalisation as an entry point into the analysis of change in political communication practices and as a way of engaging in a more historically informed and more detailed investigation of the underlying causes of change and the ways in which such change is conceived and explained.

The professionalisation of political communication suggests:

> a process of adaptation to, and as such a necessary consequence of, changes in the political system on the one side and the media system on the other and in the relationship of the two systems. These changes follow from the modernisation of society, which is a development that is still going on and will take place in similar political systems sooner or later. Professionalisation in this sense is a general and not culture-bound concept. Its actual appearance and the degree of professionalisation in a given country are however dependent on a country's

specific social and political structures and processes (see Holtz-Bacha in this volume).

Professionalisation, as understood in this book, thus refers to a process of change in the field of politics and communication that, either explicitly or implicitly, brings about a better and more efficient – and more reflective – organisation of resources and skills in order to achieve desired objectives, whatever they might be. There are two main reasons why this understanding of professionalisation is preferred to any others: the first relates to the difficulty of calling those specialist occupations that feature prominently in this volume, e.g. pollsters, strategists, public relations personnel, 'professionals'; the second reason is that the specialisms and the specialisation of knowledge can be traced back at least to the early part of the twentieth century and so confirms the gradual and cumulative nature of these developments. Both reasons are briefly addressed below.

The meaning of professionalism

One important reason why professionalisation can be used to connect apparently disparate areas of change is that it draws attention to a process of continuous change and 'improvement'. Rather than signifying momentous change and tectonic shifts, an analysis that emphasises continuous change forces us to inquire into how organisations and individuals engage with, and adapt to, their ever-changing environments. If we applied this to the discussion of election practices, for example, it would lead us to conclude that what we are currently observing, and have experienced over the last 150 years, is but a lengthy process whereby – and in response to changing media and socio-political circumstances – political parties continually review and reform their practices to meet different circumstances. The same would be true of governments that sought to 'improve' their communications practices by creating a more professional communications organisation to deal with the media and to control the flow of news. In this latter case, improving practices may enable governments to deal more adequately with the process of governing in a global, media-saturated world. The key point is that without such improvements, without elements of professionalisation[1], political parties and governments (and corporations, universities, etc…) would find it much harder to achieve their objectives.

But given the continuous dialogue that takes place between organisations and their environment, and practices and their objectives, there can never be a point at which practices are fully formed and beyond change. There can never be a point at which electoral practices or news management techniques, for instance, *cannot* be improved, cannot be made more 'professional'. Professionalisation can thus also be seen as a process of reflection and learning that leads to improvements and change. In this respect, to be a professional or to act in a professional manner is to engage in a set of practices that are accepted, at particular moments in time, as 'the standards of the best' and acknowledged to be the most appropriate in those circumstances. Unlike personnel in the classic professions of law and medicine, we would argue that those who work within the field of political communication – as consultants, press spokespeople, advisers, etc. – are operating with a much looser interpretation of what it means to be in that 'profession' and to be a 'professional'. They lack, for example, those elements that characterise the classic professions, such as:

> control over entry; a self-regulating code of conduct; definable bodies of knowledge, supported by a systematic body of theory; training and certification by recognizable standards that individuals are qualified in that body of knowledge; full-time employment of professionals in the field; and formal organisation of professionals into societies which defend professional standards and protect members interests (Scammell, 1997, p. 5; see also MacDonald, 1995; Friedson, 2001).

As yet, the list of specialists that deal with election campaigns and public relation activities cannot be characterised as a profession or professions – Scammell (1997, p. 7) sees those specialists as part of a process of 'commercialisation' instead – so there may be sound reasons then why it is best to deal with these specialists as if they belonged to a range of specialist occupations that operate with a fairly loose interpretation of what it means to be 'professional' in the conduct of their activities. At some future date these specialists might seek to change their status as they develop their knowledge base, training, ethical responsibilities and the like, but it is worth noting that such claims are often themselves contested. As Wilensky has pointed out, a profession 'must find a technical basis for (its claim), assert an exclusive jurisdiction, link both skill and jurisdiction to standards of training, and convince the public that [its] services are uniquely trustworthy' (1964, p. 138). Something that, at this stage, cannot be asserted.

The history of the professionalisation of communication activities
The other reason for seeing the process of professionalisation as a cumulative one whereby knowledge and skills are acquired over long periods of time is that one can trace the origin of such specialisms to the early part of the twentieth century. Stanley Kelley provides a good account of the early years of political persuasion in the US in his 1956 volume and he details how they became increasingly involved at all levels of politics, regionally and nationally. More interestingly, Kelley draws attention to the ways in which the specialisms developed and their competences:

> If… the basic trend noted was that toward an increased demand for propaganda services, we may analyze … two accompanying tendencies: first, that towards a broadened conception, on the part of the propagandist, of his aims and methods; and, second, one toward consideration of propaganda as a technical activity providing a basis for occupational specialization (1966, p. 26; See also Mayhew, 1997, ch. 8).

Whilst the history of the propagandist and public relations person could be identified in the US in 1920s and 1930s, their presence in other countries is of more recent origin.

In the UK, for example, one can begin to identify the use of a range of advisers from the immediate post-1945 period.[2] There are examples of the Conservative Party using surveys and advertisers in the 1950s and even of the Labour Party – traditionally opposed to marketing and advertising techniques – carrying out two 'small experimental survey(s) concerned largely to measure voters' attitudes toward the major issues facing the political parties' and, to a lesser extent, to assess the party's 'image' carried out in 1956 and 1957. (Abrams, 1963, p.14; see also chapter 3).

From both the US and British experience we begin to see the development of specialisms: of personnel involved in polling, or creating advertising material, of developing strategies, and so on. Alongside these developments, there is also an acquisition of knowledge and developments in related disciplines that give rise to a growth of interest in the field and of a greater appreciation of what can be done and the newer ways of achieving such objectives. Louis Harris predicted in 1963:

> As we develop pollsters who better understand the mechanics, language and Gestalt of politics, and as we develop candidates who are better informed about polls and social science research, inevitably the mating of the two professions will become more frequent and relations will be closer (1963, pp. 6–7).

These two reasons point towards a gradual growth of a set of specialist occupations in the field of government, and politics more generally, and to the accumulation of knowledge, in part as experiences spread and new techniques become possible. Our working definition, general though it is, does have merit in allowing us to see the longer-term development of specialist roles but, nonetheless, roles that have something in common. That is, the objective of persuasion and mobilisation. In this way we can connect the idea of professionalisation in discussions of improved electoral practices with the idea of professionalisation in discussions of new styles of campaigning and governance, and the idea of professionalisation as a response to changes in information and communication technologies. We can, in other words, add depth and some coherence to many contemporary uses of the idea of professionalisation in political communication. A brief digression into some of the contemporary uses will illustrate the overarching nature of our approach.

Professionalisation – as better campaigning, as a different model of campaigning and as a response to new technologies
The idea of the professionalisation of political communication is very often used to signify a host of changes in organisation, practices and thinking that lead to a more 'professional' and so less amateurish set of practices. For example, the use of opinion polls, the use of political consultants, the creation of a 'war room', and the use of focus groups, is used to illustrate what is often described as the 'modern' election campaign, and the professionalised paradigm (Blumler & Kavanagh, 1999). Maggie Scammell makes a similar point when she writes that 'all the distinctive features of modern

campaigning – political marketing, personalisation, escalating levels of technological sophistication – share a common theme, "professionalisation"' (1998, p. 255). Pippa Norris also develops these themes in her work when she concludes that 'modernisation has transformed the process of electioneering... [T]he defining features of post-modern campaigns ... are the professionalisation of campaign consultants, the fragmentation of news-media systems, and the dealignment of the electorate' (2000, p. 178). Other references to professionalisation can be found in Blumler and Gurevitch's discussion of 'the professionalisation of political communication' (1995, p. 207), in Mancini's work on the 'professionalisation of politics' (1999); and in Gibson and Rommele's work on 'campaign professionalisation' (2001, p. 40). In this way, the present – and professional – model is easily contrasted with the past – and more amateurish – model of campaigning. A good example of how these contrasts are used comes from a study by Farrell, Kolodny and Medvic (2001) in which they suggest that:

> The basic trends (in electoral communications activities) can be summarised as having involved a gradual shift from electioneering as essentially a localist, largely amateur, part-time affair directed at party loyalists to the permanent campaign of today that is personified by a focus on slick presentation, the prominent role of campaign consultants, and an emphasis on marketing of image and campaign consultants (2001, p. 12).

Whilst the above examples are principally drawn from studies of election communication, references to a process of professionalisation can also be found in other contexts. At the level of routine operational politics and news management, Jay Blumler has written of 'source professionalisation' (1990); Schlesinger and Tumber (1994, p. 67) have discussed the 'professionalisation of media relations' in relation to the interaction between governments and non-governmental organisations; and Negrine and Lilleker (2002) discuss professionalisation in the context of politicians acquiring media skills. Finally, Aeron Davis broadens the discussion in his work on the rise of 'professional public relations' in Britain as a central part of the conduct of modern political activity. As he points out, 'central government and political parties currently employ only a few percent of those in the profession (of public relations). ... it is in the corporate sector that the growth of the profession has been most impressive'[3] (2002, p. 23). Despite their meagre numbers in government, the use of professional public relations is an indication of the requirement for certain skills and for individuals to engage in certain media-related routines in way in which they did not do previously. That it may have a larger impact on the nature of governance itself is an issue that is often highlighted (Miller, 2003) but this does not negate the point that in the contemporary age, governments and public bodies also seek to communicate in a manner that is as professional as that found in the private sector. The British (Blair) government has thus sought to modernise and 'professionalise' its communications activities in order to make it better suited to deal with the existence of 24/7 media and to drive the government's agenda. (See also Chapter 3.)

At times, however, the move towards greater levels of professionalisation is linked to changes in communication technologies *per se*. Farrell et al.'s analysis (2001), referred to above, explores changes in electoral communication activities under headings that implicitly acknowledge the importance of new technologies. Furthermore, discussions of contemporary campaigning practices suggest implicitly that the use of the newer communication technologies, such as the internet text messaging and phone banks, create a more professional model of campaigning or, to put the matter more negatively, that those who do not use such means are likely to run less professional campaigns.

But stressing the primacy of technological change in efforts to explain contemporary changes in communication practices overlooks the complex set of factors that contribute to change. Indeed, it is important to note that over time political parties and governments adapt to changing technologies of communication, just as they adapt their structures and organisations to changing circumstances.

Drawing on the above discussion, we can see that the word professionalisation can be used – and has been used – in relation to, amongst other things, the employment of individuals with particular skills (e.g. political consultants, advertising experts, web designers), the acquisition and application of particular skills (e.g. polling experts making sophisticated use of qualitative or quantitative data), and the application of practices to meet particular ends (e.g. news management practices in part to satisfy the needs of the media). And often the way the word is used does not distinguish between those who, say, are employed by political parties on specific projects (e.g. elections), those who are employed by political parties on a continuous and full-time basis but who possess professional skills (e.g. party organisers and agents) and those who simply possess an appropriate albeit ill-defined level of skills but are more peripheral to the party organisation *per se,* such as politicians.

Nevertheless, taken together, these references to professionalisation appear to identify at least four sorts of transitions:

■ a transition, even sometimes a transformation, in the ways in which political parties, as well as other bodies, communicate with their particular constituencies, i.e. displaying a more professional style or manner in the ways they communicate;
■ A transformation in the nature and structure of the organisation, i.e. displaying a more professional organisational structure in how they organise their communication activities;
■ A transformation in the ways in which they use experts or 'professionals' from outside the organisation, be it a political party or government body, to lend support or direct the nature and content of communication;
■ A transformation in the labour market with the growth of occupations that focus on the development of skills and expertise in communicating politics, persuasion and mobilisation.

However, there are two obvious difficulties in such uses of the word professionalisation. The first difficulty is that such uses of the term often imply that what went on before was 'amateurish' and consequently ineffective. This can be seen in the Farrell, Kolodny and Medvic extract quoted above (p. xx): here we find a very broad-brush approach to change that purposely highlights the differences that they seek to identify. Unfortunately, the broad-brush approach exaggerates differences and can overlook significant continuities in practices and activities. So, for example, what are the key distinguishing characteristics between the amateur and the professional campaign: is it the personnel, their part-time as opposed to their full-time nature, their knowledge base, or the organisation of the campaign? Or a combination of all of these? And does this point to continuities rather than breaks in the transformation of parties and electioneering practices?

The second difficulty is linked to the above: who and what has become more professional, and what criteria are actually used to differentiate the professional from the non-professional? Is it to do with practice or theory, and what level of practice or theory? Is professionalisation a process of simply making communication more effective through updating and enhancing the modes for delivering a political message (so that everyone can become a professional)? Or is it related to the employment of those skilled in 'professional' communication activities – public relations experts, image consultants, data analysts, etc – to manage the campaign? And can the term also be applied to elected representatives?

Given the difficulties of identifying those characteristics that would allow us to distinguish between an amateur campaign and a professional one, or a professional communicator from an amateur communicator, in a way that does not raise further problems, it may be best to treat the phrase as a general descriptor of a whole series of changes that have taken place over time that lead to what is perceived to be a more efficient and more sophisticated use of personnel and facilities for organisation and communication. From the perspective of the political party, *the professionalisation of political communication can be deemed to be the process of adaptation by which they change their structures and practices in order to meet new and continually changing circumstances and their use of experts in order to achieve their goals.* To give an example: political parties in the twenty first century have to find ways to cope with the web and its potential. Devising strategies to meet that objective, and adapting their practices to do so, is part of a process of change and, in our understanding, of professionalisation of their activities. The critical point, as far as our analysis is concerned, is that, over time, political parties have always sought to adapt to their environment – e.g. to deal with the press, radio, television, polling data, or quantitative data – and that, consequently, it is inappropriate to think of earlier periods as being less professional than later ones since the contexts and circumstances are always different. It may be, therefore, that the professional organisation is the organisation that never stands still; it is also an organisation that is reflective.

Our task, then, is to identify and account for that process of change but, at the same time, to be more precise about the aspects of organisations that are becoming professionalised. In other words, rather than seeing all contemporary practices as underpinning a process of professionalisation, we explore the socio-political contexts within which different practices and different experts come to be used in specific organisations to achieve specific objectives. In our case, the objective of winning political power and using that power to achieve political goals.

HOW SHOULD PROFESSIONALISM AND PROFESSIONALISATION BE ANALYSED?

If, as has been argued, the word professionalisation is most likely to refer to a process of change, it is a process of change that, either explicitly or implicitly, brings about a different and more efficient organisation of resources and skills in order to achieve desired objectives. It suggests a higher stage or a development of – or an improvement on – what went on before. This could be in relation to the operation of communication facilities (a more skilful use of television), campaigning techniques (better use of polling data or better targeting of voters, for example), the re-organisation of political parties themselves (as in centralisation), the re-organisation of government communication systems (as in the creation of a centralised communication directorate to co-ordinate publicity) and even in respect of media-politics relations (as in news management techniques).

But one area in which there has been extensive consideration given to some of these issues is in relation to political parties and the ways in which they have changed in response to a number of factors, including the challenge on new communication technologies and changing campaigning practices. As Maggie Scammell has suggested, one can identify two 'senses in which modern "professionalisation" is claimed to be qualitatively different (from the past): specialisation and displacement.'

- *Specialisation* 'is largely driven by technology and, of course, the money to hire the expertise. This is partly a quantitative argument, which is saying roughly, that the degree of specialisation has accumulated to the point where campaigns qualitatively become altered' (1998, p. 256).
- With *displacement*, 'party strategists have been displaced by non-party 'professional' strategists. Employed at first for their expertise with the technologies (arising from specialisation), the professionals become increasingly central to campaign strategy and even policy-making' (1998, p. 256). This too has an impact on the conduct of campaigns, although it also has a wider impact on political parties themselves. With the professionalisation of the political communication process, 'experts' take over tasks that were formerly accomplished by party members under circumstances in which the ideological profile of any political party has decreased quite significantly, or is continually decreasing in line with the objectives of the professionals/experts.

Of these two senses of the word, it is the latter – displacement – that has come in for greater academic scrutiny and, usually, within a broader analysis of changes in the nature and organisation of political parties themselves. For example, some of the political science literature makes a distinction between the nature, purpose and organisational structure of the traditional 'mass party' and the nature, purpose and organisational structure of the more contemporary 'catch-all party' (Kirchheimar, 1966), or of the 'electoral-professional party' (Panebianco, 1982; see also Mair, 1998). Simplifying the argument somewhat, in the former, traditional party bureaucrats are essentially in control of the party, whereas in the latter, professionals (pollsters, marketing specialists, consultants, media advisers) drawn from outside have come to locate key positions, often 'replacing party leaders in key campaign roles' (Sabato, 1981, p. 7).

In a recent paper, and drawing on the Italian experience, Mancini has also made the distinction between an era in which party bureaucrats mobilised and administered election campaigns and one in which a 'culture of marketing' has established itself at the centre of a party organisation with marketing specialists offering both executive and strategic support to the running of election campaigns[4] (2002). (See also Lees-Marshment, 2001; and Farrell & Webb, 2002.) The political party then becomes little more than an organisation permanently oriented towards electoral contests; it ceases to be a policy-making forum as those functions are increasingly the preserve of party elites.

There can be little doubt that professionals from outside of political parties have come to play an important role in the conduct of elections (see Plasser & Plasser, 2002; Sabato, 1981; Thurber & Nelson, 2000), but these sorts of changes can perhaps only make sense in the context of the development of political parties *themselves* (and the extent to which different communication and political systems can give rise to the employment or use of different specialists or communication practices[5]). To deal only or mainly with communication and election related changes (e.g. hiring of consultants/ professionals) independently of other changes is not only to privilege them but also to minimise the importance of these other changes. Political parties are no different from other organisations in which change has taken place. In fact, what they have in common with other organisations is the belief that change – in structures, procedures, and personnel – may create an organisation that is better suited to deal with immediate problems and objectives. A change of party leader, for example, usually has momentous repercussions for the political party: new structures are usually created, new personnel are brought in (and old ones removed), new policies are developed, new lines of responsibility are established, and so on. All of this happens because of the belief that the change will create a better organisation (and one that also reflects the new leader's views on what that should be like and its likelihood of success).

Changes in the makeup of political parties therefore come about for a whole series of reasons and those reasons are much more complex than either technological forces (e.g. television, the internet) or the use of experts *per se*. It comes about because they believe that by reforming themselves they will improve their chances of persuading and mobilising voters, for example. It is this larger question that needs to be addressed and one can address this by coming to the topic from writings on the development of political parties (or the governmental apparatus), rather than from writings on communication, and specifically electoral communication, *per se*.

POLITICAL PARTIES AS ORGANISATIONS: ORGANISATIONAL CHANGE AS PROFESSIONALISATION

At the beginning of the twentieth century, Max Weber explored the changing nature of political parties through, in part, his analysis of processes of bureaucratisation. The modern forms of political party organisation, he argued, 'are the children of democracy, of mass franchise, of the necessity to woo and organise the masses, and develop unity of direction and the strictest discipline' (Weber, quoted in Mair, 1998, p. 34). Although the objective of 'wooing and organizing the masses' may be no different in the contemporary era, political parties are forced to approach their tasks in different, and more 'modern', ways. This would include not only using contemporary communication technologies and campaigning practices but also those who are skilled in their use.

In this sense, the appointment of permanent officials and technical experts – professionalisation as either 'specialisation' or 'displacement' (Scammell, 1998) – is part of a process that takes place in the cycle of organisations. Critically, these changes are not specific to technological developments (new media of communications), or improved knowledge (about polling, say), though these are clearly factors that are a force for bringing in those with technical skills. Changes come about as organisations seek to adapt to their environment, be it an election defeat, the need to woo voters, the need to target voters, to collect information on supporters, new communication technologies, new practices and ideas, or whatever. This would, in its own way, be true of governments who may also seek to make changes in their organisational structure to meet specific as well as generalised aims.

Mastropaolo uses Weber's ideas to develop a more thorough analysis of the contemporary state of political parties in which a professionalisation of politics takes place along two separate lines of development: on the one hand, there is the continuing need to administer or run the party, whilst on the other, there is a need to mobilise the party and its supporters (Mastropaolo, 1986). In the former case, the party bureaucrat is charged with assuring the continuation of the party organisation, and the professional politician progressively assumes duties in the administration of public affairs. But the task of mobilising the party leads to the creation of a new breed of political professionals who are principally charged with the use of the means of mass communication. Obviously, roles can overlap but the 'new' professionals direct their energies towards connecting politics with the public or citizenry. And the more independent the media, the greater the dependence of the political party on professionals, i.e. those who can help it communicate with the outside world. Although such 'new' political professionals may not necessarily have an exclusive relationship with one political party, this is still a rare occurrence as most usually align themselves with particular parties and candidates who are close to their own ideological positions (see Kolodny, 2000).

Most political parties in Western democracies now use professionals in some capacity to help them organise themselves before, but more usually during, election campaigns. Whether we adopt Maggie Scammell's framework that draws attention to a displacement of party bureaucrats or Mastropaolo's suggestion that the party professionals are now employed to run parties as election vehicles, it remains the case that the focus of interest is still fairly narrowly defined. The focus is, in the main, on a small number of high profile actors – the professional political consultants – 'who have become prime and semi permanent sources of information and insight for political reporters, and [they] are rewarded with an uncritical press and frequent, beatific headlines' (Sabato, 1981, p. 4).

Whilst there is nothing untoward with focusing on such individuals and the 'dark arts' often associated with them, that focus inevitably overlooks the fact that a process of professionalisation – defined very generally as adaptations to meet key objectives – might have also infected others within organisations, be they party bureaucrats, politicians or government departments. To give a concrete example, there is a history of professional consultants being employed by British political parties to train parliamentary candidates and Members of Parliament to deal with the media. Whilst this is clear evidence of outsiders playing a part in enhancing the electoral prospects of politicians, it also demonstrates that political actors are themselves going through a process of professionalisation. The same would be true in respect of the professionalisation of the whole governmental publicity machine (see Davis, 2002), as well as of political parties themselves as they undergo change and employ new staff (see Webb & Fisher, 2003).

A further consideration is that the specialisation of tasks may be a far more significant dimension of professionalisation than has been alluded to in the past. Whilst high profile experts have attracted much attention, the fact that political parties and candidates can buy specific services such as polling expertise and data, call centre services and data, on a contractual, out-sourcing basis, suggests that parties can change in such a way that they retain their core activities as political organisations, but can then employ others to run campaigns. This, in essence, lies at the root of Johnson's distinction between consultants as strategists and others who sell services (specialists and vendors) (2000, pp. 37–42) need no longer rely on foot soldiers to collect information or deliver leaflets, nor need they rely on local party organisations. Centralisation of policy making and election planning become viable alternatives to grass roots organisations with members heavily involved in running elections.

We need, therefore, to understand the process of professionalisation in a much more complex way, and in a way that acknowledges that political parties change their organisational structures over time and as they confront new challenges. They are never static – or at least, never static if they wish to survive and thrive. But these changes are multifaceted: parties use all available technologies; parties change as their membership structure changes; parties change as their resources change; and they change their campaigning in line with new practices.

This way of approaching the topic is implied in Peter Mair's work on the changing nature of political parties in Europe. As he puts it:

> …as the age of the amateur democrat has waned, and as the less grounded and more capital-intensive party organisations have come increasingly under the sway of professional consultants, marketing experts, and campaigners, they have clearly improved both the pace and the extent to which they can adapt to changes in their external environments. These may not be attractive parties, especially in the eyes of those who mourn the passing of the golden age of the mass party; they may even be seen as quite unrepresentative parties; but, in these terms at least, they are certainly more effective (1998, p. 11).[6]

This is not the place to discuss in detail Mair's analysis of the transition of parties from amateur parties to 'cartel parties' though it is important to note that his depiction of the 'electoral-professional' party is a party that is a *professionally* run political organisation with tenuous links to a (declining) membership. Such developments are the outcome of numerous forces (see Table 1) and this suggests that we need to explore the professionalisation of political communication within the context of the professionalisation of political parties themselves as they continually adapt to change. As Plasser and Plasser acknowledge, 'professionalisation and its concomitant orientation of strategic vote management … probably represents one of the most momentous reaction strategies of political parties in the long run' (2002, p. 310). It is not simply a reaction to specific or particular changes.

The wider context in which such changes – e.g. the use of consultants – takes place is therefore critical and it must not be ignored: socio-political change (e.g. dealignment), economic change (e.g. changes in the labour markets) and technological change (e.g. onset of ICTs) affect the existence of all organisations and forces them to review their objectives and their practices. And as one looks at changes in the ways political parties, governments and organisations communicate with their external environments, one is struck by the speed and frequency by which ideas and practices get revised: mediated mass election campaigning has now been joined by targeted local niche electioneering which had up until recently been out of favour; communication practices used whilst in opposition are now deemed unsuited to parties in government, and, finally, spin – once admired – is now derided.

Table 1: The models of party and their characteristics (adapted from Mair, 1998, pp. 110–111).

Characteristics	Elite party	Mass party	Catch-all party	Cartel party
Time-period	19th century	1880–1960	1945–	1970–
Degree of social-political inclusion	Restricted suffrage	Enfranchisement and mass suffrage	Mass suffrage	Mass suffrage
Principal goals of politics	Distribution of privileges	Social reformation (or opposition to it)	Social amelioration	Politics as profession
Nature of party work and campaigning	Irrelevant	Labour-intensive	Both labour-intensive and capital-intensive	Capital-intensive
Principal source of party's resources	Personal contacts	Members' fees and contributions	Contributions from a wide variety of sources	State subventions
Party channels of communication	Inter-personal networks	Party provides its own channels of communication	Party competes for access to non-party channels of communication	Party gains privileged access to state-regulated channels of communication

However, this vision of a world in turmoil can be misleading since there are also continuities: there are some commonly understood ideas about 'what works' on television or in the press that can often be applied across decades and media. But even these may need to adapt to changing circumstances. The advice given by Joe McGinniss (1970) to the Richard Nixon team in the 1968 presidential campaign probably differs little from what contemporary consultants would offer a candidate running for president in 2004. It included advice on what types of curtains, chairs, members of panels, and sets one should use whilst making a television broadcast, although allowances would have to be made for changes in fashion. Similarly, one could argue that those who appear in the audio-visual media must always look sincere, friendly and trustworthy! So, there are continuities but there are also moments of rapid and radical change to what is seen to 'work' and 'not work': judgments often made by experts and professionals as they monitor changing times.

Practices in the field of political communication are clearly not distinct from practices in other fields of public communication and persuasion. But, in respect of political parties, it creates a momentum for change in order to meet the objectives of electoral victory. Such change is undoubtedly implicated in what Andrew Wernick refers to as 'the competitive logic of electoralism'. As he has observed:

> the transformation of electoral politics into a public relations game is a long-term process which has had structural causes. Not only has this process been propelled, at key moments, by the whole-scale borrowing of techniques from the sphere of commercial marketing. It has also responded to long-term changes in the socio-cultural character and composition of the electorate. In both these respects, moreover, what has ultimately pushed it along is the competitive logic of electoralism itself (1994, p. 142; see also Mayhew, 1997, Ch. 7).

WHO ARE THE PROFESSIONALS?

It should be obvious from the above discussion that in respect of political and campaign communication the professionals most commonly referred to are those individuals employed by political parties for their specialist skills. These would be the pollsters, political strategists, advertising experts and media experts whose tasks are to provide political parties with the specific skills that might be required, particularly at election times. Sabato defines political consultants as campaign professionals who are 'engaged primarily in the provision of advice and services (such as polling, media creation and production, and direct-mail fund raising) to candidates, their campaigns, and other political committees' (1981, p. 8; but see also Johnson, 2000). Plasser and Plasser's Global Consultancy Project, for example, focused on 'political consultants and leading party and campaign managers' (2002, p. 8).

Depending on the nature of the political system and/or the nature of the marketplace for such skills, such specialists might be employed for the duration of the campaign, might be employed for longer, might be employed in an advisory capacity and/or as volunteers. Where elections take place at regular intervals, as in the US, there is clearly a job market for such individuals, and they can use their skills in local, state and federal elections. Where elections of significance take place less frequently, it is likely that the pattern of employment will be different and there may be a greater propensity to volunteer to work for the party rather than to be employed by it, or to be employed by it for specific periods only. What role such specialists play within the political party may also differ from one political system/party to another. They might just be 'specialists' offering their skills or they could come to 'displace', to use Scammell's word, the traditional party bureaucrats and so begin to alter the nature of the political party itself.

If, however, the process of professionalisation refers to more than specific individuals with specialist skills, then it should also be possible to observe how political parties themselves have undergone change. One recent example of this comes from Britain where the Labour Party has begun to recruit, train and employ 'professional organisers'. Under the 'Trainee Organiser Scheme', as it is known, the Party recruits individuals who spend time in the party and get 'intensive training. If they are successful, they will have the chance to work for the party as professional organisers until after the next general election' (Labour Party, 2003, p. 28). As with the attempts to improve the government's communications network, the strategy is to generally professionalise practice – i.e. make it more efficient in achieving one's objectives. A similar process is to be found in Italy: party employees undergo a training period during which they learn the skills of public speaking and appearing on television and their communication skills are assessed. This is not only happening within Forza Italia; in a recent municipal election in Bologna (2004) the Democratici di sinistra (formerly the Communist party) organised training courses for activists and members. (See also Plasser & Plasser, 2002, pp. 306–310.)

As well as identifying who the professionals are, it is also critical to identify where they fit in the organisational structure of political parties, and what they do. Are there different kinds of professionals, some of whom play a more strategic role than others? Have professionals taken key decision-making powers away from party bureaucrats? Do they share responsibilities with them or do they defer to them? Do professionals give shape to political ideas or do they alter the political ideas when they give shape to them? Do they alter the political character of political parties?

Answers to questions such as these not only provide a deeper understanding of the place of the professionals within political parties but also of the way political parties have sought to change themselves in order to adapt to changing circumstances. In effect, one begins to touch on the processes by which political parties become professional in their search for elusive voters.

A final set of questions must relate to the degree to which such changes have impacted on aspects of political communication. There may be at least two separate sets of considerations here. On the one hand, practices in communication, including political communication, may have changed in response to the availability and use of newer technologies. In which case, those who can best use those technologies of communication become key employees within political organisations. On the other hand, and principally because political organisations rarely own or control the means of communication, they turn to those who can best advise on their use. In this latter case, one can think of examples that range from those who simply offer advice to politicians on how to dress or deal with the media, to press officers who act as the point of contact between political organisations and media organisations.

As with political consultants more generally, one could argue that there are many reasons why such communication advisers are being used. Those reasons would range from their particular skills, e.g. designing a web site, to their ability to help political organisations present a more positive public presence, e.g. managing the news media. And, as with political consultants, there are issues about whether communication consultants play a key role in setting out policies, for example, or whether they are mere functionaries in the sense that they carry out functions determined by others. Obviously, the answers are bound to provide subtler accounts of what takes place within organisations but the questions posed illuminate the range of skills that political parties – and governments, and universities – need to engage with their publics.

SUMMARY AND IMPLICATIONS

The above discussion can be summarised as follows:

- professionalisation should be understood as part of a process whereby individuals continually reflect upon practices in order to improve them so as to achieve specific objectives;
- that process has infected all walks of life, including political parties who are also responding to changes in their environment, e.g. enlarged suffrage, new means of mass communication, weakening traditional allegiances, etc;
- governments, like political parties, are also responding to changes in their environments, e.g. the need to establish their legitimacy or to communicate to their citizens;
- specialists – public relations experts, polling experts, communication advisors, and so on – are often employed to help organisations (political parties, governments, universities) to achieve their objectives;
- if parties have similar objectives, i.e. to gain political power, it may be that they will begin to adopt not only similar practices but also similar structures to achieve their goals. Political parties may be more alike than in the past;
- such specialists are usually referred to as professionals because of their specialist skills, their full-time status as specialists or a combination of both;
- specialists (professionals) employed by political parties or by governments in certain capacities may 'displace' non-specialist employees, may work alongside them or may defer to them. There is probably no set pattern;
- a process of professionalisation, whereby individuals acquire ever more sophisticated skills to deal with their changing environments, is always in process and touches both specialists and others, such as politicians;
- under the condition of 'reflexive modernity', it is not only the specialist who reflects on their work. All organisations, and individuals within them, are continually reflecting on their work in order to adapt to their environment and achieve their objectives.

In the chapters that follow these themes are explored in a range of countries.

NOTES

1. Leon Mayhew (1997) uses the word 'rationalisation' to describe a similar idea.
2. There is evidence that politicians did receive some advice on how to use different communication media in the 1930s. (See Cockett, 1992)
3. Davis quotes 1998 figures which suggest that only 0.7 % of Institute of Public Relations members are employed in, or by, central government. (2002, p. 22)
4. One of the issues that does require some attention is the relationship between the professional cadre and the party hierarchy. Who makes strategic decisions? Who exercises control? Who is in charge, and who follows?
5. For example, as time cannot be bought for political spots on British television, it is less likely that there will be a 'market' for the skills required to produce the sorts of 'polispots' common elsewhere.
6. Interestingly, Larry Sabato has argued that 'the decline of political parties (in the US) created opportunities for consultants...' (1981, p.10), and that other factors, such as demographic changes, migration, etc... helped to contributes to their rise. (1981

REFERENCES

Abrams, M. (1963) 'Public Opinion Polls and Political Parties', *Public Opinion Quarterly,* XXVII, Spring, pp. 9–18.

Blumler, J. (1990) 'Elections, the media and the modern publicity process', pp. 101–113 in M. Ferguson (ed) *Public Communication. The New Imperatives,* London: Sage,

Blumler, J. & M. Gurevitch (1995) *The Crisis of Public Communication.* London: Routledge.

Blumler, J. & D. Kavanagh (1999) 'The Third Age in Political Communication: Influences and Features', *Political Communication,* 16:1, pp. 209–230.

Cockett, R. (1992) 'The Party, Publicity, and the Media', in A. Seldon & S. Ball (eds) *Conservative Century. The Conservative Party since 1900.* Oxford: Oxford University Press.

Davis, A. (2002) *Public Relations Democracy.* Manchester: MUP.

Farrell, D. & P. Webb (2002) 'Political Parties as Campaign Organisations', pp. 102–128, in R.J. Dalton & M.P. Wattenberg (eds) *Parties Without Partisans. Political Change in Advanced Industrial Democracies.* Oxford: OUP.

Farrell, D.M., R. Kolodny, & S. Medvic (2001) 'Parties and Campaign Professionals in a Digital Age', *Press/Politics,* 6:4, pp. 11–30.

Friedson, E. (2001) *Professionalism, The Third Logic,* Cambridge: Polity Press.

Gibson, R. & A. Rommele (2001) 'A party-centred theory of professional campaigning', *Press/Politics,* 6:4, pp. 31–43.

Harris, L. (1963) 'Polls and Politics in the United States', *Public Opinion Quarterly,* XXVII, Spring, pp. 3–8.

Johnson, D. (2000) 'The Business of Consulting', in J.A. Thurber & C.J. Nelson (eds) *Campaign Warriors: the Role of Political Consultants in Elections.* Washington, D.C: Brookings Institution Press.

Kelley, S. (1966[1956]) *Professional Public Relations and Political Power.* Baltimore: John Hopkins.

Kirchheimer, O. (1966) 'The Transformation of the Western European Party Systems', pp. 177–200 in J. LaPalombara, & M. Weiner, (eds) *Political Parties and Political Development.* Princeton, NJ: Princeton University Press.

Kolodny, R. (2000) 'Electoral partnerships: Political consultants and political parties', pp. 110–132 in J.A. Thurber & C.J. Nelson (eds) *Campaign Warriors: the Role of Political Consultants in Election.* Washington, D.C: Brookings Institution Press.

Labour Party (2003) 'The Professionals', *Inside Labour.* London: Labour Party. June 2003.

Lees-Marshment, J. (2001) *Political Marketing and British Political Parties: The Party's Just Begun.* Manchester: Manchester University Press.

Macdonald, K.M. (1995) *The Sociology of the Professions.* London: Sage.

Mair, P. (1998) *Party System Change. Approaches and Interpretations.* Oxford: Clarendon Press.

Mancini, P. (1999) 'New Frontiers in Political Professionalism', *Political Communication*, 16:1, pp. 231–245.

Mancini, P. (2002) 'Political Professionalism in Italy'. (Paper given at a meeting of the European Science Foundation 'Changing Europe, Changing Media').

Mastropaolo, A. (1986) *Saggio sul Professionismo Politico.* Milan: Angeli.

Mayhew, L. (1997) *The New Public.* Cambridge: Cambridge University Press.

McGinnis, J. (1970) *The Selling of the President.* London: Penguin.

Miller, D. (2003) *Commercialisation of Government Communication.* (http://www.gcreview.gov.uk/evidence/miller.pdf at 29th November 2004).

Negrine, R. & D. Lilleker (2002) 'The Professionalisation of Political Communication: Continuities and Change in Media Practices', *European Journal of Communication,* 17:3, pp. 305–324.

Norris, P. (2000) *A Virtuous Circle.* Cambridge: Cambridge University Press.

Panebianco, A. (1988) *Political parties: organization and power.* Cambridge: Cambridge University Press.

Plasser, F & G. Plasser (2002) *Global Political Campaigning.* London: Praeger.

Sabato, L. (1981) *The Rise of Political Consultants. New Ways of Winning Elections.* New York: Basic Books.

Scammell, M. (1997) *The Wisdom of the War Room* Joan Shorenstein Center for Press/Politics, John F Kennedy School of Government, Research Paper 13.

Scammell, M. (1998) 'The Wisdom of the War Room: US Campaigning and Americanisation', *Media, Culture and Society,* 20:2, pp. 251–276.

Schlesinger: P. & H. Tumber (1994) *Reporting Crime. The Media Politics of Criminal Justice.* Oxford: Oxford University Press.

Thurber, J.A. & C. Nelson, (2000) (eds) *Campaign Warriors.* Washington D.C: Brookings Institution.

Webb, P. & J. Fisher (2003) 'Professionalism and the Millbank Tendency: the Political Sociology of New Labour's Employees', *Politics,* 23:1, pp. 10–20.

Weber, M. (1969) *The Theory of Social and Economic Organisation.* New York: Free Press.

Wernick, A. (1994) *Promotional Culture.* London: Sage.

Wilensky, H.L. (1964) 'The Professionalisation of Everyone?' *American Journal of Sociology,* LXX (2), pp. 137–158.

3

PROFESSIONALISATION IN THE BRITISH ELECTORAL AND POLITICAL CONTEXT

Ralph Negrine

INTRODUCTION

'In a competitive world parties shun modern methods at their own risk' (Butler & Rose, 1960, p. 4).

'Modern politics require an efficient and professional central office machine' (Socialist Commentary, 1965, p. xiii).

The election victory of New Labour in 1997 triggered off an enormous amount of interest in its election campaign and in the roles played by its advisers. And, as more and more information began to seep out about its organisation for the election, it became clear that there was a story to tell: a story about levels of preparedness and organisation apparently not seen before, about a centralisation and control of activities that was unheard of, about a general orientation to the election that displayed a very sophisticated understanding of what needed to be done to win. The fact that some of its tactics had been borrowed from overseas – the Clinton election campaign being one such source – added to the sense that British election campaigns were converging very rapidly with those of the US, and probably of other media-centred democracies.

The importance of the role of professionals in the 1997 election cannot be doubted, although one has to qualify that comment by noting that Labour's victory came in the wake of 18 years of Conservative governments that became progressively more and more unpopular. Nevertheless, the use of professionals confirmed their place in the electoral landscape in Britain as overseas. But it would be too simplistic to suggest that election campaigns at the end of the twentieth century represented something that was utterly different from what had gone before. Certainly, there were differences between elections in the 1990s and ones earlier on in the twentieth century, but the differences were perhaps less dramatic than at first appears. As Dominic Wring writes in the conclusion to his analysis of political communication and party development, 'while there have been major changes in the way campaigns are now conducted, there are some significant continuities in practice and theorizing.' (2001, p. 51). The task is not only to identify some of the differences and continuities, but also to pay attention to the subtleties and complexities of change.

This chapter will attempt to set the use of professionals in recent British elections in a longer historical context and to use that discussion as background to a consideration of the issues and questions raised in Chapter 2 and identified above in respect of change and continuities. In the course of this discussion, three related themes will emerge and these remind us of certain continuities in the lives of political parties, continuities that derive from their desire to gain power on the back of a continually changing socio-political and communications environment. The three themes can be summarised as follows:

■ a constant desire amongst political party leaders to restructure and centralise the organisation of their parties in order to improve their electoral strength. Wring identifies 'a managerialist conception of electioneering' (2001, p. 39) with British elections in the 1950s though it would probably be possible to argue that the desire to manage and control parties and their interface with the electorate goes back much further;
■ as different technologies come to the fore, political parties seek to familiarise themselves with them and to exercise some means of control over how they are used for political communication. This practice would apply to the press, radio and film just as much as it applies to the medium of television and the internet;
■ over the last century or so, there has also been a growing tendency to employ, or seek help or advice from, those who are skilled in the many aspects of communicating to the public, be they public relations agents, polling agencies or advertisers. Indeed, the more 'mediated' the political (election) process, the more likely that such 'outsiders' will be employed in order to provide expertise across a wider range of areas (see Chapter 2, above, and also Kelley, 1956). Critically, the position of such advisers within a political party and within the political process is rarely uniform. As Martin Harrop has argued, the professionals who inhabit political communication processes and structures occupy 'a role that is more subtle and varied than commonly assumed' (2001, p. 68).

Although these themes emerge frequently, this chapter will also aim to address the question of whether the professionals – whoever they may be – have come to displace more traditional party bureaucrats/ employees.

The increasing use of professionals from outside political parties, as well as the professionalisation of political actors themselves, can be seen as part of the desire to control the conditions under which political parties compete against one another in order to gain advantage. As Lord Windlesham put it, perhaps cynically – drawing on the work of Stanley Kelley – 'in a competitive situation anyone seeming to offer special knowledge or special skill that might conceivably lead to electoral advantage is likely to be looked on with favour' (1966, p. 246).

One of the key points that I would like to emphasise is that many of the changes we are exploring in this volume are part of the process of adaptation of political parties to their environment and not specific to any particular era. Professionalisation is about the acquisition and exercise of skills to manage change: change in practices and structures, change in the ways in which individuals and groups see things and define what works and what does not; it is about adaptation to a constantly changing economic, political, technological and cultural landscape and it is about finding ways to exercise control over that change. Those who are able to, or make claims to, manage the process of change are the professionals. In the context of political communication they are the opinion pollsters, the political advisers, the advertisers, the trainers of politicians, media employees (journalists, broadcasters, film makers), and sometimes also academics who offer advice to political organisations based on their working experiences. Each, in their own way, claims to offer insights into how the electorate behaves and what needs to be done to gain their support. In the much larger picture of how governments communicate, each can offer advice on how to sustain governments in power; in the context of pressure and lobby groups each can offer insights into how to advance arguments, and so on[1] (Kelley, 1956; Davis, 2002).

In this chapter I want to argue that by looking at the changing nature of political parties over the last 70 years or so we can better understand their perceived need to constantly re-organise themselves in order to improve their prospects of winning elections. This process of re-organisation can be subsumed under the heading of 'professionalisation' as it highlights the increased attention paid to a more methodical (and so less amateurish) way of dealing with the interface between parties and the electorate. With developments in forms of mass communication and the means of mass persuasion, political parties were/are also forced to turn to those with the appropriate skills who could help them get their messages across. As Kelley concluded, 'technological advance has made political communication a highly technical, if not a professional, field' (1956, p. 104).[2]

But turning to history for illustrations of developments brings with it a particular problem, namely, how does one make a judgement about the significance or importance of events? For example, it appears that the Conservative party first employed a full-time public relations adviser in 1946. Does this fact make subsequent appointments less significant or does it point to the need to be more precise about the roles of those external advisers who were employed by political parties so that one is able to identify changes in roles and duties? This becomes a more acute issue in respect of assessing *degrees* of professionalisation: how does one determine whether practices in one era are more or less professional than practices in another era? In looking at a long period of change, such issues reoccur and force us to question our interpretations of change within political parties and in the way they interface with the electorate.

Part One of this chapter will provide a number of examples from the recent past that illustrate some of the ways in which political parties have used experts and professionals. Whether these changes lead to a more professional party is discussed in Part Two. As well as offering a summary and conclusion, Part Three will explore the theme of professionalisation in the context of governmental activities and political actors, more generally.

ACCOUNTING FOR CHANGE IN BRITAIN – LESSONS FROM HISTORY

Studies of the history of British political parties often emphasise the ways in which they have changed in response to external events such as the enlargement of the franchise, the emergence of a mass electorate, and even controls on corrupt practices. As Bob Self has argued:

> …as a direct consequence (of an enlarged franchise from about 2.5 million in 1868 to 7.9 million in 1891), parties were obliged to devise cheaper and more effective means of wooing, winning and mobilising voters through new organisational structures and novel forms of propaganda and appeal … existing organisations were transformed from cadre parties into something akin to mass membership bodies (2000, p. 21).

These transformations and the development of more 'powerful centralised and centralising party bureaucracies, to control and direct the party in the country' (Self, 2000, p. 21) were often uneven: much depended – then, as now – on who was in charge of the party and on the relationship between the main political party actors (leaders, party chairmen, etc.). An equally important point to note in the context of developments in party organisation is that organisational change often was – and continues to be – a response to either electoral defeats or the prospect of defeat. Such life-transforming events are usually seen as good grounds for change and for reasserting control over the environment that political parties inhabit by creating better and more efficient organisational structures, collecting better intelligence, and making better use of both.

We can get a glimpse of these forces at play in the histories of both the Conservative and Labour Parties in the immediate post-1945 period. What these examples show is not only the increasing attention paid to issues of organisation *per se* but also the use of experts and professionals within political parties in the pursuit of electoral success.

The Conservative and Labour Parties in the 1950s: the importance of organisation and the use of experts and professionals

Passing comment on the Conservative Party in the 1950s, H. H. Wilson (1961) has written that Lord Woolton 'completely reorganised the Central Office and the Party organisation, in the process also vastly increasing the power of the Central Office' (Wilson, 1961, p. 93). He also made 'professional advertising and public relations men … key figures in the Central Office, rapidly improving techniques and strengthening reliance on a manipulative approach to politics' (Wilson, 1961, p. 94). For example, Woolton appointed Toby O'Brien in 1946 as a public relations consultant to the party and he was put 'in charge of publicity' (Woolton, 1959, p. 344). Although O'Brien's role seems to have been one of establishing good relations between the press and the party (Pearson and Turner, 1965, pp. 227–9), he represents an early example of a professional from outside the party – albeit someone who also wanted a political career – hired to help the party position itself in the country. Other experts also played a part in the 1950 and 1951 elections. As Lord Woolton explained: '… we also used to the full the latest devices of science – the radio and television. We had, many months before the (1951) election, created a "school" for training speakers to use these new media for propaganda – and they needed training' (1959, p. 361). The trainers were, one must presume, experts and professional in their areas.

Nevertheless, the role of such outside professionals in the elections of 1949, 1951 and 1955 was quite limited even though the advertising firm Colman, Prentis and Varley was already involved in advertising campaigns. As Butler and Rose commented, advertisers were not part 'of a long-term programme of … image-building. When the (Conservative) party was returned to power in October 1951 the advertising stopped; the importance of long-term campaigning was not then recognised' (1960, pp. 18–19).

By the next general election, in 1959, things had changed quite considerably with the creation of an apparently better organisation and by more intensive use of advertisers. This time the Party was guided by Lord (Oliver) Poole, its chairman since 1955. Lord Windelsham's analysis of the Conservative Party in this period illustrates both the organisational advances made by the Conservatives but also the poor state of its main rival, the Labour Party:

> With a businessman's belief in professionalism, not always found in political organizations, he (Lord Poole) employed professional public relations men to supervise publicity and Press relations. … It is worth noting that, with the exception of television broadcasters, the Conservative Party made little use of party members volunteering to lend their professional skills to the cause, preferring to raise money to pay established companies whose continued existence and reputation were a surer guide to competence (Windlesham, 1966, p. 51).[3]

In contrast, the Labour Party simply did not have the organisational structure that would have enabled it to exploit many aspects of modern campaigning. It lacked a 'first-class public relations department' that would have allowed it to run a modern election campaign in the age of television, and it had neither an effective 'central office organization, (or) finance' (Abrams, 1962, pp. 4–5).[4]

These examples illustrate very clearly that political parties draw on a range of skills that were becoming widely available and recognised (e.g. advertising, public relations, polling) but that existed outside the parties themselves. Just as advertisers were beginning to exert their influence on the sale of goods, so politicians were becoming aware of the application of advertising and, more generally, public relations skills to the field of politics in the US. Its use in the British political context then comes as no surprise; if anything, the surprise is that it was used so little in the immediate post-1945 period, something that could be explained by a number of factors that made the British context different from the US: the short duration of election campaigns; the absence of a constant series of elections that would permit the development of a profession of political consultancy; the prohibition against television and radio political advertising and a certain ideological aversion to anything that either smacked of sale and/or Americanisation. In such circumstances, it was only the press (and posters) – and to a much lesser extent the party political broadcasts – that could really be used as media for political advertising and mass persuasion, although one could clearly become sophisticated in how they could be used, something that had already been appreciated when the parties employed experts in communication, either advertisers or those familiar with the new media. (See Cockett, 1992, for a discussion of the use of advertisers and those 'expert' in the use of radio in the inter-war period.)

Whilst the use of such experts and professionals, i.e. advertisers and radio and television producers, to run press and poster campaigns and to help produce the party political broadcasts was reasonably well established by the late 1950s (Harrison, 1965, pp. 172–179), the use of polling information by political parties – and hence the use of the now ubiquitous pollsters – to guide electoral activity dates from the late 1950s onwards (see Abrams, 1963, p. 12). By 1962, for example, the Labour Party's Director of Publicity was 'taking regular advice from a panel of consultants including Dr Mark Abrams and a number of Labour supporters from leading London advertising agencies' (Windlesham, 1966, p. 247). By then, however, the Labour party had moved ahead of the Conservatives in respect of its organisation and organisational skills.

A number of things help to account for this change. The first was the election defeat of 1959, the third defeat in a row for the Labour Party. The second is the response to that defeat which emphasised the need for change in politics as much as structures.[5] The third factor was that the Labour party began the process of change soon after the 1959 defeat, so that by 1962 it had created an organisational structure that brought together advertisers and researchers in order to exploit the lessons of research in the pursuit of

The Professionalisation of Political Communication

power. Significantly, the publicity group began to feed findings into 'general matters of tactics and presentation' (Butler & King, 1965, p. 70). The difference between this structure and that of the Conservatives was highlighted in the study of the 1964 election: Labour's publicity advisers were 'an integral part of (its) election planning. Neither Colman, Prentis and Varley (or anyone else working for the Conservatives) were regarded as performing more than ancillary services...' (Butler & King, 1965, p. 91). A fourth, and related factor, was that the Conservative party was suffering from a lack of direction, whereas the Labour party 'was remarkably unquarrelsome in 1963–64, and its propaganda effort was not upset by internal party wrangles' (Rose, 1965, pp. 378–9).

As we shall see presently, the 'integrated' model – a publicity organiser aided by professionals (usually but not necessarily only volunteers), feeding into a campaign committee, and under the control of the party leader – has some interesting parallels with the 'Mandelsonian' model of the 1980s and 1990s (discussed below). In other respects, it highlights two issues of concern here:

- the first is that it is possible to argue – on the evidence drawn from the above examples – that the better organised a political party becomes, the greater the likelihood that it would seek to exploit expert/professional (outside) help. We can see this in the context of both the Conservative and Labour Party's actions in the 1950s and early 1960s, although one has to concede that the Labour Party was less comfortable with using the means of modern advertising within its campaigns. Nonetheless, those who wished to make it a successful party did not shy away from using all the tools that could be made available. As Socialist Commentary forcefully argued, in the policy-making process one needed not only to generate policies but to understand their consequences in the public world, and that required analysis, surveys, projections, and the like; that is, a professionally informed overview of policies and their implications. (1965, p. xv). And if publicity was to be 'engaged in at all, this must be done professionally; it must take advantage of all the appropriate media' (1965, p. xviii).
- the second point is more complex but perhaps more significant in relation to the broader discussion of professionalisation and changes in political party organisation. The outside experts employed – at least in the 1950s – worked under the direction of both political actors (e.g. party leaders) and paid party officials. They did not direct the nature or content of campaigns, except that there were often fine distinctions to be made between the formation and communication of policies. Having examined the 'communication of policy' in the Conservative Party in the late 1950s, Lord Windlesham makes the following observation:

  ... in political communication as well as in commercial advertising the way in which a message is presented may alter the effect it will have, those who have a professional skill in methods of presentation may come to influence or even determine the form and content of the political message as well as the way in which it is presented (1966, p. 53).

This obvious tension was undoubtedly one of the reasons why the Labour Party was more reluctant to use all available means to court voters, but *not* using all the modern means available was also recognised by certain members of the Labour Party as a great impediment to its progress. Herein lie many of the tensions that have perpetually confronted the Labour party: desire for change and modernisation as against continuity and tradition; old methods of working as against the newer ones; newer forms of organisation as against older ones, and most dramatically, a continuing attachment to old principles as against adapting them to meet new circumstances. All these tensions play themselves out as the Labour Party modernised itself in the run-up to its victory in the 1997 general election, creating in the process a veritable model of a professional party.

New Labour and the 1997 election
The Labour Party lost both the 1979 and 1983 elections having run campaigns that many – including its own advisers – considered particularly weak and structures-less; it was no match for the Conservative party.

> The Conservative election campaign in 1979 was professionally planned and executed; perhaps it was the most professionally run Conservative campaign ever. The party hierarchy was aware of the need for professional research (both quantitative and qualitative), for proper analysis of that research and for sophisticated use of the information so gained in the planning and execution of the pre-election and election political propaganda (Rathbone, 1982, p. 43).

According to Tim Bell, Conservative party advertisers were directly linked, via Gordon Reece, the party's Director of Public Relations, to the 'controlling group' of four, chaired by the party chairman. The 'agency was able to see virtually any relevant piece of information (they) wanted concerning party policy or party research' (1982, p. 11). Labour, by contrast, had multiple centres of control and direction, and no real strategy (Delaney, 1982).

The 1983 election also proved to be disastrous for the Labour Party. It had done little public opinion research and there had been little forward planning (Grant, 1986, pp. 83–84), but this may have been a reflection of the political turmoil that it was itself undergoing. As a consequence of that, and in no small measure because of the election of a new leader (Neil Kinnock), 'a total overhaul of its [Labour's] approach to campaign and communications was an early priority….' (Shaw, 1994, p. 54). That overhaul included the setting up of a single body – the Campaigns and Communications Directorate – to coordinate 'all campaigning and communications functions'. In October 1985, Peter Mandelson took over as Director of Campaigns and Communications. He urged 'even greater disciplined communications and expertise in projecting key policies to target audiences', and he called for an agreed communications strategy, a cohesive presentation of messages and proper use of outside professional support (Shaw, 1994, pp. 55–6; see also Gould, 1998).

The Shadow Communications Agency (SCA) was set up as a unit that would 'draft strategy, conduct and interpret research, produce advertising and campaign themes, and provide communications support as necessary' (Gould, 1998, p. 55). The research – both qualitative and quantitative – was fed into the campaigning process and into the party as it embarked on the process of modernising itself and of making itself more relevant to the Britain of the 1980s and 1990s.[6] It was 'largely a volunteer team of advertisers, headed by Philip Gould and Chris Powell, and was essentially an addendum to the Director, to whom it reported' (Butler & Kavanagh, 1992, p. 46). At its first formal meeting were members of advertising agencies, advisers from the MORI polling agency, market researchers, political consultants, party officers/employees (Peter Mandelson, Patricia Hewitt from the leader's office) and politicians (Gould, 1998, p. 57). In the run-up to the 1987 election the American political consultant Joe Napolitan also 'started to help Neil Kinnock (the Labour leader)' (Gould, 1998, p. 162).

Although the SCA provided research and advice, did it initiate policies or merely implement policies decided elsewhere? Did the experts and professionals, in other words, play a critical role in policy development? Butler and Kavanagh suggest that 'the policy review was initiated from the top of the party' rather than in response to grass roots demands, and that the SCA was a unit that provided the ammunition that party modernisers could then use to initiate change (1992, pp. 53–4; see also Shaw, 1994, pp. 54–5; and Gould, 1998, pp. 88–89). And the modernisers did change the party: from the 1980s through to the mid 1990s, old policies and positions were abandoned in favour of new ones as the (New) Labour Party re-positioned itself. With the Conservative government entering a period of crisis after its return to power in 1992, the Labour Party began to move ahead in the polls.

The organisational changes introduced in the 1980s and carried through into the 1990s, alongside the major review of policies, transformed the Labour Party and made it electable once again. Its organisational structure allowed it to focus its activities of converting disenchanted Conservative voters, on targeting key and marginal seats (e.g. Operation Victory, Operation Turnout), using new techniques to target voters and opinion leaders (e.g. phone banks, rapid rebuttal, the internet) and, more generally, adopting strategies that would enable it to get its message across to voters in a clear and simple way. Success in 1997 was repeated in 2001 aided, in part, by the weakness of any opposition. With no credible opposition in 2001, it was highly unlikely that New Labour was ever going to lose the general election. And, in both these elections, research for the purpose of electoral advantage was integrated into the party organisation (see Cook, 2002).

In many ways, the campaigns fought by New Labour in 1997 and 2001 can be seen as the templates for contemporary elections. They created a structure that achieved success and delivered a style of politics that suited New Labour's condition and its need to recreate itself as a trusted party. It allowed for a centralisation of power under the control of a party leader, and for a level of coordination of activities across the country that others may have simply dreamed of. So, it is not surprising to note that others have now adopted some of the practices. For example, the Conservative Party has now begun to exert greater control over its constituencies in order to ensure that there is a uniformity of practices that will be to its advantage (see Watt, 2004).

The elections of the 1990s and of the new millennium provide us with two general lessons that need to be addressed, albeit briefly. The first of these is that the outsiders – the experts, advisers, polling professionals, and others – do not recreate political parties and policies as much as feed into a process that is already taking place. For the Labour Party, the lost elections of 1983 and 1987 offer a background to the desire for change, as the discussion above described. The 'modernisation project' carried on into the 1992 election, although it stalled under the leadership of John Smith (leader 1992–1994). After Smith's sudden death in 1994, Tony Blair's election as leader in 1994 gave the 'project' added momentum. The fact that the process did stall under Smith shows how political considerations – personalities, principles, and traditions – mediate the power of the professional advisers. In Blair, the modernisers found someone who saw the need for change in the same way that they did, and who was willing to move ahead as fast as they did (or faster).

The other lesson is that for change to take place it is critical to have the right organisational structure (and the right staff). In this respect, it is interesting to note two things: the Labour campaigns post-1987 were run away from the party's traditional head office, so symbolically creating a new locus of power away from the traditional party base (in 1997, for example, it was run from Millbank); secondly, and as Philip Gould has acknowledged, rebuilding Labour required not only a new set of principles but also a 'new campaigning organisation' (1998b, p. 6). The campaign was 'structured around a war-room in which all campaign operations and all campaign personnel were in the same physical space; opposition activity was constantly monitored; attacks were instantly rebutted; dialogue with the electorate was constant. From top to bottom, voter feedback was built into the system' (1998b, p. 7).

The centralisation of the campaign and the skilled use of professionals enabled the Labour Party to come to power after many years in the wilderness. But it has also raised questions about the power and influence of the unelected outsiders who work in the shadows and who serve the centralised power structure. Have they taken over? Have party bureaucrats been displaced? Have politicians lost control over parties? Have political principles been abandoned?

All these questions simplify a very complex picture of change, as the above discussion shows, but they do need some consideration. The next section offers some thoughts on these questions.

THE PROFESSIONALS: WHO ARE THEY?

The discussion above – and the examples used – lend support to the view that political parties organise themselves in such a way as to try to manage and control the electoral environment. The individuals cited above – Lord Woolton, Oliver Poole, and Peter Mandelson, amongst others – represent individuals at the vanguard of a process of change, but they are individuals who tend to work within the remit that their elected political masters permit. This last point is also true for those like Philip Gould, New Labour's pollster, who has helped the party during its project of change.

Given the evolving nature of British political parties into increasingly centralised parties with a very small membership and consequently financial base, and that modern politics is highly mediated, it is perhaps understandable that those in charge of them will seek to hire outside professionals to aid them in their quest for electoral success. In the British context, and given that elections take place every 4 or 5 years, the pattern seems to be that parties employ the services of outsiders rather than employ them within the party as permanent full-time employees. Here one would include the pollsters, advertisers, and consultants who come to the aid of the party as elections loom. Sometimes advisers take on more permanent roles but as advisers to individuals as, for example, Gordon Reece for Margaret Thatcher or Amanda Platell, head of media, for William Hague. The positions of these advisers become inextricably tied up with those of the politicians they serve.

There probably are several advantages to having outsiders come to the help of the party at intervals rather than be employed permanently by the party. One advantage is clearly that of minimising costs. Hiring or using advisers full-time would be expensive in itself and there may be few such professionals who would seek to devote all their energies – and the resources of their own organisations if they are experienced heads of polling or marketing agencies – to one client. Another advantage is that outside professionals can be used to establish campaigning units separate from the party's general organisation and usually working to the leadership; the party organisation can thus be bypassed. A third advantage is that such arrangements allow for both change and continuity – one can hire and dismiss advisers much more easily than one can permanent staff and they can be used to reinforce the fact that the political centre remains the dominant partner in the relationship.

Such organisational structures also ensure that politicians and party bureaucrats work in conjunction with expert/professional advisers but usually retain overall control of election strategies, for better or worse. A good example of this comes from the Conservative Party's election campaign in 2001. Whilst the data collected for that party's campaign pointed in one direction, key people in the party overlooked the data or imposed their own interpretation on it. As Andrew Cooper, the party's then opinion researcher, observed in his account of the 2001 campaign, 'the overwhelming information' collected was 'ignored' (Cooper, 2002, p. 102).

One other point to note about advisers in the British political context is that, by and large, they are politically committed. Some become politicians: Peter Mandelson, Patricia Hewitt and Charles Clarke all became Labour MPs and Ministers; while others continue with their work but remain allied to particular parties. Philip Gould and Maurice Saatchi are good examples of this and both continue to offer advice to the Labour and Conservative parties respectively. A younger generation of advisers may be less committed: the Conservative Party's short-lived marketing director, Will Harris – he stayed in post a mere nine months – had voted for Tony Blair in 1997.[7]

If there is an aversion or antipathy to the use of experts/professionals, it is an aversion that grows out of a fear that they are leading the political party rather than lending it their support, skills, and knowledge. This can be seen in the reluctance of the Labour Party to embrace the 'new tools' of polling and advertising in the early 1950s, but it was overcome in due course: it used the medium of television to great effect in the late 1950s, just as it used the lessons of advertising and polling post-1983 (see Gould, 1998). In many important respects, then, political parties are rarely averse to using new means of communication or persuasion to gain electoral advantage. The way they have embraced the internet is a good example in support of that point.

A final point to make in relation to experts and professionals is that the nature of the relationship between 'insiders' and 'outsiders' has oscillated over the last half century. Harrop (2001) has suggested that in the immediate post-war period, campaign professionals, principally advertisers, were called upon to help the political parties (mainly the Conservatives) to advertise their policies, but that in the mid-1960s, both advertisers and pollsters became more acceptable within political parties, although their role 'remained ancillary' (2001, p. 61). From 1965 onwards, one begins to see a more fully integrated campaign being run with campaign professionals almost at the heart of all activities, with either campaigns under the direction of advertisers (e.g. Saatchi) or under the full control of the party (e.g. 'Mandelsonian' model). Equally significant for Harrop is the fact that different eras have seen different types of professionals being favoured: in the 1960s and 1970s the opinion pollsters, in the 1980s the qualitative researchers and the advertising agencies vying for ascendancy. In the 1990s, the changes taking place are taking place, according to Harrop, within the political parties, with the parties once again calling in help from outsiders.

Recent developments within the Conservative Party throw much light on the above discussion. With the forced departure of the Conservative leader, Iain Duncan Smith, the new leader, Michael Howard, lost no time in restructuring the party organisation in order to create a framework that was more in line with his principles and views: out went the professional servants of the old leader, in came new ones, and in came Maurice Saatchi with an expectation that he will bring with him his own team. Is this the model of the professionalised party in control of all political communications but always at the ready to hire other professionals when the need arises? Is this a variant of the Mandelsonian Labour model that the Conservatives are now adopting? Is this a model in which party bureaucrats are displaced? Is the Conservative Party learning from its own past or from the Labour model? Will a new model be established?

These questions are easier to pose than answer but they highlight the complex relationship between the parties and the advisers, many of whom play an on-going role within their organisation. It may be that, as in other walks of life, it is no longer enough to do things: one must make an effort to publicise the activity for public consumption (and approval). Blair government's efforts to modernise, dare one say to 'professionalise', the government's communications activities is one such example. 'The task' of the Mountfield working group, which was set up in September 1997 after New Labour came to power, 'was to consider proposals to respond to concerns about how far the GIS (Government Information Service) was equipped in all areas to meet the demands of a fast-changing media world and to build on the skills and resources of the career GIS.' In addition to recommending better 'co-ordination with and from the Centre, so as to get across consistently the Government's key policy themes and messages', it recommended that, in its own opaque language, 'the practice and procedures of all Government Press Offices (be brought) up to the standards of the best, geared to quick response round the clock…' (www.gics.gov.uk/handbook/context/0600.htm as at 30.12.03). In other words, there was an acceptance that there should be, what the Phillis Review into government communications called, 'a professional approach to communications across government' (www.cabinet-office.gov.uk/reports/commrev/ pdf/pmguidance.pdf).

Reasons for change include a belief that the needs of government in the age of '24/7' media are significantly different from those of governments in a less demanding media environments, and that new communication technologies also lead to the generation and use of new practices. And central government, like political parties, has to respond to these. Unlike parties, though, central government can spend considerable sums on such communication activities, and the extent of employment of advisers and spin-doctors within government departments – and across other state agencies – testifies to this (Davis, 2002, pp. 20–22). Suggestions that the Labour government has used outside professional consultants and public relations advisers to bypass the traditional – and politically 'neutral' – sources of government publicity and communication are now common (Miller, 2003: White, 2002) and underline the point that in media centred democracies communicating with voters is critical, as is using the latest methods and the most skilled professionals to do so.

Equally significant are the sums of money spent by government in what one could call 'propaganda' activities in the period prior to an election to alert voters to how well it was doing in government, as well as the sums spent by government on advertising agencies and consultancies to promote its other activities. Figures released recently show that the Labour Government 'was second only to Proctor & Gamble in the amount it spent on advertising in 2003, up ... to £138m...' (Wintour, 2004, p.3). This figure has grown over the years. In 1992, the government had only spent £53 million in advertising (at 1992 prices) though this was only a point along a rising curve (Deacon and Golding, 1994).

Overall, then, we are now seeing a process whereby political organisations seek to get their messages across efficiently and in a manner considered to be professional – or what is understood to be professional in the current period. And like those organisations, politicians are themselves also aware of the need for their own activities to be of a professional standard; hence the need for training and support in handling the media. In other words, as more and more political activity is mediated, those who wish to communicate to the public seek ways to ensure that their communication activities are appropriately undertaken for maximum effect. It is all part of what Deacon and Golding refer to as 'a central activity of modern statecraft' (1994, p. 7).

CONCLUSION

Professionals, as this chapter has shown, have long been involved with political parties. That involvement has taken many forms: individuals becoming part of the political organisation and playing a significant role within it, e.g. O'Brien, Mandelson, but still pursuing a political career; individuals brought in from outside to run the organisation for a period of time, e.g. Lord Poole, Lord Woolton; individuals hired, or volunteering, to give advice and assistance, e.g. pollsters, television and media 'trainers'. The variety of the arrangements suggests that there is a particular type of relationship that exists between those who exercise political power and those who assist, a relationship whereby those who assist play a role, undoubtedly an important one, within a framework that is set out by political circumstances. Advisers, experts or professionals do not create the policy or the party but help the party give itself a form. As Patrick Seyd commented on New Labour's organisation during the 1997 election, the model used by the party was a top-down 'electoral-professional' one 'in which policymaking and campaigning were increasingly professionalised and run by MPs and full-time officials, and members' role was to assist...' (1998, p. 69). That sense of the political centre holding the reins aptly sums the relationship between political actors and advisers, at least in the British context.

What are the implications of this for the idea that political communication has become more professional or is undergoing a process of professionalisation? The argument that has been developed in this chapter, and in Chapter Two, suggests that political parties employ experts or professionals in order to gain advantage. The examples given in this chapter lend support to the point that such developments are by no means new: training politicians to deal with the media, providing sophisticated polling data, producing professional-looking political broadcasts, and so on, are all examples of how political parties adapt to meet new challenges and seek ways to better persuade and mobilise. At times those new developments are beneficial, as Scammell has argued in

The Professionalisation of Political Communication

relation to focus group research. It creates a means of direct communication between 'ordinary citizens' and politicians (Scammell, 1995). At other times, the use of experts has been criticised for distancing the citizen from the political process and for simply creating a better system for propaganda and manipulation.

The real point is that one can never stop political parties, or governments, or universities or corporations from using the best means available to communicate with the public at large. That they will turn to those who are professional at those things is not surprising. They would in fact be failing in their duties if they did not. Does this lead to a process of professionalisation or something different, a gradual long-term adaptation to change and the use of the most modern and best techniques to communicate with a media-saturated and media-savvy public?

NOTES

1. Discussions around this topic in the early part of the twentieth century would use such phrases as 'manipulating public opinion', 'engineering consent', and 'experts in propaganda'. See Kelley (1956) in particular.
2. Kelley also acknowledges that changes in news values force politicians to turn to those who know how to use the media to obtain coverage. (1956, p. 103)
3. H. H. Wilson credits Lord Woolton with the introduction of advertising and public relations. See quote above, p. 3.
4. Drawing on American experience, Stan Kelley quotes an extract from a Californian Senator written in 1910: 'Three things ... imperatively and immediately necessary with us' money, organization, and a 'publicity bureau in charge of a skilled and competent newspaper man.' (1956, p. 28)
5. It is not surprising to note that title of the chapter on the Labour party in the study of the 1964 election is 'The modernization of Labour'.
6. After the 1959 defeat, a number of senior Labour politicians had arrived at similar conclusions. They noted that 'the Labour Party had failed to adapt its traditional doctrines to the needs and aspirations of an increasingly prosperous group of would-be middle-class voters who had decided the result of the election.' (Windlesham, 1966, p. 85)
7. He is reported as expressing a desire to continue to work for the party on a consultancy basis.

REFERENCES

Abrams, M. (1962) 'Professionalism in Politics', *Socialist Commentary,* April 1962, pp. 3–5.

Abrams, M. (1963) 'Public Opinion Polls and Political Parties', *Public Opinion Quarterly* XXVII, Spring, Princeton University Press, pp. 9–18.

Bell, T. (1982) 'The Conservatives' Advertising Campaign', in R. Worcester & M. Harrop (eds.) *Political Communications The General Election of 1979.* London: George Allen & Unwin

Butler, D. & D. Kavanagh (1992) 'Labour: Seeking Electability', pp. 43–66 in D. Butler & D. Kavanagh *The British General Election of 1992.* Basingstoke: Macmillan,

Butler, D. & A. King (1965) *The British General Election of 1964.* London: Macmillan.

Butler, D. & R. Rose (1960) *The British General Election of 1959.* London: Macmillan.

Cockett, R. (1992) 'The Party, Publicity, and the Media', in A. Seldon & S. Ball (eds) *Conservative Century.* Oxford: Oxford University Press.

Cook, G. (2002) 'The Labour Campaign', pp. 87–97 in J. Bartle, S. Atkinson & R. Mortimore *Political Communications: The General Election Campaign of 2001*. London: Frank Cass.

Cooper, A. (2002) 'The Conservative Campaign', pp. 98–108 in J. Bartle, S. Atkinson, & R. Mortimore *Political Communications: The General Election Campaign of 2001.* London: Frank Cass,

Davis, A. (2002) *Public Relations Democracy*. Manchester: MUP.

Deacon, D. & P. Golding (1994) *Taxation and Representation: The Media, Political Communication and the Poll Tax*. Luton: John Libbey.

Delaney, T. (1982) 'Labour's Advertising Campaign', in R. Worcester & M. Harrop (eds) *Political Communications The General Election of 1979*. London: George Allen and Unwin

Gould, P. (1998) *The Unfinished Revolution*. London: Little Brown.

Gould, P. (1998b) 'Why Labour Won in Crewe', pp. 3–11 in B. Gosschalk & J. Bartle (eds) *Why Labour won the General Election of 1997*. London: Frank Cass.

Grant, N. (1986) 'A comment on Labour's campaign', pp. 82–88 in I. Crewe & M. Harrop *Political Communications: The General Election Campaign of 1983*. Cambridge: CUP.

Harrison, M. (1965) 'Television and Radio', pp. 156–184.in D. Butler & A. King (eds) *The British General Election of 1965*. London: Macmillan,

Harrop, M. (2001) 'The Rise of Campaign Professionalism', pp. 53–70 in J. Bartle & D. Griffiths (eds) *Political Communication Transformed. From Morrison to Mandelson*. Basingstoke: Palgrave,

Kelley, S. (1956) *Professional Public Relations and Political Power*. Baltimore: John Hopkins Press.

Miller, D. (2003) *Commercialisation of Government Communications*, Submission to the Government Communications Review Group. www.gcreview.gov.uk/evidence/miller/miller.pdf

Mountfield Report (www.gics.gov.uk/handbook/context/0600.htm as at 30.12.03)

Pearson, J. & Turner, G. (1965) *The Persuasion Industry*. London: Eyre and Spottiswoode

Phillis Review (www.cabinet-office.gov.uk/reports/commrev/pdf/pmguidance.pdf as at 30.12.03)

Rathbone, T. (1982) 'Political Communications in the 1979 General Election Campaign by one who was in it', in R. Worcester & M. Harrop (eds) *Political Communications: The General Election of 1979*. London: George Allen and Unwin

Rose, R. (1965) 'Pre-election public relations and advertising', pp. 369–380 in D. Butler & A. King (eds) *The British General Election of 1965*. London: Macmillan.

Scammell, M. (1995) *Designer Politics. How Elections are Won*. Basingstoke: Macmillan.

Self, R. (2000) *The Evolution of the British Party System: 1885–1940*. Harlow: Longman

Seyd, P. (1998) 'Tony Blair and New Labour', pp. 49–74 in A. King, D. Denver, I. McLean, P. Norris, P. Norton, D Sanders & P. Seyd *New Labour Triumphs. Britain at the Polls*. Chatham, New Jersey: Chatham.

Shaw, E. (1994) *The Labour Party since 1979: Crisis and Transformation*. London: Routledge.

Socialist Commentary (1965) *Our Penny-Farthing Machine*. Labour Archives: Manchester University.

Watt, N. (2004) 'Fox threatens to deselect poor Tory candidates' *The Guardian*, 13th February 2004.

White, V. (2002) *Tony in Adland*, Panorama. May 2002. For transcript see http://news.bbc.co.uk/hi/english/static/audio_video/programmes/panorama/transcripts/transcript_26_05_02.txt

Wilson, H.H. (1961) *Pressure Group. The Campaign for Commercial Television*. London: Secker and Warburg.

Windlesham, Lord (1966) *Communication and Political Power*. London: Jonathan Cape.

Wintour, P. (2004) 'I've only £200,000 to make case for Europe – minister', *The Guardian*, 7th August 2004, p.3.

Woolton Lord, (1959) *The Memoirs of the Right Honourable, the Earl of Woolton*. London, Cassell.

Wring, D. (2001) 'Political Communication and Party Development', pp. 35–52 in J Bartle. & D. Griffiths (eds) *Political Communication Transformed. From Morrison to Mandelson*. Basingstoke: Palgrave.

PROFESSIONALISATION OF POLITICS IN GERMANY

Christina Holtz-Bacha

This chapter develops the argument that professionalisation of political communication is a process of adaptation to and, as such, a necessary consequence of, changes in the political system on the one side and the media system on the other, and in the relationship of the two systems. These changes follow from the society, which is a development that is still going on and will take place in similar political systems sooner or later. Professionalisation in this sense is a general and not culture-bound concept. Its actual appearance and the degree of professionalisation in a given country are, however, dependent on a country's specific social and political structures and processes. In Germany, the professionalisation of politics, and the way politics presents itself to the public, has been going on for several decades but is still in progress. Thus, this chapter will first give a general outline of the changes that affected Western societies in similar ways and Germany in particular. This will lead to an analysis of the consequences for the relationship between the two systems and discuss what that all means for political communication and for electoral campaigning in particular.

SOCIAL CHANGES LEADING TO CHANGES IN THE POLITICAL SYSTEM AND IN THE MEDIA SYSTEM

The sociological concept of modernisation is used to describe recent changes in Western societies. Modernisation is closely connected with individualisation, which stands for the weakening influence of once powerful social structure variables. Traditional social structures have lost their meaning for the individual and thus their integrating function. Social variables no longer prescribe individual behaviour in a binding way that, for example, allowed prediction of electoral decisions with high probability. Instead, the individual has gained new liberties for his or her decisions in life. Life has thus become a matter of individual decisions, which has, at the same time, led to new uncertainties. These developments have had consequences for the political system and for political communication.

The classical models of electoral behaviour, namely the Columbia and the Michigan models, were more or less built on social structure variables. Through the connection of these variables and political predispositions or party identification, political behaviour was conceived as being rather stable. Parties and politicians knew who their clientele was and how to speak to them. Changes in society and the dissolution of old orders must, therefore, also have consequences for the applicability of these models. (Cf. also Holtz-Bacha, 2002.)

In fact, findings from several Western democracies have shown party ties to be weakening. Voter volatility, as expressed in increasing numbers of floating voters, and voting abstention has been attributed to the so-called dealignment process. In addition to the differentiation of society, the mass media and the increasing level of education are supposed to have fuelled dealignment.

While these changes have been occurring, we have also observed an increasing importance of the mass media, followed by the emergence of new structures in the media market. Both have contributed much to the change in the conditions in which politics is made and presented to the public. Among the relevant developments in the media system and the role that media play in society is the establishment of television as the medium most consumed by media users, and where they get a great deal of their political information.

Commercialisation is the term that describes the more recent changes of the media market, which was initiated by opening up the broadcasting market for commercial stations. In most West European countries, this happened during the 1980s. commercialisation means that economic criteria have become more important for decisions in the media than journalistic ideals. In addition, the differentiation of the media market in general, and of the television market in particular, increased the number of channels available to the audience. These developments all had consequences for the mediation of politics. In the commercialised media world, politics – just as other media products – has to hold its own in the market, its success being measured by audience shares. The multi-channel environment on the one hand holds the potential for a fragmentation of the audience, meaning that the audience is distributed over the multitude of channels. Individual channels no longer have the big audience shares that were common in the monopoly situation and that took on an integrating function in society. On the other hand, the multitude of channels has made it easier for the individual viewer to compose his or her own special television menu. This also means that it has become easier to switch channels and thus to avoid politics on television.

These developments altogether challenge the political system, forcing it to adapt to the changes in society and in the media market. On the one hand this means coping with social differentiation, new values and unpredictable voters. On the other, a commercialised media system and fragmented audiences compel the political system to make greater efforts to gain the media's and the public's attention. The professionalisation of politics is thus an inevitable consequence of these trends, particularly visible in election campaigns where the share of power is at stake and communication efforts increase.

The mediatisation of politics, in the sense that politics is 'continuously shaped by interactions with the mass media' (Mazzoleni & Schulz, 1999) on the one hand and the politicisation of the media on the other, has led to the emergence of an 'interpenetration zone' (Münch, 1997) between the political system and the media system. This is where the interaction between political public relations and political journalism takes place and thus political logic and media logic meet and mix. Both the subsystem of the political system (political PR/publicity) and the journalism subsystem (political journalism) still act under the constraints of their own system and according to their logic, but through interaction and in order to achieve their goals, also integrate the logic of the other. Actors on the part of the political publicity subsystem are politicians who present themselves to the public as well as to their communication managers and experts. Actors on the part of the journalism system are political journalists. Political actors and journalists both have their own specific interests but are dependent on each other for their attainment and therefore try to strategically influence the other side (cf. Esser, 2003).

So, with increasing difficulties in addressing the citizens, and the voters in particular, and with the growing importance of the mass media, which was fostered by the introduction of television and gained even more speed by its commercialisation, political actors reacted by actively trying to shape the media's presentation of politics according to their own needs and to their own advantage. To increase their chances of success, they started to adapt to the rules of the media and to perfect the packaging of politics. In any case, this describes a process that developed over a longer period of time and is still going on and, due to the influence of systemic variables, happens in different countries in different ways and at different speeds.

CHANGES IN THE MEDIA SYSTEM
The post-war history of the German media system was marked by two developments. The first was the introduction of television during the 1950s. The diffusion of the new medium was somewhat slow. Television was only fully established when it reached complete household coverage around 1980. The second *caesura* was the opening up of the broadcasting market for commercial stations in the 1980s. This has led to quick and far-reaching changes affecting those who provide the broadcasting content as well as those who consume it.

Public broadcasting had a monopoly until 1984, when it had to face fierce competition as private channels appeared on the scene. Due to the size of the population and the potential of the advertising sector, Germany has become one of the most competitive broadcasting markets in Western Europe. The average television household, independent of technical equipment, today receives 38 channels. Therefore, audience fragmentation is a characteristic of the German television market. The most popular channel, which in 2003 was the commercial station *RTL*, has an average market share of less than 16%. However, the public television stations altogether still reach more than 40% of the market. The competitive environment has drawn public television, although conceived of as being independent of economic reasoning, into the commercialisation process. This gave rise to the convergence hypothesis that predicted an increasing similarity of content, whichever the direction of assimilation.

Results from several studies show that differences still exist in the way public and commercial television present politics. Commercial channels tend to present political matters to a greater extent as 'infotainment', packaging the political subjects in an entertaining manner. Findings, meanwhile, also indicate a turn in German public television towards 'infotainment'. Differences are still apparent for the structure of actors. Political actors have a better chance of appearing on the public programmes, while private actors are seen more frequently on commercial programmes. Not surprisingly, there is also a contrast between both systems according to the issue's level of reference: Public stations prefer events and issues that affect society as a whole, or refer to a particular level of reference, such as institutions or problems with effects for particular groups of society. Commercial stations instead prefer to deal with issues referring to an individual, private level (Krüger, 1996; 2001; cf. also Greger, 1998).

On the other hand, the commercial media are supposed to be more autonomous *vis-à-vis* the political system. While under economic pressure, and thus more audience-oriented, commercial broadcasting – as the private press – is less dependent on politicians than public service broadcasting, where politicians have kept their option to directly or indirectly influence decisions over content and personnel.

CHANGES IN THE POLITICAL SYSTEM

Until the early 1980s, politics was made by only three parties. Since Germany's representational electoral system usually leads to coalition governments, the small Free Democratic Party (FDP) acted as kingmaker for either the Christian Democratic Union (CDU/CSU) or the Social Democratic Party (SPD) and thus achieved an importance disproportionate to its size (for a complete overview, cf. Holtz-Bacha, 2004b). The party landscape became more competitive when the Greens entered the scene. The new party on the left of the political spectrum made it over the 5% threshold and took seats in the Bundestag for the first time in 1983. In the long run, this opened up the possibility of a new coalition, particularly for the SPD. After unification and the first all-German election in 1990, the established parties had to deal with another newcomer when the Party of Democratic Socialism (PDS), the successor of the former GDR state party, made it into parliament. In particular, the most recent national election in 2002 has shown that the two big players among the German parties, CDU/CSU and SPD, are highly dependent on the electoral performance of the smaller parties that can help either one into government. Christian Democrats and Social Democrats came out of the election with exactly the same percentage points and the red-green coalition could only continue to govern because of the success of the Greens.

At the same time, the election in 2002 has again confirmed the emergence of the 'unpredictable voter'. Voting decisions are made late in the campaign or are changed during the course of the campaign. Since the beginning of the year 2002, the SPD had been much less popular than their top candidate, the incumbent chancellor Gerhard Schröder, and only made up ground during the final weeks of the campaign. Two weeks before Election Day, the number of undecided voters was estimated at 25–35%. Finally, the turnout rate, which traditionally had been high in German national elections, is gradually decreasing. In 2002, 79.1% of the voters actually cast their vote, which was 3.1% less than 1998. Across the board, parties have lost partisanship. Although somewhat later than in other Western democracies, dealignment has by now also been diagnosed for Germany (Dalton, 2002, pp. 184–185). In addition, Germany – as many other countries – suffers from a general disaffection of citizens towards the political system. The image of politics has deteriorated, parties and politicians seem to be all the same, and voters express feelings of inefficacy.

Finally, the increasing dependence of the political system on the media, as well as the media's increasing economic pressure have led to changes in the relation between politicians and journalists. Their close relationship has often been described as a symbiosis, where both sides benefited from each other. The journalists got the information they needed to fulfil their public task and also basked in their proximity to power. Politicians, always in need of attention for their issues and for themselves, could easily push their agenda and get their topics through to the media and framed in a way that was beneficial to their own interests. In particular, after the German parliament had moved from Bonn to Berlin, the fruitful symbiosis was diagnosed as having mutated into a parasitic relationship, where one partner exploits the other for their own benefit. Journalists started to lament being instrumentalised by politicians, whereas politicians complained about the way they were treated by the media. The change in the relationship between politicians and journalists was often attributed to the 'new Berlin Republic', referring to the new conditions for political actors and the media in Berlin. However, the emergence of the 'Berlin republic' probably simply coincided with broader developments as outlined here earlier: commercialisation of the media is one sure reason for the rougher climate between journalists and politicians, changes in the way politicians present themselves to the public and the journalists' impression of becoming part of the political staging game are another (cf., Holtz-Bacha, 2004a).

CAMPAIGNING WITH TELEVISION

The elections of the 1970s are usually called the first television elections in Germany. Until then, campaigns were dominantly print-oriented although political advertising went on television as early as 1957. 'The 1976 German federal elections constituted a turning point in how the political parties perceived the mass media'. This statement was made by Max Kaase (1986), who associated this development with the fact 'that the 1976 federal elections were the first in which Elisabeth Noelle-Neumann applied her spiral of science theory to the analysis of the political process in Germany (p. 97). According to Noelle-Neumann, the climate of opinion, which individuals perceive by directly observing their environment and through the use of the media, influences opinion formation at the individual level, thus having an effect on the election outcome. Based on data from the 1976 national elections, Noelle-Neumann (1977) identified a 'double climate of opinion' in Germany. In that year, the number of voters intending to vote for the then-governing parties, SPD/FDP, and the opposition parties, CDU/CSU, was about the same throughout the summer right up to Election Day in October 1976. However, the chances of victory accorded to the CDU/CSU dropped continually – a development that was seen most dramatically when analysing regular television viewing figures. Since the Christian Democrats fell just short of the absolute majority in 1976, the obvious conclusion was that the election had been decided on television (cf. also Kaase, 1989). Noelle-Neumann (1980) named two reasons why television created the impression that the SPD/FDP would win the election. First, left-liberal sympathies are greater among journalists than in the general population. As such, they evaluated the situation differently: 'The journalists did not manipulate, that's simply how they saw the situation' (p. 232). Second, the climate of opinion transmitted by the media was nourished by optical and verbal signs of public opinion (pp. 237–239). For this latter claim, Noelle-Neumann referred to a study done by Kepplinger (1980), who analysed 'optical commentary' during television coverage of elections. He found that the opposition candidates were portrayed to their detriment and the government candidates to their benefit. This optical commentary was picked up by people who watched a lot of television, and they started to see Kohl, who was the chancellor candidate of the CDU/CSU, as heading towards defeat in the election.

Political actors were quick to take up the spiral of science theory and revise their strategies accordingly. The campaign manager of the CDU, Peter Radunski, capsulated the reactions at that time with his now often quoted phrase, 'Elections can be won and lost on television' (1986 p. 131), which also led him to propagate the idea of the Americanisation of campaigning. Convinced that it had become the most important medium, campaigners started to focus on television and embarked on two broad strategies. On the one hand, they moved towards a more proactive communication management to enhance the chances for their messages being taken over by television as frequently and as much unchanged as possible. On the other hand, they began to closely watch what was reported and who appeared, and for how long, on television. As a consequence, television stations came under considerable pressure and reacted with strictly balanced but bloodless reporting in order to avoid being accused of slant and possibly affecting the outcome of elections. In the case of the CDU/CSU, this also had an impact on their media policy. The party increased its efforts to allow commercial broadcasters to enter the market.

Even at that time, the engagement of outside expertise for campaigning was not new in Germany. Since the first post-war election in 1949 the major parties had worked with agencies, which were mainly hired for designing the advertising material, or with market research institutes, which took care of the polling. Gradually, parties started to work with more than one or two agencies: a differentiation process that was speeded up when television began to take the leading role in election campaigns. In 1976, the CDU hired six agencies for different parts of the campaign. Survey research was also used to develop the party's controversial slogan 'freedom instead of socialism', and to test the acceptance of candidate posters for their chancellor candidate, Helmut Kohl. In the same year, Kohl engaged the Director General of the Austrian public television channel ORF, Gerd Bacher, as his personal campaign adviser, which can also be regarded as an indicator for the increasing focus on individual candidates.

Some of the parties established long-term cooperation with certain advertising agencies. These were usually agencies that did not have a special profile for political advertising. Parties were clients just like any other company. With elections only coming up every four years and Bundestag elections being the only national elections besides the European Election, the German political system does not provide enough of a basis for the emergence of agencies that specialise in political advertising. Länder elections, let alone community elections, both held every four to five years, also do not guarantee a steady and by no means a big income for the agencies, because the regional units have less money available for campaigning than the national party organisation.

While outside expertise underwent specialisation, parties at the same time tended to centralise their campaign organisation. For the first time in 1965, the SPD concentrated their campaign management on just a few people to make the decision process more effective. However, although more and more campaign tasks were delegated to outside marketing experts, the main responsibility for the whole campaign stayed with the parties and their campaign managers.

CAMPAIGNING UNDER THE CONDITIONS OF THE DUAL BROADCASTING SYSTEM

While political communication during the 1970s gradually took into account that television had taken the lead among the mass media and started to adapt to its logic, the late 1980s saw another turning point. Although commercial television went on air in 1984, it only started to play a role for election campaigning in the 1990s. When, during the 1989 European Election campaign, party ads appeared on commercial channels, the Länder, which have the legislative competence for broadcasting in Germany, realised that they had forgotten to regulate electoral advertising on commercial channels, which was done at the next opportunity. Nevertheless, Germany then became one of only a few West European countries that allowed parties to purchase broadcasting time for their political advertising on commercial channels in addition to the free slots that parties get on public television. The following elections showed that only the bigger parties were able to pay for additional advertising time. This finally torpedoed the principle of equal opportunity for all parties, which the Constitutional Court always insisted upon, but was in fact already called into question by graded allocation of advertising time to parties according to their strength. Thus, the emergence of commercial channels offered new and less restricted outlets for party advertising but to the disadvantage of smaller parties (for a general overview, Holtz-Bacha, 2001).

Only in 1994 did campaigners and commercial channels actually come closer to each other. Parties reckoned on commercial television and the commercial channels themselves started to pay attention to the campaign. It took until the election of 1998 for the new conditions of the dual broadcasting system to really have an effect on how the campaigns were designed: The trend to personalisation and entertainisation seemed to be the obvious consequence of the commercialised market. Yet another challenge was the Internet, which established itself as a campaign channel at about the same time and provided for another medium to address voters directly.

The 1998 campaign was soon characterised as being different from the campaigns before. Americanisation was the keyword of public discussion, and for several reasons Americanisation was particularly diagnosed for the SPD campaign. In fact, the style of the campaign became an important issue as it unfolded. However, looking back at earlier campaigns, this was by no means the first time that Americanisation had been diagnosed in Germany but had in fact been repeated again and again since the election in 1961 when Willy Brandt, running as the chancellor candidate of the SPD, adopted features of the 1960 Kennedy campaign (cf. Lieske, 2003). Nevertheless, scientific observers had the impression that another stage of professionalisation was reached in 1998 where nothing was actually new but everything was a little more sophisticated than before. The dominant features of the campaign were centralisation and specialisation, personalisation, and entertainisation.

Centralisation and specialisation were demonstrated at their best by the SPD's campaign headquarters Kampa. The Kampa was set up as a central unit along the lines of Clinton's War Room in the 1992 U.S. presidential campaign, as well as of Blair's campaign headquarters during the 1997 British general election. The party's executive manager, Franz Müntefering, together with his chief of staff, Mathias Machnig, headed the Kampa, working there with a team of about 70 mostly young people. About two thirds of them came from inside the party, the others being professional marketers from outside. The SPD sought advice from U.S. and British experts for the organisation of the campaign headquarters, as well as for the campaign in general. SPD representatives had been close observers during the recent campaigns in the U.S. and in Great Britain, and later, campaigners met with professionals in both countries and invited them to Germany (cf. Bergmann & Wickert 1999, p. 476).

While the whole campaign – mobilisation, media and advertising campaign – was centrally organised from campaign headquarters, the Kampa made extensive use of outside expertise by hiring a total of eight agencies to handle specialised campaign tasks. The Kampa was divided into ten departments. One of them organised *Offensive 98*, targeting 32 constituencies selected for intensified campaigning. This is linked to Germany's electoral system, which is a personalised proportional system giving each voter two votes – one for the party, the other for a (regional) candidate. The 32 constituencies targeted by *Offensive 98* were mainly constituencies where the CDU had won in 1994 against the SPD with only a slight margin. The campaign in these constituencies was designed according to detailed findings from survey research and supported by appearances from high-ranking party representatives. Polling in general, supplemented by tests of advertising material in focus groups, played a prominent role in the 1998 campaign. Early surveys provided the basis for an analysis of the starting position. Repeated surveys during the campaign allowed for control and possible changes of strategies. Members of the polling institutes hired by the SPD were constantly present at the Kampa.

In addition to being the campaign headquarters, and thus securing central planning and appearance, the Kampa fulfilled a symbolic function. The image of a centralised campaign management pulling the strings demonstrated professionalism to the party members and the public. This was important for a party that four years earlier had found it difficult to show unity and to back its top candidate, and that, in early 1998, had two candidates who – more or less openly – competed for the nomination as the Social Democratic chancellor candidate. Demonstrating fighting power with the Kampa provided members with the confidence of victory and gave the electorate, as well as the competing parties, the impression of competence. This function was further emphasised by the SPD's main campaign slogan: Until the nomination of the chancellor candidate, the party ran the slogan 'Wir sind bereit' (We're ready), which changed to 'Ich bin bereit' (I'm ready) as soon as Gerhard Schröder was nominated.

Parties, when confronted with the weakening of party ties based on social position or partisanship, try to avoid polarising issues in their campaign. The two big German parties in particular, though having developed out of religious and class cleavages, today present themselves as catch-all parties. Again, following the model of the British Labour Party and *The Third Way*, the SPD in 1998 labelled its course *Die neue Mitte* (The New Centre). Despite its vagueness, the party tried to position itself with this slogan in the middle of the party spectrum and thus attract voters suspicious of the left. Similarly, the SPD made innovation one of its main campaign issues. An innovation congress held in mid-1997, even before the Kampa was set up, was the first attempt at active agenda-setting for a modern party and was, at the same time, safe because it was about an undisputed topic.

While professionalisation is usually associated with campaign management, it is overlooked – although often discussed – that modern campaigns also require professionalised candidates. The heavy emphasis of modern campaigns on individual candidates, even where parties dominate the political system, goes hand in hand with professionalisation and places great demands on the candidate. When Gerhard Schröder was nominated as the SPD chancellor candidate in 1998, he was the fifth to challenge the incumbent chancellor Helmut Kohl. Schröder was officially nominated with a perfectly staged 'coronation' at a party convention in mid-April, which the media compared to a sports event or the Oscar awards night. For this and other events, the party hired a specialised events agency (cf. Holtz-Bacha 1999, p. 9).

Even before he became the chancellor candidate of his party, Schröder was known to be an apt 'telepolitician' who knew how to use the media. He was described as an 'instant politician who dissolves easily in any media format' (Kurt 1998, p. 574; translation by the author). This quality made it easy for him to grasp the necessities of a modern election campaign and to follow the scripts for his appearances. While experts like the former CDU's campaign manager, Peter Radunski, always complained about the candidates not complying with the requirements of modern campaigns and the recommendations of their consultants, Schröder was probably the first German chancellor candidate who easily and seemingly happily indulged the media campaign.

More than previous SPD chancellor candidates, Schröder succeeded in maintaining a television presence throughout the campaign. While the opposition candidate in Germany has a traditional disadvantage compared to the incumbent chancellor, who enjoys a bonus because whatever he does is newsworthy (cf. Semetko & Schoenbach 1994, p. 132), Schröder got more television time than earlier challengers to Kohl. In addition, he was much more favourably evaluated than Kohl (cf. e.g. Schneider et al. 1999; Caspari et al. 1999).

Among the media adaptation strategies of the German parties, and often regarded as an obvious consequence of the commercialised media world, is a trend towards 'entertainisation', or in other words, the attempt to make politics entertaining and to sell politics through entertainment. In 1998, campaigners contributed to this trend with appearances on the more entertaining television programmes. With their generally high ratings, entertainment programmes not only offer politicians the opportunity to reach a wide audience, but also allow them to reach viewers who are not normally interested in politics. Moreover, it is an inadvertent audience, because viewers tune in to be entertained, and do not expect political information. Appearances on entertainment programmes such as talk shows, late night shows, quiz shows, or soap operas, have thus become a more and more important element of campaign strategies. Although again not new, this trend became more obvious during the 1998 campaign and was one reason for the extended debate about the new style campaign (Holtz-Bacha, 2000).

While the 1998 SPD campaign was praised as being highly professional and also proved to be successful with the voters, things turned out to be different for the election campaign in 2002. This again proves the fact that context factors play an important role and provide specific conditions for each campaign. In particular, the SPD, having been in government since 1998, had to go into the campaign as the governing party while the CDU this time was the challenger. Kampa 02 now found an effective counterpart in the CDU's Arena 02. Unlike Kampa, Arena 02 was part of the CDU headquarters and not a separate unit.

In addition to the challenge of having to campaign as the incumbent, the SPD had to deal with the fact that its popularity shrank sharply in early 2002. The CDU took the lead in the polls early in 2002 until about two weeks before Election Day on September 22. However, while the SPD struggled around 35%, its top candidate, Chancellor Gerhard Schröder, was much more popular. The gap between him and his party amounted to 15% and more. Against this backdrop, even if the party had not planned a personalisation strategy before, it would have been forced to focus on the chancellor. Schröder himself declared that the election would be a decision between 'him or me' soon after the Christian Democrats had chosen the Bavarian prime minister Edmund Stoiber as their chancellor candidate. In fact, personalisation and, to an extent not known before, privatisation became the main characteristics of campaign 2002 (cf. Holtz-Bacha, 2003; Schulz, 2003; Wilke & Reinemann, 2003).

Since Stoiber was known to be a conservative hardliner and a controversial candidate for voters in North and East Germany, and for women in particular, Schröder's claim also aimed at a polarisation on issues. The CDU, however, did not fall for the provocation. It was the accomplishment of Stoiber's personal adviser Michael Spreng, a former tabloid journalist, to get rid of the candidate's conservative image and move him more to the middle of the political spectrum. To make him appear somewhat softer and eligible for women, his wife, daughters and even grandsons served an important function during the campaign. On the other side, as a counterpoint to Stoiber's purportedly conservative ideas about the role of women in society, Schröder's wife was brought into the campaign to represent the modern woman, having been a single mother before her marriage, mastering a dual role in the family and her profession.

Not just because of his personal disadvantages as a candidate, Stoiber pushed what was called his competence team, a kind of a shadow cabinet, and tried to campaign on issues and on one issue in particular – and that was jobs. Therefore, Schröder's attempt at campaigning on his personal popularity and drawing Stoiber into a personal battle did not fully succeed. As a consequence, Schröder either had to counter the jobs issue or had to distract attention from this uncomfortable problem. The issue was countered by reproaching the CDU with speaking ill of the country. The opportunity to distract attention was delivered by heaven in form of the floods in East Germany at the end of August, which worked to the advantage of the chancellor, who knew how to use the situation. In order to hold onto the new popularity until Election Day, another topic had to be pushed, which was found when the United States started to discuss openly a possible attack on Iraq. By making clear that the German government did not support the plan and would refuse any involvement in Iraq, the SPD successfully campaigned on peace and Anti-Americanism.

Thus, the campaign in 2002 has demonstrated that – beyond personalisation – issues do play a role. Parties and candidates can do a lot for setting their own agenda, and that is what active communication management is for. However, for one player and his/her issues there is always a challenger who may try to push another issue. In addition, there are real life issues, for instance the economic situation, and there are unexpected issues that have to be dealt with. So, if professionalisation is defined as the process by which the conveyance of politics is adapted to the challenges of social and political change and of changes in the media system, professionalisation is also the art of adapting to more specific challenges that come up during a campaign and that cannot be planned for.

This short overview, as well as the confrontation of the two most recent electoral campaigns in Germany, shows that each campaign is different. There is not a steady development of certain techniques and strategies. Instead, campaigns are shaped by systemic and context factors that provide for variance across time and across countries.

CAMPAIGN MODE TAKING OVER DAY-TO-DAY POLITICAL COMMUNICATION?

While campaigns sharply bring to the fore the characteristics of strategic communication and how this is targeted to the media with the help of experts, and campaign mode is said to replace governing mode, day-to-day political communication still follows somewhat different rules. Nevertheless, over the years, the tactics and strategies that proved their worth in campaigning have been taken over and by now are clearly visible in the communication efforts of parties and political institutions. This is fostered by the fact that Germany is literally involved in a permanent campaign because, at least on the Länder level, there is always an election coming up somewhere that also has relevance for the national government. On the other hand, the German political system, and federalism in particular that provides for a distinct decentralisation of power, prevents campaign style from dominating regular political communication.

The 16 Länder are represented in the Federal Council (Bundesrat) that, in addition to the Bundestag, is the second chamber on the national level that takes part in the legislative process. More than 50% of the national laws cannot be passed without the consent of a majority of the Federal Council. The Federal Council can have a different majority from the Bundestag, meaning that the majority of the Federal Council supports the opposition in the Bundestag. Over the years, the existence of opposed majorities in the two chambers has led to a higher level of polarisation that had to be reconciled with the requirements of cooperative politics, which are seen as characteristic of Germany:'In practice, the outcome was a combination of confrontation and cooperation, and hence, the coexistence of competition, partisan struggles and majority rule together with consensus formation through compromises or unanimity in decision-making' (Schmidt, 1996, p. 73). These features of the political system lead to distinct patterns of political communication in Germany. Communication management of the government always has to take into account the interests of the coalition partners in the government, the interests of the parliamentary parties, namely the parties of the governing coalition as well as the opposition parties, and the interests of the 16 Länder governments, in particular those where their own party has a majority. Against this backdrop, government communication becomes a delicate matter. On the one hand, it is to present the achievements and plans of the coalition government, but this makes it difficult for the coalition partners to sharpen their individual profile. On the other hand, the government must seek to trigger support for its actions in the parliament, at least by its own parties, but the government also often needs support from the opposition and the Länder. These complex relations would rather suggest clandestine coordination but in fact are, more often than not, fought out in the media. 'Going public' rather than backstage negotiation lies in the interest of all actors who seek to present themselves to the electorate and to gain public support for their own stance, and thus to strengthen their position *vis-à-vis* the other side (cf. Pfetsch, 2003, pp. 74–75). Thus, although government communication in Germany is to a great extent aimed at coalition building, the polarisation of two blocs, the red-green coalition, which has been in government since 1998, and the Opposition parties CDU/CSU and FDP, as well as the need of the parties to polish their individual images, has led to a shift from the old political logic to a more media-centred approach of news management. This strategy is particularly attractive for the opposition parties because they have to work against the traditional bonus that the government enjoys with the news media.

The systemic background and party competition help to explain why news management in Germany has still been diagnosed as following a political or party-centred strategy as opposed to the media-centred style of news management that is characteristic of the United States. Party-centred news management is primarily 'determined by the aim of informing the public, legitimizing decisions, mobilizing public and political support, creating trust in government performance, and by the executive's need to make its message compatible with the institutional prerequisites of the political process' (Pfetsch, 1998, p. 70). Accordingly, research has shown that party and government communicators, who are in charge of conveying politics to the media and the wider public, see themselves as part of the political system, providing a service for politicians and the media. Issue- and image-centred objectives rank higher than instrumental and strategic aims. The relation between political speakers and journalists was still marked by a great need for harmony on both sides, thus calling for consensus rather than confrontation. This is maintained and fostered by personal networks and background circles. (Cf. Pfetsch, 2003; Tenscher, 2003.)

However, research also hints at changes in the German political communication culture. The confidential and non-public communication channels seem to lose their relevance while a growing distance between political speakers and journalists is observed, which has also been regarded as an indicator of a professionalisation process on the part of the speakers. Thus, the political communication system, where representatives of the political system and the media system meet, has developed into a web of symmetric and asymmetric, cooperative and controversial relations of subsystems that are independent of each other but nevertheless lose their autonomy (Tenscher, 2003, p. 342). In fact, changes in the way journalists see their own role also indicates the gradual dissolution of the formerly close ties between German politicians and journalists. While German journalists always emphasised their political role, they have more and more come to accept an entertaining role as well. This trend can in particular be observed among the younger generation of journalists who grew up in the commercialising German media system. One of the more obvious indicators for the changing relation between journalists and politicians is the waning of the traditional gentlemen's agreement between the two sides that once protected politicians in their private sphere (cf. Holtz-Bacha, 2004a).

All of this has had consequences for the political system. Politics today has to struggle for attention and is therefore forced to take the logic of the media into account and even more so the logic of entertainment. For many, the election of Gerhard Schröder, who became known as the 'media chancellor', seemed to mark the transition from old-style communication that regarded the media as a means to inform the public and create popular consent, to news management that sees the media as its target. In fact, his openness to the media, his appearances in television shows early in his first term, and the way he instrumentalised his private life for image building, have caused heated debates. However, on the one hand, it is obvious that he set a trend. Other politicians adopted his strategies, which supports the view that Schröder was simply among the first who accepted the necessities of the media society and exploited them to his advantage. However, the instrumental use of the private for campaign purposes seems to have tempted the media to push further the boundaries about what is acceptable coverage of politics and politicians.

CONCLUSION: PROFESSIONALISATION AT TWO SPEEDS?

Although Germany has reached a certain degree of modernisation, which has brought about new challenges for the mediation of politics, the outcome as far as professionalisation is concerned is ambiguous. Professionalisation in the sense of adapting to the challenges of an unpredictable electorate and a diversifying media system could long be observed in electoral campaigns. The process was speeded up first by the establishment of television as a campaign channel and later by the commercialisation of the media system. Over the years, more and more campaign tasks have been given into the hands of outside marketing and polling experts but are still decided and organised by campaigners who come from inside the parties and thus have a political background, learning 'on the job' in election campaigns.

Although the same conditions apply for day-to-day political communication, the special features of the German political system prevent the marketing orientation to take over in the same way as is visible in campaigns. The communication experts, who are in charge of conveying politics to the media and the electorate, are part of the political system and remain in the background. Their relationship with journalists in the political communication subsystem is still very much characterised by cooperation for mutual benefit. Only recently have researchers found some indications of the symbiotic relationship coming to an end. Strangely enough, the growing distance between communication officers and journalists is due to boundary-crossing by both sides: Journalists feel under pressure by sophisticated strategies on the part of the political actors – politicians themselves or their communication experts – and fear losing their discretionary power and thus their credibility, while at the same time political actors are under the impression of being forced onto the defensive by journalists, who are not content with what is being offered to them or try to play with political power themselves.

Therefore, professionalisation of politics in Germany could be said to proceed at two speeds. When it comes to campaign communication, professionalisation has come far and progresses quickly, but the process is more restrained where routine political communication is concerned, because the constraints are more effective where politics is *made* rather than just *represented*.

REFERENCES

Bergmann, K. & W. Wickert (1999) 'Selected aspects of communication in German election campaigns', pp. 455–483 in B.I. Newman (ed) *Handbook of Political Marketing*. Thousand Oaks, CA: Sage

Caspari, M., K. Schönbach, & E. Lauf (1999) 'Bewertung politischer Akteure in Fernsehnachrichten', *Media Perspektiven*, pp. 270–274.

Dalton, R. J. (2002) *Citizen politics. Public opinion and political parties in advanced democracies*. 3rd edn, New York: Chatham House.

Esser, F. (2003) 'Wie die Medien ihre eigene Rolle und die der politischen Publicity im Bundestagswahlkampf framen – Metaberichterstattung: ein neues Konzept im Test', pp. 162–193 in C. Holtz-Bacha (ed.) *Die Massenmedien im Wahlkampf. Die Bundestagswahl 2002*. Wiesbaden: Westdeutscher Verlag

Greger, V. (1998) 'Privatisierung politischer Berichterstattung im Fernsehen? Zur Veränderung der Akteursstruktur in politischen Informationssendungen von 1986 bis 1994', pp. 251–282 in K..Imhof & P. Schulz (eds.) *Die Veröffentlichung des Privaten ? die Privatisierung des Öffentlichen*. Opladen: Westdeutscher Verl

Holtz-Bacha, C. (1999) 'Mass media and elections: An impressive body of research', pp. 39–68 in H.-B. Brosius & C Holtz-Bacha (eds) *German Communication Yearbook*. Cresskill, NJ: Hampton

Holtz-Bacha, C. (2000) 'Entertainisierung der Politik', *Zeitschrift für Parlamentsfragen*, 31, pp.156–166.

Holtz-Bacha, C. (2001) *Wahlwerbung als politische Kultur. Parteienspots im Fernsehen 1957–1998.* Wiesbaden: Westdeutscher Verlag,

Holtz-Bacha, C. (2002) 'The end of old certainties: Changes in the triangle of media, political system, and electorate and their consequences', *Ethical Perspectives,* 9 pp. 222–229.

Holtz-Bacha,C. (2003) 'Bundestagswahlkampf 2002: Ich oder der', pp. 9–28in C. Holtz- Bacha, (ed), *Die Massenmedien im Wahlkampf. Die Bundestagswahl 2002.* Wiesbaden: Westdeutscher Verlag.

Holtz-Bacha, C. (2004a) 'Germany: How the private life of politicians got into the media', *Parliamentary Affairs,* 57, pp. 41–52.

Holtz-Bacha, C. (2004b) 'Germany: The "German model" and its intricacies', pp. 9–27 in J. Roper, C Holtz-Bacha & G. Mazzoleni *The politics of representation.* New York: Peter Lang.

Kaase, M. (1986) .'Massenkommunikation und politischer Prozeß', pp. 357–374 in Kaase, M. (ed) *Politische Wissenschaft und politische Ordnung. Analysen zu Theorie und Empirie demokratischer Regierungsweise. Festschrift zum 65. Geburtstag von Rudolf Wildenmann.* Opladen: Westdeutscher Verlag,

Kaase, M. (1989). 'Fernsehen, gesellschaftlicher Wandel und politischer Prozeß', pp. 97–117 in M. Kaase & W. Schulz (eds) *Massenkommunikation. Theorien, Methoden, Befunde.* Opladen: Westdeutscher Verlag.

Kepplinger, H.M. (1980) 'Optische Kommentierung in der Fernsehberichterstattung über den Bundestagswahlkampf', pp. 163–179 in T. Ellwein (ed) *Politikfeld-Analysen 1979. Wissenschaftlicher Kongreß der DVPW 1.-5. Oktober 1979 in der Universität Augsburg. Tagungsbericht.* Opladen: Westdeutscher Verlag.

Krüger, U.M. (1996) 'Boulevardisierung der Information im Privatfernsehen', *Media Perspektiven,* pp. 362–374.

Krüger, U.M. (2001) 'Die Boulevardisierungskluft im deutschen Fernsehen. Programmanalyse 2000: ARD, ZDF, RTL, SAT.1 und ProSieben im Vergleich', *Media Perspektiven,* pp. 326–344.

Kurt, R. (1998) 'Der Kampf um Inszenierungsdominanz. Gerhard Schröder im ARD-Politmagazin ZAK und Helmut Kohl im *Boulevard Bio'*, pp. 565–582 in H. Willems & M. Jurga (eds) Inszenierungsgesellschaft. Opladen: Westdeutscher Verlag.

Lieske, S. (2003) *Deutscher Wahlkampf made in USA? Eine qualitative Analyse der deutschen Wahlkampfliteratur und der Berichterstattung deutscher Printmedien zur Frage der Amerikanisierung von Bundestagswahlkämpfen.* Mainz: Unpublished Master's Thesis,

Mazzoleni, G. & W. Schulz (1999) "Mediatization' of politics: A challenge for democracy?' *Political Communication,* 16, pp. 247–261.

Münch, R. (1997) 'Elemente einer Theorie der Integration moderner Gesellschaften. Eine Bestandsaufnahme', pp. 66–109 in W. Heitmeyer, (ed.) *Was hält die Gesellschaft zusammen?* Frankfurt a. M.: Suhrkamp.

Noelle-Neumann, E. (1977) 'Das doppelte Meinungsklima. Der Einfluß des Fernsehens im Wahlkampf 1976', *Politische Vierteljahresschrift,* 18 pp. 408–451.

Noelle-Neumann, E. (1980). *Die Schweigespirale. Öffentliche Meinung ? unsere soziale Haut.* Munich: Piper.

Pfetsch, B. (1998), 'Government news management', pp. 70–93 in D. Graber, D. McQuail & P. Norris (eds) *The politics of news. The news of politics.* Washington, DC: CQ Press

Pfetsch, B. (2003). *Politische Kommunikationskultur. Politische Sprecher und Journalisten in der Bundesrepublik und den USA im Vergleich.* Wiesbaden: Westdeutscher Verlag.

Radunski, P. (1983) 'Strategische Überlegungen zum Fernsehwahlkampf' pp. 131–145 in W. Schulz & K. Schönbach (eds) *Massenmedien und Wahlen.* Munich: Ölschläger.

Semetko, H.A. & K. Schoenbach (1994).*Germany's unity election. Voters and the media.* Cresskill, New Jersey: Hampton.

Schmidt, M. (1996) 'Germany. The Grand Coalition State', pp. 62–98in J.M. Colomer (ed) *Political institutions in Europe.* London: Routledge.

Schneider, M., K. Schönbach. & H. Semetko (1999). 'Kanzlerkandidaten in den Fernsehnachrichten und in der Wählermeinung', *Media Perspektiven*, pp. 262–269.

Schulz, W. (2003) 'Kanzler und Kanzlerkandidaten in den Fernsehnachrichten', pp. 57–81 in C.Holtz-Bacha (ed) *Die Massenmedien im Wahlkampf. Die Bundestagswahl 2002.* Wiesbaden: Westdeutscher Verlag,.

Tenscher, J. (2003) *Professionalisierung der Politikvermittlung? Politikvermittlungsexperten im Spannungsfeld von Politik und Massenmedien.* Wiesbaden: Westdeutscher Verlag.

Wilke, J. & C. Reinemann (2003) 'Die Bundestagswahl 2002: Ein Sonderfall? Die Berichterstattung über die Kanzlerkandidaten im Langzeitvergleich', pp. 29–56 in C. Holtz-Bacha (ed) *Die Massenmedien im Wahlkampf. Die Bundestagswahl 2002* Wiesbaden: Westdeutscher Verlag,), text missing?

5

THE SWEDISH MODEL BECOMES LESS SWEDISH

Lars W. Nord

The Swedish Prime Minister Göran Persson, has officially stated that he is no friend of advanced opinion polls. Most marketing firms during the national election campaign in 2002 failed to predict the success of the ruling Social Democratic Party. After the surprising outcome of the election, the Prime Minister said he obtained a better and more reliable picture of public opinion by walking down the main streets in the City of Stockholm. If people smiled and nodded at him, his party was on its way up. If people looked away from him or ignored him, the opinion climate was the other way around. These observations during a brief walk a few blocks from the Prime Minister's Residence to the Government Office gave Persson, according to him, much more useful information than analysing complex opinion data from numerous polls conducted by statistical experts and marketing companies.

This story is, however, much more of an anecdote than a true description of political communication practices in Sweden today. It would be ridiculous to imagine the party in government not using sophisticated methods when analysing opinion trends and evaluating public preferences. In times of globalisation and modernisation there are definitely good reasons to believe that advanced communication practices are adopted in most countries usually referred to as the most well-established democracies in the world (Swanson & Nimmo, 1990; Bennett & Entman, 2001).

Nevertheless, international trends probably do not explain everything when it comes to political communication practices in a nation. Distinct features in individual countries such as the nature of political systems, media structures or public opinion still matter, which is why it is productive to consider the interplay between international trends and national traditions in this field (Swanson & Mancini, 1996; Pfetsch, 2001; Nord, 2001a; Plasser & Plasser, 2002).

The objective of this chapter is to describe and analyse the political communications processes in Sweden and the degree of professionalisation in terms of specialisation of tasks, the increased use of experts and the management of the campaign (Lilleker & Negrine, 2002). Following an introduction about both the political system and media systems in Sweden, a discussion about the probable causes of the changing natures of communication practices at both national and party level is offered. The last part of the chapter is dominated by a discussion about the concept of professionalisation in Swedish communication practices and its possible explanations and effects.

FROM STABILITY TO VOLATILITY – IN MEDIA AND POLITICS

Sweden was not the first democracy in the world, but can probably be described as one of the most stable. From the full emergence of democracy around 1920 the same five political parties – the Social Democrats, the Conservatives, the Liberals, the Centre Party and the Leftist/Communist Party – formed the Swedish Parliament, the Riksdag, for about 70 years. Even more astonishing, one single party, the Social Democrats, has dominated Swedish politics during this same period. The Social Democratic Party ruled for an uninterrupted period of 44 years from 1932 to 1976. Political power has shifted somewhat in recent decades, but the Social Democrats still dominate the political scene and have been in power for the last ten years. From an international perspective this one-party dominance in a multiparty democratic system is unique, and the powerbase has relied both upon a strong relationship with the labour union movement and a regular pattern of class-based voting behaviour in Sweden (Hadenius, 1995; Holmberg, 2000).

At the present time, political stability has not disappeared from Swedish politics, even if it is much harder to achieve due to crosscutting cleavages. Opinion shifts are more dramatic than ever. A huge majority of the political parties have reached historical all-time lows or all-time highs in voting results during the four most recent elections in Sweden: 1998 (national parliament), 1999 (EU parliament), 2002 (national parliament) and 2004 (EU parliament).

Thus, the former political stability is to some extent challenged by a more volatile public opinion (Asp & Esaiasson, 1996; Holmberg, 2000). These changes must be viewed from a societal context where the welfare state, characterised by a huge public sector and high taxes, has gradually been replaced by more market-oriented policies based on the conditions of the international economy. This process has been more evident and thorough since Sweden joined the European Union in 1995, and has not been affected by the referendum decision of 2003 to stay outside the single currency area.

The Professionalisation of Political Communication

If the political system has gone from stability to volatility, the same can be said about the media system. A party press system dominated the print media during most of the last century. Newspapers were affiliated to political parties, sometimes owned by political parties, and both news pages and opinion pages were often coloured by these close attachments. Diversity was thus maintained through different and easily recognised political opinions in different newspapers. The highlight of the party press system was the introduction of the press subsidy system in the 1970s, where the second-ranking newspaper in circulation in an area received governmental support in order to maintain competition in the regional market (Nord, 2001b).

When broadcast media appeared on the scene, public service broadcasting systems were established. In contrast to the printed media, diversity was supposed to be reached by well-defined rules for the public service broadcast companies, aimed at guaranteeing objective and impartial news reporting. As with the party press, public service media could be described as channels for political information with close connections to, and dependence on, the political system (Hadenius, 1998). However, recent years have seen dramatic changes on the national media scene where deregulations and technological advances have introduced more market-oriented broadcast media companies. At the same time there have been enormous changes in the newspaper market, which has seen a market-driven development with more owner concentration, joint ventures and take-overs with both vertical and horizontal integration processes taking place (Hvitfelt, 2002).

Another important feature of these media changes is within the political de-alignment process. The consolidation of professional values among publishers and journalists has enabled media companies to become much more independent of the political system. As political loyalties are now articulated much less in public, media interest in showing party affiliations has decreased dramatically. Thus, a party-related media system has to a large extent been replaced by an independent and market-oriented media system. All the main actors in the Swedish political communication system now have to adjust to new conditions where marketing logic and highly volatile public opinion are distinctive features.

MEDIA DEMOCRACY AND NEWS MANAGEMENT

In a party-based democracy public debate is naturally linked to the activities of the political parties and their performances in the public sphere. Party congresses, town hall meetings, parliamentary debates and policy platforms are central to the opinion formation processes. Citizens evaluate the political parties by joining party activities, discussing with party members and reading party-produced political information or advertisements. Of course, the media plays an important role in these opinion processes, but in a party-based democracy the main function of the media is to be a channel for information by reflecting upon political party positions and giving space to different ideological views. In this model the media system is more or less attached to the political system (Mazzoleni & Schulz, 1999).

Most modern democracies, however, show rather limited similarities with the above-described conditions of political opinion formation. On the contrary, media is central both as an arena and an actor in the most advanced democracies (Pharr, Putnam & Dalton, 2000). Party-based communication practices are becoming less important as party loyalties become eroded and party identification is reduced (Dalton & Wattenberg, 2002).

At the same time, and maybe as an effect of these de-politicisation processes, more articulated professional journalistic values and more politically independent media organisations are becoming more important in shaping the public discourse (Mazzoleni & Schulz, 1999; Bennett & Entman, 2001; Schulz, 2001).

Sweden is no exception to this rule. In recent decades, a political power shift in opinion formation capacities from political parties to media organisations has become evident. Leading political scientists have described this development as a process of mediatisation and as the most outstanding political power shift in Swedish society during the last century (Esaiasson & Håkansson, 2002). The changes taking place have different explanations, but there are good reasons to consider both the depoliticisation of the Swedish political culture and the modernisation and commercialisation of the Swedish media system. Taken together, these processes deeply influence the role of citizens in political communication (Asp, 1986; Asp & Esaiasson, 1996; Strömbäck, 2001; 2004).

In terms of citizen communication behaviour, Sweden is undoubtedly a media-centred democracy. According to recent national surveys, about 80% of the population rely mostly on the media, and particularly on television, for their political information (Table 1). Personal information and personal experiences play a marginal role in this aspect.

The fact that television is central to political information processes in Swedish democracy does not, however, offer the political parties any noticeable advantages in using television as a direct channel of communication. This is impossible for two main reasons. First of all, political advertisements are prohibited, both in public service broadcasts and in commercial channels. Thus, one of the most distinctive features of modern political campaigns does not exist in Sweden. It is also unlikely that it will exist in the near future, as there is a political majority in the parliament supporting the belief that political ads actually reduce the quality of public discourse, given their often superficial and negative character. Of course, political ads reach Swedish viewers through cable and satellite from TV stations based abroad, but they play only a marginal role in political communication aspects.

Secondly, no free broadcasting time is made available to political parties in either television or radio during the election campaign. The fact that not even public service

Table 1. Primary sources of political information among Swedish citizens (percentage)

Source		
Personal experiences	7	
Personal communication	14	
Media communication	79	
– TV		55
– Radio		10
– Newspapers		23
– Internet		2
Total	100	

Source: Demobarometer 2002. N =1 147.

companies allow such political party presentations is unique to Sweden. Instead, the tradition in public service media is to have journalist-led questioning and special programmes with party leaders in the final weeks before the elections and a final debate between the party leaders two days before Election Day. It is obvious in recent years that these final debates have also become more 'mediatised', including a freer journalist-moderator role and with less interest in formal procedures, such as giving exactly the same time to each politician or following a pre-scheduled speech list (Esaiasson & Håkansson, 2002; Nord & Strömbäck, 2003).

To sum up, Sweden could be described as a media-centred democracy, where neither political adverts nor political party programmes are allowed in television. The most effective direct channels of communication with citizens are thus excluded from political campaigns in Sweden. In such systems, media consultants will probably not proliferate very quickly (Gibson & Römmele, 2001). This leaves the political parties with a dilemma, and they have to try other strategies to set the agenda. Television is felt to be necessary to achieve this, but they have no guaranteed access to it and cannot rely on any set conditions.

Successful TV strategies thus require careful media management and the ability to achieve publicity. Without adverts and party programmes it is vital to appear favourable in both the TV news and ordinary programmes. Thus, there is a constant battle within the news, where political parties and other organisations are busy creating newsworthy political stories and the media companies are as busy trying to evaluate the real newsworthiness of these stories (Nord & Strömbäck, 2003). This obviously gives room for more dramatic and superficial political news focusing on the political game and scandals, as confirmed in recent content analyses of national political news in Sweden (Strömbäck, 2004).

So even if political parties cannot be involved in direct communication activities in television, they certainly need both professional skills and financial resources in the field of news management. The need to utilise free media to maintain voters' support thus becomes a daily priority of government and party workers.

When it comes to changes in communication practices at the party level, these can be examined both by analysing the people working with communication within the party organisations and the techniques used by the parties in their communication activities. In both these aspects, Sweden has been traditionally viewed as a typical multi-party democracy with a proportional electoral system, where voting was mainly class-based and predictable and in which party meetings dominated campaign activities.

However, some reviews of Swedish party practices over the last few decades have shown signs of change. They indicated a greater interest in conducting opinion polls and developing media strategies, even if these changes were small and not evidence of a complete modernisation or 'Americanisation' of political communication practices. Instead, national characteristics seemed to co-exist with some adoption of international trends (Asp & Esaiasson, 1996; Petersson & Holmberg, 1998; Nord, 2001a).

To analyse the recent development in this area a set of qualitative interviews with political party officials was conducted in 2002 and 2003 by CPRC, Centre for Political Communication Research (Nord & Strömbäck, 2003; Nord 2004). Representatives from all seven parties in parliament were interviewed and asked about their communication practices.

THE PARTY IS OVER, OR IS IT?
The results of the interviews confirm that the political parties in Sweden are slowly adapting to new communication practices, as there are more people working with such activities than previously, and there are now more opinion polls and focus groups conducted. In general, all the political parties now behave in a similar manner. About ten years ago, only the biggest parties with huge resources admitted to some use of opinion polls and media strategies, while the other parties denied any use of such communication practices. The number of people working with PR and media-related activities also varied significantly (Petersson & Holmberg, 1998). Today, all party representatives confirm their use of marketing techniques and admit the need for professional skills in this field. Although Swedish political parties are still to some extent driven by ideological compassion and issue-orientation, more political marketing considerations are becoming obvious within the existing party communication strategies.

The overall figures concerning party employees, however, shows a general decrease of party officials between 1993 and 2003 (Table 2). But this trend is more evidence of centralisation than of demobilisation of the political parties. Most of the party jobs that

Table 2. Personal resources in political parties 1993 and 2003

	1993		2003		1993–2003	
	Total	Media & Opinion	Total	Media & Opinion	Total	Media & Opinion
Social Democrats	602	2	429	7	– 173	+ 5
Conservative	155	5	113	9	– 42	+ 4
Centre Party	145	7	97	12	– 48	+ 5
Liberals	40	8	45	7	+ 5	– 1
Christ Democrats	1	1	30	6	+ 29	+ 5
Leftist Party	24	0	35	4	+ 11	+ 4
The Greens	10	0	60	5	+ 50	+ 5
Total	977	23	809	50	– 168	+ 27

Source: Personal interviews 2003/2003 (Nord 2004). The table shows the total number of people employed by the party and the number of people mainly occupied with media, PR and political marketing activities.

have disappeared were at regional and local levels, and within the three parties with the biggest organisation (the Social Democrats, the Conservatives and the Centre party). In the other four parties there has been a significant increase in party officials. Overall, differences between parties have diminished and central administration has been consolidated, while the party organisation at regional and local levels has been dismantled. This indicates an increased emphasis on professional and skilled party officials.

As Sweden is one of the few countries in Europe which holds national and local elections on the same day, the centralisation process affects campaign activities at the local level. There is less money spent on local campaigns and the process is less personal as the majority of political posters are centrally produced. The highlight of the local campaign is often a visit by a Party Leader or a Cabinet Member. Central campaign practices assume even greater importance as local voting is also, to some extent, influenced by national voting.

The development is further illustrated by the number of people employed with responsibility for opinion and media activities. During the period from 1993 to 2003 the numbers have more than tripled in most parties. The exceptions to this are the Liberals and the Greens where the changes have been more modest. The general rule is now, however, to employ people in (and also between) election campaigns to conduct party opinions polls, handle media relations, work with the party website and, in some cases, administer focus groups and voter segmentation analyses. They are paid by the party organisation and they usually have both an academic background and some experience of political work within the party.

The overall trend of more people working within the party communication business is probably more widespread than the above table shows. Consideration must also be given to the fact that the ruling Social Democratic Party has access to huge communication resources outside the party organisation. There are about 25 Social Democratic ministers in the government, each with their own staff, including press secretaries and assistants. These employees are not officially integrated within party activities but play an important role, not least at election times, preparing the leading politicians with arguments and media advice. The press departments within the government have developed substantially over recent years, particularly within the Prime Minister's Office.

To conclude, there are more party people than ever engaged in modern communication practices. At the same time, the majority of party officials still work within traditional areas such as recruiting and training party members and articulating and consolidating political interests of the party supporters. The fact that both party identification and party membership have been going down has not yet affected internal party work. Despite a more volatile electorate, it appears that it is easier for officials to depend on organisational competence rather than on political marketing skills. The main explanation for this may be because of the system of public financing, based on voting figures, whose aim is to maintain the existing party structure. All parties in the parliament receive the majority of their income from the fiscal budget, while member fees or private money offer only a marginal contribution (Nord, 2004).

Marketing tools have been used regularly in Swedish party politics during recent decades (Petersson & Holmberg, 1998). The breakthrough was during the 1980s and 1990s and there has been no real increase in the number of polls since. All political parties use opinion polls every year, even if they are more common in election years. However, there are different levels of interest in opinion polls. While Social Democrats and the Non-Socialist Opposition Parties each conduct a number of polls annually and have at least one person employed to prepare and analyse the polls, the Left party and the Greens only buy a few questions in an external survey (Table 3).

The steady level of party opinion polls may be surprising but can be explained by the fact that many other polls exist in public life. Many leading media companies publish monthly polls about party support or confidence in party leaders. There is empirical evidence that polls have been used more and more frequently in political news reporting (Strömbäck, 2004). As well as media polls, there are a great number of polls conducted by interest organisations, lobbyists, private companies and public authorities, all aimed at influencing public opinion and setting the political agenda.

Table 3. Regular use of political marketing tools 1993 and 2003.

	1993				2003			
	Polls	Focus groups	Voter segment.	Opp. mapping	Polls	Focus groups	Voter segment.	Opp. mapping
Social Democrats	Yes	Yes	Yes	Yes	Yes	Yes	Yes	Yes
Conservatives	Yes	Yes	No	No	Yes	Yes	No	No
Centre Party	Yes	No	Yes	No	Yes	Yes	Yes	Yes
Liberals	Yes	No	No	Yes	Yes	No	No	Yes
Christ Democrats	No	No	No	No	Yes	No	No	No
Left Party	No	No	No	No	No	No	No	No
The Greens	No	No	No	No	No	No	No	No

Source: Personal Interviews 2002/2003 (Nord & Strömbäck 2003 and Nord 2004). The marketing tools are opinion polls, focus groups, voter segmentation analyses and mapping of political opponents.

These opinion polls are, at least in their public versions, less extensive than the party opinion polls but they can nevertheless be used as complements when analysing opinion trends. Thus, internal party polls are often mainly designed to further elaborate the nature and origins of public opinion among different voter segments.

Finally, exit polls are conducted in Sweden. Due to voluntary restrictions accepted by parties, marketing companies and media, they are, however, only published after the voting procedure is completed.

Another important tool used to gain greater understanding of opinion formation and attitude change is the focus group. Most parties use this method, particularly the Social Democrats and the Centre Party, who both conduct focus groups five or more times annually. The focus groups are mainly used to complement the opinion polls. Thus, the parties most engaged in polling are also the ones most interested in setting up focus groups. These parties are also the only ones to pay attention to voter segment analysis or to the mapping of political opponents during election campaigns.

The number of political marketing activities indicates that a few people are involved in these activities and quite modest personnel resources are used here. Among the larger parties the same people are responsible for all marketing tools, and no special departments exist for different analytical instruments. The professionals working with these tasks usually possess all-round skills rather than being experts in any one particularly communication field.

The professionals in the parties not only analyse internal polls and focus groups, but are also responsible for the evaluation of official statistics and other surveys conducted by universities, institutes or marketing firms. There is no doubt that the analysis of such data is discussed very seriously in leading circles within the political parties. It does, however, remain unclear to what extent polling data is actually considered when election platforms or media strategies are decided: in interviews after the last national election in 2002, only two of seven Party Secretaries openly admitted the importance of this polling (Nord & Strömbäck, 2003).

As well as opinion analysis, most professionals in the parties are occupied with media management. They are members of the Party Leader Staff (Press Secretaries) or are planning media activities, writing press releases or opinion articles and following the media coverage of political affairs. Media professionals advise Party Leaders and Government Members about media performances and stage media events.

The leading politicians themselves, however, are still recruited using traditional values such as ideology, competence, management, compassion, charisma and experience. One of the basic ideas about political leadership in Sweden has been formed by seeing the benefits of having a unifying political leader who appeals to the electorate but who, above all, is capable of handling conflicts within the internal party arena (Strömbäck, 2002).

Officially, this idea still exits. In reality, however, media skills are undoubtedly taken into consideration when new party leaders are elected. As a result of a more volatile electorate and media-centred communication processes, the ability to turn in a good media performance becomes more and more essential (Hvitfelt & Nord, 2000). It is thus impossible to think of a new political leader who does not possess considerable media skills. All today's top politicians are not only media talented, but are also professionally media-trained in order to feel comfortable with different types of media exposure. This professionalisation of politicians is not very controversial within the political parties, as it is often looked upon as a key to electoral success in a media-centred democracy.

A new but growing group of professionals is occupied with web activities such as campaigning and mobilising supporters on the net. Sweden is one of the countries in the world where the Internet is most developed (Norris 2000). Recent surveys show that about 70% of Swedish households have access to the Internet and use of the net is growing in all age groups, even if it is still young people who are the most frequent visitors to web sites (Nord, 2002).

But the Internet has not played any significant role in political mobilisation or in election campaigns. The pattern in Sweden is similar to many other EU countries where only a small group of politically interested citizens visit the party or the candidate web sites (Carlson & Djupsund, 2001; Nord, 2002). There are reasons to believe that the Internet will become more important in political communication in the future, as it has become in the US, but it still has to prove its capacity to mobilise new groups of citizens and renew democracy in countries such as Sweden.

A PROFESSIONALISATION 'LIGHT'?

The overall picture of changing communication practices in Sweden is thus mixed. Media is becoming more important both as an arena and an actor in the political communication process. As a reflection of partisan de-alignment, a volatile electorate and limited possibilities for direct communication, news management is more important than ever. All these facts should encourage a professionalisation and an increased marketing-orientation of the political parties.

Such changes are, as noted above, undoubtedly taking place within most political parties in Sweden. The transformation process is, however, rather slow and does not at all correspond to the dramatic changes taking place within the electorate and the media system. Some activities are centralised, more polls are used and more people are working with media and public relations, but parties still spend more resources on internal affairs than on voter mobilisation and opinion formation.

It is, however, reasonable to believe that changing practices will become more obvious in the not too distant future. Some political scientists have predicted that, if the recent development continues, the Swedish parties will run out of members around 2013 (Petersson et al., 2000). Whether this is a true prediction or not, sooner or later the parties will have to adapt more completely to a situation where media and voters are more important for survival than are members and supporters.

Of course, there have been significant international impacts on political communication in Sweden. In 1995 Sweden joined the European Union, and this 'Europeanisation' has of course, to some extent, been affecting public discourse, introducing a new political level in Sweden. But more important than the formal membership was perhaps a more gradual process beginning in the early 1990s when broadcast media was deregulated and newspapers became more independent and commercial. These media trends were definitely inspired by structural media changes in Europe (Hadenius, 1992). An internationalisation of political communication thus took place several years before Sweden became a member of the EU. The national media system now looks quite similar to a North/Central European standard, sometimes described as The Democratic Corporatist Model and characterised by external pluralism in the press and in broadcasting systems with substantial autonomy (Hallin & Mancini, 2004).

However, most communication practices are American in origin, and most political consultants in Sweden have visited the US during election times to learn more about marketing tools and media strategies. Occasionally, American experts have also played minor roles as advisers in Swedish election campaigns. Therefore, when it comes to single methods and practices, it is accurate to talk about an American influence in Swedish politics.

On the other hand, differences in the political systems, the media systems and the electorates actually oppose the thesis of 'Americanisation'. A multiparty-based, parliamentary democracy with a proportional electoral system and with strong traditions of public service media and partisan interests among citizens is not easily adaptable to American practices (Hallin & Mancini, 2004). The similarities that have appeared between Sweden and the US are thus probably better explained by a more general modernisation of communication practices taking place in all advanced democracies due to similar technological and sociological developments in each country (Swanson & Mancini, 1996; Negrine & Papathanassopoulos, 1996; Nord, 2001a).

It is reasonable to describe Sweden as a country where professionalisation of political communication has taken place, but a somewhat 'lighter' version has been adopted than in other comparable countries. The parties have more people working with communication issues than ever before and most modern practices in political marketing are used, especially during election campaigns. However, the parties are still characterised by a value-based or ideological organisational structure. The campaign party has not as yet replaced the party of ideas or the issue party, but all parties are gradually becoming more market-oriented and more professionalised. A similar party trend is also well documented in the neighbouring Nordic countries of Denmark and Norway (Heider & Svåsand, 1994; Jönsson & Larsen, 2002). An apposite term for this development is perhaps 'hybridisation', meaning a development in political communication where different national systems show both converging and diverging trends in communication practices (Plasser & Plasser, 2002).

There are several reasons why this process has not kept pace with current changes in domestic political culture and conditions of opinion formation:

First of all, Sweden has a multiparty political system and a basically proportional and party-based electoral system. Thus a possible global diffusion of American campaign and marketing techniques based upon a two party system and candidate-centred first-past-the-post electoral system is less likely to occur.

Secondly, the political parties still thrive on party platforms and action programmes in their campaign activities, while officially they are playing down political marketing practices because of the negative attitudes among party members. Most parties were founded as popular movements and this has probably encouraged a non-professional party 'self-image' in Swedish political culture. Political professionalisation in such political systems develops closer to party structure and environment (Mancini, 1999).

Thirdly, the special rules regarding televised politics exacerbates this situation. Usually, a great deal of professional competence is required in the production of political advertisements for TV and for party broadcasts. As these phenomena do not exist here, it reduces the need for professional skills in these fields, while on the other hand more experts on news management are required.

Fourthly, the traditional media structure in Sweden can still be described as 'politics-friendly'. Even if most newspapers are now more or less independent of political parties and there is a dualistic broadcast system, most of the national media still pays a great deal of attention to political affairs, particularly during the run up to an election. Polls, power plays and scandals are becoming more frequent news items, but much time and space is nevertheless spent on more serious political coverage (Strömbäck, 2004). It is worth noting that Swedish tabloids are much more serious than most of their European counterparts and the biggest commercial TV station is still operating under public service-like conditions. Media is free and operating on the market, but the political coverage is not basically market-oriented.

A DEMOCRATIC DILEMMA

As communication processes are decisive for politics in modern democracies, the conditions and characteristics of these processes thoroughly affects the quality of democracy (Swanson & Mancini 1996; Blumler & Kavanagh, 1999; Bennett & Entman, 2001). As the professionalisation of party politics increases, in terms of the number of marketing experts and the usage of new techniques in the parties, they will probably focus more on strategies for maximising voter support and media attention than keeping up with issue-orientation, ideology positioning and public concerns. The fact that party identification is declining and the electorate is becoming more volatile further endorses this development. Dramatic opinion shifts in voter support for political parties stresses the need for professional skills in evaluating public opinion when politics becomes more a question of survival than a question of substance.

The risk associated with the ongoing process of professionalisation is thus a further weakening of the position of political parties. Of course parties sometimes have to disappear if they become obsolete, but at the same time it is difficult to imagine a strong democracy completely without political parties, basing their legitimacy on the ability to articulate common interests in society, set the agenda, make coherent decisions and implement these decisions. If parties in the future are reduced to become only voting mobilisation organisations, then party-based democracy is surely at stake.

In another scenario, however, it can be argued that an increased ability to interpret and analyse public opinion could actually offer essential contributions to democracy. From a political marketing perspective, politics is always the result of public needs and existing preferences among citizens. Thus, political parties further adapting to such needs and priorities should have excellent prospects of becoming successful in terms of public support and in obtaining parliamentary seats. In this case marketing tools, news management and professional skills could be seen as a form of precision work which improves democracy.

Perhaps the most realistic scenario lies between these two extremes. It is more likely that professionalisation will neither kill existing parties nor give them unlimited success. Instead, it is reasonable to think that the professionalisation process poses considerable conflicts for the parties regarding their objectives: they can either become more professionalised and accept the new conditions for campaigning and opinion formation, or they can remain as a consolidating party organisation and balance internal interests within the party. In the first case, they risk party unity and coherence in politics. In the second case, voter support and political influence are in jeopardy.

This is probably why Swedish politicians and party officials have so far been afraid to declare their use of modern communication practices. They have to try to maintain a careful balance between the different interests of their parties. Everybody loves a winner, but while the winning strategies remain largely unacceptable within the domestic political culture, these modern practices sometimes have to be couched in traditional rhetoric.

This probably explains why the Swedish Prime Minister appears to be keener on counting smiles in the streets rather than looking at the percentages obtained in opinion polls in his analysis of public opinion.

REFERENCES

Asp, Kent (1986 *Mäktiga massmedier*. Stockholm: Akademilitteratur.

Asp, Kent & Peter Esaiasson (1996) The Modernization of Swedish Campaigns: Individualization, Professionalization and Medialization, In David L. Swanson & Paolo Mancini (eds *Politics, Media and Democracy – An International Study of Innovations in Electoral Campaigning and Their Consequences*. Westport: Praeger.

Bennett, W.L. & Robert M. Entman (2001) *Mediated Politics – Communication in the Future of Democracy*. Cambridge: Cambridge University Press.

Blumler, Jay & Dennis Kavanagh (1999) The Third Age of Political Communication: Influences and Features, *Political Communication*, 16, 3.

Carlson, Tom & Göran Djupsund (2001) Old Wine in New Bottles? The 1999 Finnish Election Campaign on the Internet, *The Harvard International Journal of Press/Politics*, Vol. 6, 1.

Dalton, Russell J. & Martin P. Wattenberg (2002) *Parties without Partisans – Political Change in Advanced Industrial Democracies*. Oxford: Oxford University Press.

Esaiasson, Peter & Nicklas Håkansson (2002) *Besked ikväll!* Stockholm: Stiftelsen Etermedierna.

Gibson, Rachel & Andrea Römmele (2001) Changing Campaign Communications: A Party-Centered Theory of Professionalized Campaigning, *The Harvard International Journal of Press/Politics*, 6: 4.

Hadenius, Stig (1992) Vulnerable Values in A Changing Political and Media System: The Case of Sweden, in Jay G. Blumler (ed) *Television and the Public Interest – Vulnerable Values in West European Broadcasting*. London: Sage.

Hadenius, Stig (1995) *Svensk politik under 1900–talet*. Stockholm: Tiden.

Hadenius, Stig (1998) *Kampen om monopolet – Sveriges radio och TV under 1900–talet*. Stockholm: Prisma.

Hallin, Daniel C. & Paolo Mancini (2004) *Comparing Media Systems – Three Models of Media and Politics*. Cambridge: Cambridge University Press.

Heidar, Knut & Lars Svaasand (1994) *Partierne i en brytningstid*. Bergen: Alma Mater.

Holmberg, Sören (2000) *Välja parti*. Stockholm: Norstedts.

Hvitfelt, Håkan (2002) En ny medievärld, in Håkan Hvitfelt & Gunnar Nygren,(eds) *På väg mot medievärlden 2020*. Lund: Studentlitteratur.

Hvitfelt, Håkan & Lars Nord (2000) Sådana politiker vill folket ha, in Håkan Hvitfelt & Karvonen, Lauri (eds) *Nygamla opinioner*, Sundsvall: Demokratiinstitutet.

Jönsson, Rasmus & Ole Larsen (2002) *Professionel politisk kommunikation – en stuide av 20 dages valgkamp*. Köpenhamn: Akademisk Forlag.

Lilleker, Darren G. & Ralph Negrine (2002) Professionalization: Of What? Since When? By Whom? *The Harvard International Journal of Press/Politics*, 7: 4.

Mancini, Paolo (1999) New Frontiers in Political Professionalism, *Political Communication*, 16: 3.

Mazzoleni, Gianpietro & Winfried Schulz (1999) 'Mediatization' of Politics: A Challenge for Democracy? *Political Communication*, 16: 3.

Negrine, Ralph & Stylianos Papathanassopoulos (1996) The 'Americanization' of Political Communication: A Critique, *The Harvard International Journal of Press/Politics*, 1:2.

Nord, Lars W. (2001a) Americanization v. the Middle Way: New Trends in Swedish Political Communication, *The Harvard International Journal of Press/Politics*, 6:2.

Nord, Lars W. (2001b) *Vår tids ledare*. Stockholm: Carlssons.

Nord, Lars W. (2002) *IT och demokrati*. Lund: Studentlitteratur.

Nord, Lars W. & Jesper Strömbäck (2003) *Valfeber och nyhetsfrossa – politisk kommunikation i valrörelsen 2002*. Stockholm: Sellin.

Nord, Lars W. (2004) *Hur professionella är de svenska partierna?* Sundsvall: Demokratiinstitutet.

Norris, Pippa (2000) *A Virtuous Circle: Political Communications in Postindustrial Societies*. Cambridge: Cambridge University Press.

Petersson, Olof & Sören Holmberg (1998) *Opinionsmätningarna och demokratin*. Stockholm: SNS.

Petersson, Olof, Gudmund Hernes, Sören Holmberg, Lise Togeby & Lena Wängnerud (2000) *Demokrati utan partier?* Stockholm: SNS.

Pfetsch, Barbara (2001) Political Communication Culture in the United States and Germany. *The Harvard International Journal of Press/Politics*, 6: 1.

Pharr, Susan J., Robert D. Putnam & Russell J. Dalton (2000) Trouble in the Advanced Democracies? *Journal of Democracy*, 11: 2.

Plasser, Fritz & Gunda Plasser (2002) *Global Political Campaigning – A Worldwide Analysis of Campaign Professionals and Their Practices*. Westport: Praeger.

Schulz, Winfried (2001) Changes in the Mass Media and the Public Sphere, in Slavko Splichal (ed) *Public Opinion and Democracy – Vox Populi – Vox Dei?* Cresskill, NJ: Hampton Press.

Strömbäck, Jesper (2001) *Gäster hos verkligheten*. Stehag: Symposion.

Strömbäck, Jesper (2002) *Medialiserat politiskt ledarskap*, Stockholm: Institutet för Mediestudier.

Strömbäck, Jesper (2004) *Den medialiserade demokratin*. Stockholm: SNS.

Swanson, David L. & Dan Nimmo (1990) *New Directions in Political Communication*. Newsbury Park: Sage.

Swanson, David L. & Paolo Mancini (1996) Politics, Media and Modern Democracy: Introduction, in David L. Swanson & Paolo Mancini (eds) *Politics, Media and Democracy – An International Study of Innovations in Electoral Campaigning and Their Consequences*. Westport: Praeger.

The Professionalisation of Political Communication

6

From Accommodation to Professionalisation? The Changing Culture and Environment of Dutch Political Communication

Kees Brants and Philip van Praag[1]

Every country has its own examples of how its government successfully or dismally handled a crisis that prominently featured in the media. In spite of its long held image of consensual politics and Lowland dullness, the Netherlands is no different. In 2001 and 2002, for example, the issue of drug trafficking from the West Indian ex-colonies of Aruba and Curacao, the scale of which was well known to both police and Ministry of Justice, suddenly exploded in public. It was not so much the issue of drugs, but the authorities' way of dealing with this particular problem that appears to have aroused the ire of some opposition politicians and the media. In order to avoid case overload of police and prosecution, those caught smuggling cocaine (often by swallowing drug-stuffed condoms) at Schiphol Airport, simply had the goods impounded and were then sent back again. The media, well informed by unnamed immigration sources, framed the news as a failure of law-enforcement. The resulting public debate forced an irritated minister, against his will and better judgement, to introduce stricter rules and more severe penalties. The subsequent overload of courts and jails not only prompted protest by judicial and prison authorities, but also resulted two years later in a return to the send-back policy.

This story seems to indicate, or at least to hint at, a number of issues. Firstly, that decision makers sometimes feel that media frames, with their specific problem definition, assumed cause and dramatised effect, forces them to act at a time and in ways which are not of their own choosing. Secondly, that there is a substantial mistrust between political and media actors. From a more symbiotic relationship of mutual dependency and understanding, politicians now blame the media for hyping and sensationalising complex social issues while the media can barely hide their irritation over the ways governments try to control the news output in order to reduce uncertainty about media publications and control possible image damage. Thirdly, providing information and managing news has become an art in itself, and more than that, a profession with many practitioners. Information officers, media strategists and political advisors now surround the minister, the party leader, the political elite, watching over what they say, how they say it and where. Fourthly, next to the institutionalisation of political news management, the means of reducing uncertainty and managing the news also take different forms. Apart from overt formats of interaction, like press conferences, releases and briefings, there is a more or less covert form in which off-the-record briefing, spin doctoring and leaking are used to get a story across, to frame an occurrence or a person in specific ways and to influence journalists as to their choice of news selection, news values and news angle.

All this seems to indicate a trend towards stricter control of political communication, in the Netherlands as elsewhere, from a traditional relationship of mutual understanding and respect to one of professionalisation and mistrust. The question is, however, to what extent such claims are actually corroborated by empirical evidence – a question this chapter tries to answer by sketching the recent changes in and between media, and in political news management. And if there is a trend, how one would evaluate the characteristics and effects of this new political communication culture.

CHANGES IN THE POLITICAL COMMUNICATION ENVIRONMENT
The Netherlands has always been renowned for its specific form of consociational democracy. 'Pillarisation', accommodation and pacification were the labels for an arrangement of peaceful co-existence between disparate groups within a vertically segmented society, living apart together in potentially conflictual 'pillars' based on religion or ideology.[2] Though each of these 'pillars' had their own separate associations (ranging from trade unions to the school system), as well as media and political parties, the elites of the different pillars pacified and accommodated potential conflict through often secret and usually invisible negotiation and compromise. The result was consensus and paternalism at the top, and tolerance, or rather, acceptance of each other's culture at the bottom (cf. Lijphart, 1975). For a long time, the media were contained in, and reinforced, this pillarised structure through a system of interlocking directorships. They performed within a *partisan logic*, whereby government and political parties set the agenda and the media, as lapdogs, functioned as a platform for the political elite, merely communicating their opinions and decisions to the rank and file of the pillars. Through this symbiotic, though somewhat one-sided partisan relationship, they created an almost closed political communication system.

As such, pillarisation as a social and political system did not survive the roaring Sixties. Though it still resonates in the consensual and pragmatic political culture of 'poulder politics', loyalty within the pillars, obedience towards the political elite, the culture of secrecy and the inherent paternalism all came under pressure. In the following decades, the landscape of politics, media and the populace changed substantially. The electorate, leaving the Catholic and Protestant churches in droves, began to float, switching in the first instance from the party of their own pillar to others of similar persuasion. The self-evidence of the righteousness of the political elite was rocked. The media severed their direct links with political parties and distanced themselves from the intimate symbiosis and dependency these entailed. The partisan logic was replaced by a *public logic* in which the media still very much respected decision makers and parties as the actors setting the political agenda, but from a more critical distance and without closely identifying with them. In a public logic the media appear as watchdogs, performing in the public interest and from a sense of responsibility for the well being of the political system and the democratic process.

Since the end of the 1980s, several dramatic changes in politics, media and the public have left their traces on the form and style of political communication. Firstly, in the domain of politics. With the disappearance of ideology and religion as the dominant indicator of party policy, differences in stance or policy solutions became blurred. The number of floating voters grew at every election and, especially at second order elections, the number who turned-off completely increased as well. Party membership fell to one of the lowest in Europe (Mair & Van Biezen, 2001), but at the same time, membership of single-issue movements, albeit often in the form of 'check book activism', grew to one of the highest in Europe (Sociaal en Culturel Planbureau, 2000). The rise and sudden death of populist politician Pim Fortuyn, nine days before the 2002 elections, had an even more dramatic effect on the existing political communication culture. His naming and blaming of immigration policies, the anti-establishment sentiments he professed in his debates with other politicians and with the media elite, his alignment with the assumed plight of the ordinary people, made him an instant, though controversial, success and a regular guest in talk and current affairs shows. Through the magnifying glass of television his adversarial tone, style and culture, that until then was considered anathema in the Netherlands, gained momentum and further popularised anti-political cynicism.

The changes in the media are characterised by concentration, commercialisation and competition. The newspaper press was hit by waves of mergers, resulting in three publishers owning 90% of the market today, one of them being a UK financial investor, and in the number of independent dailies falling from more than sixty after the Second World War to just under thirty in 2004. With 'de-reading' and competition from television, the press is in dire straights and anxiously looking for new, and especially young, audiences. Television, where the pillarised structure continued to exist though the political 'colouring' disappeared, saw the introduction, in 1989, of commercial television. The number of national commercial stations quickly grew to six, drastically fragmenting the broadcasting landscape that already knew three national public and dozens of regional and local television channels. The result was not only a growth in the entertainment and infotainment offered, but also, in absolute terms, an increase of informative programmes: commercial channels need news shows for reasons of competition and 'brand image', reaching a sizeable or target group audience. The development from a supply market, in which media producers decide what is relevant, to a demand market dominated by what the public is interested in, also led to a fragmentation and loss of audiences, a dramatic effect in a commercialised market where high ratings are both paramount and rare. This had political consequences too: to reach the same size audience as in the mid 1980s a politician had to appear in as many programmes and channels as was physically possible. Finally, competition leads to forms of 'pack' journalism – covering what the others cover, interviewing who the others interview – as well as a search for scoops and originality – covering what the other don't yet have.

The changes in relations between the media and the public are closely linked to and have their effect on those of politics and media, and the relation between the two. The de-pillarisation resulted in a strengthening process of individualisation, with a further declining belief in values inspired by religion or ideology and increasing consumerist behaviour, also *vis-à-vis* politics. 'What's in it for me?' became a key question at the ballot box or when evaluating politics and policies. At the same time, the interest in party and governmental politics is waning, especially among the young. With the remote control in their hand, they zap along the more informative programmes and, more preoccupied by style, image, presentation and taste, they search for pleasure and the icons of the entertainment world.

The media-led and 'mediatised' changes in political communication in the Netherlands, a concentration and commercialisation driven more from a supply to a demand market in the media, and a growing cynicism in the relationship between media and politics and between politics and the public, inspired a shift towards a *media logic*. Different from the partisan and the public logic, the kind and content of news reporting are in this logic decided by the frame of reference in which the media make sense of, interpret and frame issues and people. The media identify less with the public interest and more with what the public is interested in, that is to say, with what they assume the public deems important and enjoyable. They set the political agenda and with it, politics becomes dependent on the functioning, the production routines and the news values of the media.

In the US-inspired discussion about this media logic, political journalism is said to profess a more interpretative, framing style of journalism, manifesting itself in a focus on conflict and scandal, on *horse race* news and *strategic game* frames, and in the centrality of cynical journalists in media reporting, leaving the politician with just enough room for a *soundbite*. The result of this style of journalism is said to be a growing cynicism among the populace versus politics and, in the end, versus the media as well (Cappella & Jamieson, 1997; Patterson, 1993). In our analysis of political reporting in the Dutch elections since 1994 we see clear indications of such interpretative journalism; not as dramatic, however, as is claimed for the US and lacking the effects on the public's attitudes (Van Praag & Brants, 2000; Brants & Van Praag, 2005). A conflict focus exists but it is not structural or dominant. The growing competition for audiences and juicy stories lead to the unearthing of more scandals and more publicity about them. Moreover, they are often framed as a failure of government control and structural 'deficiencies', forcing authorities to respond and live up to this new *media logic*.

MANAGING GOVERNMENT INFORMATION
Development and state of the art
The internal and sometimes heated discussion about and strategy of the government's public relation and communication policy is not new. Shortly after World War II it was inspired by the anxiety German propaganda had invoked. No government wanted to be (seen to be) associated with influencing the attitudes and behaviour of its citizens. Communication had to be neutral and limited to informing, explaining and elucidating those policies that had been accepted by Parliament. Moreover, providing information had to be reactive and not initiated by government. In such passive circumstances, the number of information officers per ministry could be counted on the fingers of one hand.

The spirit of change at the end of the 1960s resulted in a change from a passive to a more active policy of making things public, based on the principle of the people's right to know, and legally guaranteed by a Public Information Law (proposed in 1970 and introduced ten years later). Typical for this shift in political culture was the novelty in 1970 of a weekly press conference by the prime minister, followed by a television interview in the evening. The transition in this period from a 'pillar-controlled' partisan logic to a public logic more or less forced the government to extend and professionalise its information provision. Every ministry got its own central information and communication directorate; in 1983 with a total number of 861 full time jobs, which eight years later had risen to 1026 FTE (full time equivalent). Because of budget cuts and socio-political critique of the number of government information campaigns, the increase stagnated in the early 1990s. In 2003 the total number of ministerial PR jobs was 944 FTE (see table 1), which is around 2.5% of the total number of civil servants. It should be noted, however, that outside these numbers there is a hidden, and often substantial, number of information officers working directly for the policy and not for the information department. The ministry of Agriculture, for example, has another 40 FTE outside its information directorate (Berenschot, 2003).

The majority of the civil servants are employed to inform the public, with a growing number focusing especially on digital forms of communication. Informing the press is

Table 1. Ministerial information and communication personnel (in FTE)

Ministry	Total Employment	… of which … are press information officers
Foreign affairs	64.5	11
Justice	52	11.5
Interior	44.5	11
Education & culture	62	11
Finance	59	14
Defence	50	24
Housing & environment	80	12
Transport	71	17
Economic Affairs	77.5	17.5
Agriculture & nature	33	12
Social affairs	113	22.5
Health	57.5	11
Prime minister	180	12

The figures for press information are indicative, as they are classified differently by different ministries. *Source:* Berenschot, 2003

done by a minority, around 20% of the total workforce. The ministry of Defence stands out with around 50% involved in informing the press. In the last decade, the level of education has been increasing: with an average age of forty one, 40% is academically schooled and another 50% has some other form of higher education (Neijens, 2002, p. 285). The situation among journalists is comparable, with slightly more having university degrees.

The most important directorate is that of the prime minister, the National Communication and Information Service RVD (Rijksvoorlichtingsdienst). All information coming from the government, the royal household and – particularly important in the Netherlands – the press information during the formation of coalition cabinets, falls under the responsibility of the RVD. The director general is also chair of the Information Council, where the directors of the different ministerial directorates meet regularly to coordinate their policy. The coordinating function of the RVD has recently become more important, with a subsequent decline in the policy space of the ministries.

Establishing communication as an integrated part of policy making seems to succeed reasonably well at the top management level. Intensive cooperation and consultation between politicians, senior civil servants, strategic advisors and senior information officers has become the rule, often on a daily basis. But at the middle and lower levels of

The Professionalisation of Political Communication

the ministries, 'thinking in communication terms' is still far away. There, communication advisors are called in when policy has to be implemented and not at the time of strategic choices or in long term policy development. Where directors want a more pro-active information policy, the shop floor is still left in the dark.

From post-informing to pre-spinning

The growing importance of information and communication and the necessity felt to convince the public of the need for specific policies has prompted a changing role perception among the profession. Already in the early 1980s there was a fierce debate between the so-called *stricts* and *stretched*. The former saw their role as limited to informing, explaining and elucidating policy accepted by parliament. Influencing and persuading was considered dubious and should be restricted to those cases where a broad political and social consensus existed, as in the case of an anti-discrimination campaign, for example. The *stretched* held that once policy was accepted, all modern means of advertising and public relations should be allowed to explain that policy and to gain support for it.

Since that debate, influencing behaviour with persuasive communication has been accepted by both government and parliament. And though the *jargon* would not be used, government communication has moved from pure information-providing and more towards public relations, with minor restrictions, such as that the policy should be accepted, the issue not politically contested and that the communication should contain enough factual information to allow for independent judgement by the public. In reality, however, hard criteria are difficult to define or to uphold and persuasive government campaigns keep on stirring up debate: the campaigns are said to be too paternalistic, too moralistic and there are too many of them. The discussion took an even harder tone when, in the 1990s, it turned out that several ministries had been subsidising television programmes in order to realise or to explain their policy aims (e.g. to uphold certain traffic rules) or to influence public attitudes (e.g. improving the image of voluntary work for the army). After a public debate this covert form of informing the public and avoiding media scrutiny has been restricted.

A second, more recent, discussion took place about the question whether information should be limited to policy accepted by parliament or whether the government could also inform about (and thus possibly gain support for) policies that were still on the parliamentary drawing board. Traditionally, responsibility for discussing yet-to-be accepted policy rests with political parties, but of late they have lost prominence and have a hard time playing a dominant role in public debate. Moreover, as part of an increasing media logic, the media are more inclined to frame issues at an early phase and in ways not always in accordance with the government's focus. Press officers have shown their anger when oppositional interest groups and sympathising media started an offensive, jeopardising a certain government proposal. When a specific minister proposed a public counter-offensive, as in the case of a national congestion tax, it was met with severe criticism. At the moment standing policy is that public information campaigns for yet-to-be accepted policy are allowed, provided it is made clear where it stands in the policy process and that the importance of the issue and the intensity of the debate merit the means of an information campaign.

In communicating with the press, the division between accepted and yet-to-be accepted policy is fairly blurred, especially regarding the informal contacts with journalists. The professional role perception here differs between the practitioners, but many an information officer actively engages in framing and influencing the media agenda. Research among the thirteen departmental communication directors indicates, however, that there is little sympathy for the strong political interpretation prevalent among Anglo-Saxon 'spin doctors'. They see themselves first and foremost as ministerial advisors; only very few consider themselves primarily as communication strategists, selectively informing and, if need be, manipulating journalists (Smits, 2001, p. 327). Though spin doctoring is an issue discussed enthusiastically by political journalists (and more hesitantly by politicians), this covert form of political communication has hardly led to the same public debate as we have seen with the more overtly persuasive public campaigns.

Transparency and access
Though free publicity is still considered more important than paid publicity in most forms of political communication, the political decision makers have not been sitting back passively while the logic changed from partisan to media. Already in 1998, Prime Minister Wim Kok advocated a stronger collaboration between ministries, in order to 'soon enough sense upcoming waves of publicity and to come up with an adequate and early response' (Bakker & Scholten, 2004). While a state commission in 2001 implicitly chose a media bypass strategy by focusing more on the Internet as an alternative channel for reaching the audience (Wallage, 2001), two years later another advisory commission had been caught up by a media-logic inspired, sombre mood and propagated a stronger professionalisation of government communication, the setting up of its own newspaper, buying air time, and more image-focused personalisation in party political communication (ROB 2003, pp. 44ff). The government, however, does not intend to go this far.

At the same time, it begins to emphasise the importance of new media as instruments in informing and involving the public. The Internet especially is used for this. All ministries cooperate with the RVD in the central government site, www.regering.nl. Each of them also have their own web site and editorial board, usually allowing a limited form of interaction (consultation or response) and sometimes a more extensive form of virtual deliberation. Most ministries, however, do not yet know how to adequately deal with and respond to digitally active citizens.

One way or the other, governments and ministries do take stock of and respond to public and publicised opinion. As to the first, the RVD has introduced a public sensitivity monitor (*Belevingsmonitor*), a barometer measuring the public perception of and (positive or negative) excitement about support for issues and policies. There were high expectations about these 'ears and eyes' at their introduction in 2003, but the frequency of measurements has recently been lowered; both for budgetary reasons and because, as one minister said in passing: 'we are not masochists who every week want to be confronted with our lack of popularity'. As to the sensitivity and openness towards the publicised opinion of the media, all ministries and their press informers and spokespersons are accessible around the clock. This accessibility is more reactive, though, since a pro-active policy outside office hours is a rarity. Most departments also actively monitor the media, though only two departments perform a regular and systematic media analysis; research by the ministries is minimal anyway and if so, contracted out to commercial or university researchers. Again, research is one of the first victims when budgetary cuts take place.

MANAGING ELECTION CAMPAIGNS

Professionalisation of managing public information by the political parties is much slower in establishing itself. Since the 1960s the parties have realised the importance of television, but adjusting to the television age is another matter. Limited financial means is a considerable hindrance here. Though in the 1970s state subsidies had been introduced, it has hardly compensated for the gradual and, in all, dramatic decline in party membership. At the beginning of the 1990s, the three largest parties (Christian Democratic CDA, social democratic PvdA and liberal-conservative VVD) relied on membership dues for some 60% of their total income. State subsidies contributed about 20% and another 20% was collected by fund raising activities among the rank and file of the party and 'party taxes' on the salaries of politicians (Koole, 1994, p. 289).

Even those larger parties have had modest party offices, due to lack of funding. If the size of the salaried staff is taken as a criterion, 'the extra-parliamentary organization of Dutch political parties has scarcely become more professionalized since the early sixties' (Koole, 1994, p. 290). Party offices have even fewer staff than before, though to some extent the loss there is compensated by a rapid gain in the size of the parliamentary party staff. We see that same shift with the information and communication activities, which have moved from the party office to the parliamentary party organisation.

Election campaigns in the Netherlands have traditionally been one of the cheapest in the democratic world, partly because, until very recently, donations from business hardly existed at the national level. For the last few years the VVD has organised fundraising dinners with politicians, but the financial result of some 15,000 euros is merely 'peanuts'. According to newspaper reports, Pim Fortuyn's LPF received some 1.4 million euros from rich businessmen during the election campaign of 2003, but this was not confirmed by the party. Except for rules of transparency about gifts received, which were introduced in the mid 1990s, guidelines as to what is and what is not allowed in party sponsoring do not exist. On the other hand, following the Fortuyn turmoil, state subsidy for political parties was raised some 50%, to 15 million euros, in 2004.

In spite of an increase in the last ten years, campaign expenditure is still limited. The nine parties represented in parliament spent just over 7.8 million euros in the 2002 elections, with the social democrats in the lead with a mere 1.5 million. Since the 1989 elections they have almost tripled their expenditure. The 2002 elections saw an increase of two million euros compared to 1998, but just over half a euro per voter is considerably less than political parties spend in other European countries. In the short campaign of 2003, after the conservative Cabinet fell following internal rows with the ministers of the Lijst Pim Fortuyn, the budget of the parties dropped to 6.6 million euros.

A semi-amateur status
The level of professionalisation of the parties' campaign communication, which is thus restricted by the level of financial maneuverability, can be judged by several characteristics (Van Praag, 2000). Firstly, by the *centralisation of the campaign* and the employment of professional staff, which show a slow but gradual change. Together with the partly leader, the parliamentary party is increasingly getting a stronger say in the running of the campaign, while the party board and the rank and file are more and more sidelined. This modernisation is, however, only slightly reflected in the level of professionalisation of the campaign staff. Certainly with the smaller parties, but even with the big four, we normally find few outside experts on the payroll during elections. The campaign leader, usually a party man, is hired for the duration of the campaign, advertising is outsourced, spin doctors are still a rare breed and normally a spin-off from the party's information department, and, for media training of party leader and main candidates, a former journalist may be temporarily employed. Recently, we do see in campaigns political leaders surrounding themselves with a few trusted professionals, who have a strong say in the strategy. With declining numbers of party members, a labour-intensive campaign is no longer possible and a capital-intensive alternative beyond their means. After the 2003 elections, evaluation commissions of CDA and VVD concluded that professionalisation of their campaigns in the future would be desirable, but the limited budgets so far hinder their wishes becoming realities.

Secondly, *electoral research* is beginning to escape its amateur-like status, with the use of bench marking, strength-weakness analyses, voter-volatility testing, slogans, leader image and locating electoral target groups. Research is, however, hardly translated into campaign strategies and mostly conducted well in advance of the elections. Only the PvdA, influenced by the 1992 Clinton campaign, employs an electoral researcher since the 1994 campaign and spends about 15% of its campaign budget on research; other parties commission polling bureaus, but only on a limited scale. The Social Democrats were also the first to introduce focus groups in 1994 and to establish a long-term research strategy. In 1998 the party introduced a marketing concept in its campaign, locating and targeting voters as political consumers. With market and focus group research they tested their campaign slogan 'Strong and Social'. The other parties still use a selling or persuasion concept, aimed at convincing voters of the qualities of the party's policies and politicians.

Thirdly, *paid publicity* is considered a must in an increasing media logic, but hardly an option in light of the limited financial space of political parties in the Netherlands. In times of partisan and public logic, access to free publicity was almost limitless and while journalists might be critical, parties felt they could get their story across. That has changed. The introduction of commercial television has altered the landscape of television, fragmented the audience and partly dramatised and sensationalised the style of political television. Journalists are more conflict- and scandal- oriented, and more inclined to set the political agenda themselves. To control publicity through paid means is only a marginal option, however. Allocation of free air time to all parties participating in the elections has existed since 1959, but the audience ratings have dwindled from 40% to a mere 1 or 2%; this form of political communication has always been considered an electoral sideline. Since 1998, paid political advertising on both public and commercial channels is allowed, at the cost of the traditional newspaper advertisements. In 2002 and 2003, all parties had some paid TV advertising, including even the orthodox reformed Christian Union. Parties are now reserving some 40% of their campaign budget for party spots, but this is still far less than a professional ad campaign would need.

Fourthly, the use of *information and communication technologies*, as another form of controlled publicity, has become part and parcel of the Dutch election campaign since 2002 (Voerman & Boogers, 2005). Since the 1998 elections, the number of hits has increased fifteen fold, to 1.5 million users, while 30% of the electorate claim to regularly visit party web sites. Even the party manifestos, which used to be ignored by voters when only available in printed versions, have now become popular objects for downloading. Every party and each party leader now has its own site – with mostly volunteers doing the work – informing about policies, ideas, as well as the schedule of the party leaders' visits. More and more, ICT is also being used to personalise communication: hesitantly some politicians have started web logs (notably the VVD leader Zalm, who is also Minister of Finance), but more informative personalised sites by lower-placed candidates have become commonplace. In the US, the internet has become an important tool in fundraising, but in the Netherlands the primary function is to inform the rank and file and hopefully to convince visiting floating voters. The Christian democratic CDA used a special intranet in 2003 to coordinate and streamline the communication of all candidates.

Finally, a well considered *publicity strategy* characterises a modern, professional campaign. The larger parties nowadays seriously consider media strategies, but the means are limited again. Most parties monitor media during campaigns, tracking how the party and the leader are doing in public opinion, and they begin employing forms of news management, and use data from media monitoring to adjust their campaign strategies. Very few information officers, however, consider themselves 'spin doctors'; most of them publicly loathe the concept, but they all try it regularly, one way or the other, if only to counter interpretative frames coming from the media. There are enough examples of successful and failed attempts, but systematic research as to its saliency and success does not exist. Press officers and semi-spin doctors often come from the ranks of journalists and use their good relationship with them, but their framing strategies might be hindered by the competitive media and party environment, and the lack of negative campaigning. The short adversarial eruption during 'the year of Fortuyn' seems to have been more an exception than a new rule.

CONCLUSIONS

With the government and, up to a point, with political parties we notice an increasing professionalisation of political communication since the end of pillarisation, accommodation and media's partisan logic. Indications are to be found in the growing number of people employed in communication and with providing information to both the public and the press, and in their higher educational level. The difference between government and parties, however, is that the former, since the 1970s, has had the means to invest in the necessary apparatus, while the latter were confronted with declining membership and stagnating funds.

Professionalisation of government communication is thus further ahead than that of political parties. For the former, it is not the financial means that limit its expansion, but the professional ethics of the (older?) generations of information officers. Even now, the majority of directors of communication object to the Anglo-Saxon style of influencing the press. Political parties, on the other hand, follow the developments in the US with intense interest. During every presidential campaign, Dutch campaign managers travel to the US to see and study the Republican and Democratic strategies at close range. In the last couple of years the contacts between the Dutch and the UK Labour party has also intensified. But all this does not allow for talk of an (Anglo-) Americanisation of Dutch political communication; at best it is a curious learning, but more like a slow process of modernisation (cf. Swanson & Mancini, 1996). Most Dutch campaign professionals are aware that a consensual Dutch political culture hardly accommodates a face-value adoption of a more adversarial US and UK campaign practice. In spite of Fortuyn's tone and style in 2002, negative campaigning and attack ads are still – judging from the 2003 campaign – not done.

A beginning of centralisation is another feature observable in both government and political parties. At first there was a streamlining within the ministries, but in the last ten years coordination between the ministries has become more important, strongly propagated, and influenced by the national communication and information service,

RVD. The same picture emerges from political parties. At party headquarters a team leads the campaign, while strategic decisions are taken more and more by the party leader together with a few trusted insiders; rapid response and one single voice are paramount.

Both within and outside politics, its mediation has been criticised for threatening the quality of Dutch democracy. There is little empirical evidence that interpretative journalism is affecting the attitudes of large groups in society. The tone of political reporting is hardly cynical, certainly not compared to the US. Moreover, there are no indications of a causal relationship between changes in the style of political reporting – towards commercially driven media logic – and the (minimal) increase in political cynicism in the Netherlands in the last few years. In general, the level of trust in institutions like parliament, political parties, the police, etc. is higher than in most other comparable countries.

Media logic has influenced the behaviour of politicians, especially party politicians. It is particularly they who are sensitive to incidents, disclosures and assumed scandals highlighted by the media. It does contribute to politics' racy image, but this is hardly a threat to democracy.

Notes

1. The authors are senior fellows at the Amsterdam School of Communications Research of the University of Amsterdam. Kees Brants also holds the chair of Political Communication at Leiden University.
2. The most important were the catholic, protestant and socialist pillars, and a more loosely structured liberal-conservative sphere.

References

Bakker, P. & O. Scholten (2004) *Communicatiekaart van Nederland* [The communication map of the Netherlands]. Alphen aan den Rijn: Samson.

Berenschot (2003) *Nulmeting: structuur en werkwijze directies communicatie* [The organisation of communication directorates]. Utrecht.

Brants, K. & P. van Praag (eds) (forthcoming) *Een lang en turbulent jaar. Politieke communicatie in de verkiezingen van 2002 en 2003* [A long and turbulent year. Political communication in the 2002 and 2003 elections]. Amsterdam: Het Spinhuis.

Cappella, J. & K. Hall Jamieson (1997) *Spiral of Cynicism: the press and the public good.* New York: Oxford University Press.

Koole, R.A. (1994) 'The vulnerability of the modern cadre party in the Netherlands'. pp. 278–303 in: R.S. Katz & P. Mair (eds) *How parties organize 'Change and Adaption' in Party Organizations in Western Democracies.* London: Sage.

Lijphart, A. (1975) *The Politics of Accommodation: Pluralism and democracy in the Netherlands.* Berkeley: University of California Press.

Mair, P. & I. van Biezen (2001) 'Party membership in Twenty European Democracies', *Party Politics,* 7:1, pp. 5–21.

Neijens, P. (2002) 'Actieve communicatie over niet-aanvaard beleid: de kloof tussen overheidscommunicatie en journalistiek' [Active communication about yet-to-be accepted policy], *Tijdschrift voor Communicatiewetenschap*, 30:4, pp. 279–294.

Patterson,T. (1993) *Out of Order.* New York: Vintage Press.

ROB (2003) *Politiek en Media: Pleidooi voor een LAT-Relatie* [Politics and Media: Playdoyer for a LAT-Relation]. Den Haag: Raad voor het Openbaar Bestuur.

Smits J.H. (2001) 'Spindoctors aan het Binnenhof? Over rolopvatting van directeuren Voorlichting bij de Rijksoverheid' [Spindoctors in Dutch politics? The role perceptions of government information directors] *Bestuurskunde*, 10:7, pp. 320–329.

Sociaal en Culturel Planbureau (2000), Sociaal en Culturel Rapport 2000, Nederland in Europa. [Social and Cultural Report 2000. The Netherlands in Europe] Den Haag.

Swanson, D. and P. Mancini (eds) (1996) *Politics, Media, and Modern Democracy.* Westport, CT: Praeger

Van Praag, P. (2000) 'De professionalisering van campagnes: vastberaden maar met mate' [Professionalization of campaigns: stern but within limits], pp. 16–36 in: P. van Praag & K. Brants (eds) *Tussen beeld en inhoud. Politiek en media in de verkiezingen van 1998* [Between image and content. Politics and media in the 1998 elections]. Amsterdam: Het Spnhuis.

Van Praag, P. & K. Brants (eds) (2000), *Tussen Beeld en Inhoud. Politiek en media in de verkiezingen van 1998.* [Between image and content. Politics and media in the 1998 elections] Amsterdam: Het Spinhuis.

Voerman, G. & M. Boogers (2005) 'De opkomst van de website als campagne-instrument' [The rise of websites as campaign instrument], in: K. Brants & P. van Praag (eds) op.cit. Amsterdam: Het Spinhuis.

Wallage, J. (2001) *In dienst van de democratie* [At democracy's service]. Den Haag: Commissie Toekomst Overheidscommunicatie.

7

POLITICAL PROFESSIONALISM IN ITALY

Paolo Mancini

OLD AND NEW POLITICAL PROFESSIONALISM IN ITALY

There has been an abundance of political professionalism, in the Weberian sense, in Italy for years. It was inextricably linked with the mass political parties that were so important in this country up to a very few years ago. They were able to survive throughout recent Italian history, including during the Fascist dictatorship, thanks to the existence of a very high number of party bureaucrats who represented their backbone. Both the Christian Democrat party and the Communist party (together with smaller parties such as Partito Socialista or the right-wing party Movimento Sociale) took their strength and their capacity to affect many different parts of Italian society from the everyday work of thousands of party employees who, to use Weber's words 'were living for politics and from politics': their main skill was politics itself. They understood perfectly the party apparatus, and very often they were at the top of a network of interpersonal communications that allowed them to control the party decision making process and the gathering of consensus in support of party policies. Their role as agents of socialisation and 'living beings' in the processes of communication was essential to the party: they spread the voice of the party, they were used to find new members and to identify those who were already persuaded. They were the quintessential identification of what Farrel calls the 'labour intensive campaign' (Farrel, 1996), that is a campaign, and therefore a political debate and struggle, organised thanks to either the free or paid support of thousands and thousands of party activists. In his own work on party bureaucrats, Mastropaolo, who has adopted Weber's insights, has argued that their main function was that of 'mobilisation', that is: spreading consensus, looking for public support, advocacy in favour of particular ideological ends, and social and economical interests. (Mastropaolo, 1986).

In many cases, and at a certain point in their career, party bureaucrats could also assume a position in community government (both at the level of central government and decentralised local communities, or linked positions) so starting a new career in government that could last for their entire life as they moved from one position to another. In such cases, they were fulfilling an 'administration function' (Mastropaolo, 1986). In this new position, their role as agents of communication became less important, as they were now required to have good skills in government, in running the government apparatuses, in decision making processes. In other words, their formal and informal roles in Italian politics were a laboratory for these individuals, mainly because of the strength of the party apparatuses and their diffusion and capacity to permeate every sphere of society.

Thanks to the existence of party bureaucrats (together with a large number of activists), mass parties developed up to the beginning of the Fascist period and were able to survive the experience of Fascism, and play a very important role in the Resistance and in reestablishing democracy at the end of the Second World War. As their importance increased, so did their numbers.

In recent years, this kind of political professionalism has become much less important for a number of different reasons. The decline of party bureaucrats, which started in the 1980s, has accelerated with the appearance of Berlusconi in the political arena, as he identified more general changes that were taking place in society and that were affecting the position and the role of party bureaucrats. First of all, the dramatic transformations (secularisation, the disappearance of the previous social and economical cleavages) that affected most Western democracies (Panebianco, 1988), have led to the progressive weakening of the traditional mass parties and therefore of their communication apparatus, based on the work of party bureaucrats and activists. The links between political parties and citizens have weakened, so that the latter no longer depend on the former for their information, their beliefs and values. The influence of political parties over society has also diminished and, in the same way, their organisations have weakened to the point of no longer being able to employ as large a number of workers as they had done in the past, or to support the candidates running for a position. The decrease in party membership is the best indicator of this evolution. Two examples well illustrate this: In 1955, the PCI had 2,090,006 paid up members, in 1995 the figure was 682.290; in 1955, the DC had 1,186,785 members but in 1995 only 160,000.[1] As mass parties have decreased their role in society, mass communication has become the main agency of political socialisation.

Secondly, the Italian political system underwent dramatic changes following the scandals and the judiciary inquiries known as 'Tangentopoli' (bribery city) that caused the death of most of the parties and the arrest of many important political leaders. The apparatuses of the Christian Democracts and the Socialist Party completely disappeared, while the biggest political machine, the ex-Communist Party, changed its name and became much leaner, following the general process of secularisation and the weakening of mass parties[2]. Hundreds of party employees were fired.

Moreover, there have been changes to the electoral laws that have introduced a more personalised campaign and, therefore, the need for each single candidate to be supported beyond the help that party apparatuses, weakened as they were, could ensure. These changes have affected both the national and the local elections. At the level of national elections, a prevalent majoritarian system has replaced the proportional system, introducing competition based on single individual figures, whereas, in the past, electoral competition was based almost entirely on party affiliation. At the local level the direct election of mayors, and then of regional governors, was also introduced. One consequence of these changes is that candidates themselves now have to provide an election team previously made available through party structures. Furthermore, direct elections have opened the way to candidates from outside the world of politics and who have even more need of personal electoral teams.

Although traditional party professionals have not completely disappeared as a result of these changes, their numbers have diminished and their role has been transformed. Their traditional communication functions, derived from being at the centre of diffused and widely spread networks of interpersonal communication, or from being in charge of means of communication heavily dependent on or linked to the party, are now performed by the mass media system acting essentially on the basis of commercial logic. The exigencies deriving from the increased role of the mass media system have produced the birth of a new kind of political professionalism that is essentially linked to an array of communication tasks and skills that are the main topic of this chapter.

These changes affect both the normal, everyday political process and the specific period of campaigning. As to the former, all government and political institutions have been forced to assume an organisational structure, based on professional skills and principles, whose aim is to interact with the increased role of the mass media within the new structure of the public sphere. This point is dealt with more fully in the section on centralisation and news management. On the other hand, the disappearance of many of the old party apparatuses, together with changes in the electoral system, have increased the need for particular skills and professional figures who are able to perform the tasks once performed by bureaucrats in the party structure during the election campaign.

CENTRALISATION AND NEWS MANAGEMENT

As is well known, news management is not a new attitude of government and all other institutions playing some role in the public arena. It started with the advent of the mass media system itself and with its increased role in shaping public attitudes. In his classic book, *Discovering the News*, Michael Schudson has clearly shown how news management began in the US around 1920 (Schudson, 1978). In Italy, too, news management by the Government is not a new phenomenon, even if, in the past, it assumed the form of a relationship of subordination of the mass media system to the government, as it was able, together with political parties, to direct the choices of the media (Murialdi, 1986). Nevertheless, there is no doubt that it has become more and more important in the last few years with the commercialisation of the entire mass media system in the 1980s, and the progressive weakening of all those traditional communication structures (e.g. interpersonal communication networks) and links (e.g. press subsidies and different forms of economic support for the media) that allowed parties and governments to have direct access to the public arena. Gradually, it became clear that these structures and these links were no longer able to provide direct means of communication to their intended audiences; to reach the intended audiences, it was important to compete successfully against all other media and all other messages and therefore it was crucial to have the support of professionals with the most appropriate skills.

Such change was common to most Western democracies, but it has been even more dramatic for Italy. Up to the end of the 1980s, the links between parties and citizens were so strong that it was not necessary to consider how to reach and persuade people other than through the traditional party or groups networks. Most citizens were, more or less, strictly affiliated to existing cultural or ideological networks: their opinions were dependent on these networks and with the different subcultures into which Italian society was organised. They either got their news about public life through the existing channels of communication, which were in turn connected with their specific subcultures, or they were just not interested in such news. Their opinions were already forged and rarely liable to change. Government activity, too, was dependent on networks of communication which most of the time overlapped with party or political links. The level of involvement in political life was low, as much research has shown (Almond & Verba, 1989), and therefore the need for information from government and related institutions was also low.

At the point at which the Italian subcultures (essentially the Catholic and the Communist) began to lose their power to shape the opinions of the citizens, the government and all the other institutions playing some role within the public sphere (e.g. parties, unions, cultural and ideological groups, social movements, etc.) felt the need for new competencies and skills to ensure that their messages could compete successfully with the large number of other circulating messages. The process of secularisation and the commercialisation of the media thus had a bigger, and later, impact in Italy than in other countries because of the deeply rooted subcultures that used to shape opinion independently of the activities of the mass media.

Beyond the more general social changes, both at the level of government and party organisation, news management got a big boost from the arrival of Berlusconi. He entered the political arena just at the end of the decade of mass media commercialisation in the 1980s. He brought into the political arena all those strategies and skills that are typical of the business sector. If he brought these skills, and the people able to perform them, from his own companies, as we shall see later on, his opponents obtained the same skills from the professional market. The highly competitive communication market that suddenly replaced the public service oriented scene altered the requirements for political communication and pushed it more towards entertainment. Consequently, political debate became more dramatised and not dissimilar to other forms of television spectacles and television entertainment in general.

Italian political life itself became more dramatised and much more of a spectacle than in other countries. From being a country in which the competition for new markets (both at the level of the political market and media market) was almost completely absent, Italy became the country of political drama (Ceccarelli, 2003). When D'Alema, leader of the ex-communist party, became Prime Minister in 1999 he brought to Palazzo Chigi, the seat of government, a number a young professionals with skills and personal experiences in mass communication (Cattaneo & Zanetto, 2003). As an example of the overlap between political communication and entertainment and between the political environment and the professional market, when D'Alema resigned as Prime Minister, one of his collaborators became press secretary on the TV series, 'Big Brother', another established his own firm of political consulting, and yet another went back inside the DS party as chair of the Communication Department.

When in government, these individuals were essentially involved in spinning activity that, at that moment, was a completely new approach to Italian democracy. At the same time, they made great efforts to organise the sorts of events that would give the D'Alema government opportunities to enhance its relationships with the mass media in ways that were not part of the culture of the traditional leftists in Italy: D'Alema met Bono, leader of the pop band U2, and an important Italian singer, Giovanotti, at Palazzo Chigi; he prepared a *risotto* during a famous talk show. The centre-left government of D'Alema inaugurated another professionalised activity that would be pursued by the next Berlusconi government: TV ads were broadcast to promote the initiatives and the legislative accomplishments of the government. All these activities show a completely new attitude to the relationship between government and mass media – the same new attitude that would be even more evident in campaigning.

This new attitude and approach to the media has been substantially improved upon by the Berlusconi government that followed the D'Alema government, with an even more important role being given to its press agents, who really took on the spinning function that had not, up until then, been practiced in Italy. Building on suggestions drawn from polls and surveys, Berlusconi is able to shape media content and set the public agenda by selecting the topics, the language and the statements that very often appear to be outside the realm of politics but that give a voice to that part of the electorate – the middle class, centre-right and undecided voters – that he wants to reach and that he has come to know from survey research.

In the case of both the D'Alema and Berlusconi governments, a process of centralisation has taken place, with greater attention being given to planning the relationships with the mass media in ways that were not previously part of governmental culture in Italy. A group of individuals, skilled in the field of communication with the external support of professionals, mainly pollsters and advertisers, has begun to direct, not just the communication activities of governments and parties, but their political strategies as well.

CAMPAIGNING

The professionalisation of political communication is more evident during campaigns. Berlusconi has also been critically important in bringing about these developments. He has introduced new forms of political communication based on the marketisation, trivialisation and the ownership of the mass media. A common element in these attitudes has been a process of professionalisation. Many have spoken of Forza Italia, Berlusconi's party, as *partito azienda* (a company party) pointing out how it was established thanks to the transfer of Berlusconi's staff from his companies (essentially his advertising firm) into the new party structure: these people brought with them their business oriented and professional skills (Calise, 2000; Poli, 2001).

The idea of Forza Italia as '*il partito azienda*' highlights the issue of professionalisation. Berlusconi established Forza Italia in a very short period at the beginning of 1994, thanks to the people he transferred from his own business organisation and thanks to their professional skills. Publitalia, the company in charge of selling Fininvest air-time to advertisers, was the main reservoir for establishing Forza Italia. Some years before, Publitalia had been the main instrument in Berlusconi's victory over his television competitors, Rusconi and Mondadori, so allowing Fininvest to gain the biggest share of advertising investments (Pilati, 1987). Research on the 1994 elections by Emanuela Poli identified 60 employees of Publitalia who had moved to Forza Italia (Poli, 2001). Their skills were not primarily focused on politics but rather on communication.

The best example of this during the 1994 election campaign was that of the pollster, Gianni Pilo. He was the young general manager of the Fininvest marketing department. When Berlusconi decided to enter the political arena, he asked Pilo to conduct all the polling necessary to establish a new party. Pilo established a private company, Diacron, that carried out all the surveys that allowed Berlusconi to decide if he was the right person (in the perception of the voters) to run the country, what issues he had to put in front of the voters, and then conducted all the surveys that allowed Berlusconi to determine his political strategy. According to many observers, Forza Italia and Berlusconi himself have been the product of a marketing approach that has made it possible to identify the most appropriate leader (Berlusconi himself), his symbolic values, and his links with particular issues (Diamanti, 1994). With the results from his surveys, Berlusconi had no difficulty in identifying the right people within his firm to produce his media message. Berlusconi's victory was built on his ability to propose who the favoured leader should be, namely himself, and the topics that the voters perceived as most important. He succeeded in this thanks to the number of carefully conducted surveys carried out on his behalf.

The choice of Forza Italia's local candidates was determined by the same criteria. A group of professionals was set up to select the right candidates to win from amongst a large group of people who put themselves forwards as potential candidates. There were several criteria for selection: candidates had to be new to politics, had to be young and essentially had to be good communicators. Fifty percent of those who applied for candidacy were not chosen because they were bad communicators on television. (Poli, 2001).

There is no doubt that the main novelty Berlusconi introduced into Italian campaigning was his marketing approach that had not been used before 1994. Better than proposing to voters the ideas and the issues the party was elaborating, as in traditional Italian politics, and more generally in the traditional idea of politics related to mass parties, he asked the voters what issues and what figures they would prefer. In this sense, he transferred to the political arena the marketing culture his business firms were used to applying. In the following election, 1996, he used the same approach but this time he did not succeed because he failed to build those political alliances that he was later able to construct in 2001[3].

In 1994, surveys showed that people were tired of the old Italian politics, its language, its parties and its main figures who had been accused of corruption during the *Tangentopoli* period. This also convinced Berlusconi to focus his campaign more and more on trivialisation – mixing politics with entertainment – and presenting himself as a political outsider (Caniglia, 2000), bringing within the realm of politics many features taken from everyday life and other symbolic contexts: company efficiency, success in entrepreneurship and economics and in sport (he was, and still is, the owner of the Milan football team). Berlusconi's language, building on what the surveys were showing, became simpler and closer to everyday life. He was very successful in abandoning the old attitude of Italian politics and its discourse, addressed essentially to people already familiar with politics. As many have pointed out, Berlusconi won because he was the natural consequence of the type of society and values, consumption, success in business and sport he helped to establish with his television services (Bobbio, Bosetti &Vattimo, 1994; Mazzoleni, 1995). In this sense, he was a 'populist leader' (Meny & Surel, 2000; Mazzoleni, Stewart & Horsfield, 2003) or, even better, a 'telepopulist leader' (Peri, 2004): he won because of the 'political malaise' diffused in Italy after *Tangentopoli* and because of the volatility of the electoral vote that followed the disappearance of the previous political parties. He also personified that 'popular' imagery diffused by a commercial media system and focused essentially on entertainment, sport and their values. His attention to 'what people want', expressed through survey research, is part of this populist attitude.

Being the owner of the Fininvest group was, of course, an important ingredient in his victory, but less than usually thought. As Mazzoleni has stressed, the image of the new 'Big Brother', so diffused in Italian and foreign media, is an exaggeration: Berlusconi won because he was able, through professionalised skills, to make use of all the opportunities offered by the new mass media system. In this regard, it has to be stressed that his use of television adverts has been overestimated: after the initial period of his 1994 campaign, during which he produced an enormous number of political ads, they were forbidden by law.

As Holtz-Bacha has shown in relation to the German case (Holtz-Bacha, 2002) and by Jones in the context of the British case (Jones, 1997), campaign centralisation is another important feature of the process of political communication professionalisation. In the case of Berlusconi, this was also linked to the highly personalised campaign which he inaugurated. The manner in which he centralised his campaign was taken directly from every typical business organisation seeking to obtain the greatest profit possible by means of a centralised strategy. A good example of this in Berlusconi's case is the way that he used to meet all his consultants and all the top leaders of his party organisation on exactly the same day, Friday, and in the same place, his home headquarters, Arcore, where he used to meet with the top officials of Fininvest when he was still in charge of the company. This meeting, called 'Il Tavolo per l'Italia', (The Table for Italy), was the place where all the main decisions regarding his 2001 campaign and later campaigns were taken. There is no doubt that this is another example of 'il partito azienda' and the way in which Berlusconi managed to transfer the main principles of company management into the party organisation. He placed within his campaign organisation, and then within his party organisation, the professional people (mainly pollsters and media men) who were already working in his company.[4] In this sense, Berlusconi did not collaborate in expanding political professionalism by creating new professional figures; he used already available people to establish his marketing strategy.

In many ways, Forza Italia's candidates followed Berlusconi's path but to some degree, as we shall see later on, they also contributed to enlarging the world of political professionalism. First of all, as their leader demonstrated, they saw the importance of political marketing and therefore promoted many surveys, so making the profession of political pollsters more important in all those regions and cities in which they were running. Secondly, as they mostly came from outside the realm of politics, they needed electoral teams that actually did not exist at all. They too needed advertisers, organisers, press agents and the like.

BEYOND BERLUSCONI: THE DIFFUSION OF POLITICAL COMMUNICATION PROFESSIONALISM IN ITALY

In some ways, Berlusconi's opponents followed his path, as did the candidates of his own party. Even for his adversaries, the new-born electoral market, within which undecided voters were numerous, created the need to use new strategies and new means that had not been necessary during the *Prima republica* which was characterised by a very highly stabilised vote and by strong links between voters and parties.

First of all, his opponents, essentially the DS party and the coalition built around it, l'Ulivo (the Olive tree), made considerable use of survey research. But they also felt the need for a new way to communicate with the voters and to organise the general consensus. In the 2001 election, the general manager of the Ulivo campaign involved one of the major US consultants, Stanley Greenberg, who used to come to Italy frequently because of family connections. It is not clear what Greenberg contributed; he was in charge of some surveys and this permitted him to give some general advice on strategy. The Ulivo, too, centralised its campaign with the support of other pollsters (university professors and professionals from survey firms) in addition to Greenberg. This group also met once a week to examine the data from surveys, the press coverage and the general direction of the campaign. Nevertheless, because of the heterogeneous character of the Ulivo coalition, the centralisation of the campaign did not achieve the same results as in Berlusconi's case (Gentiloni, 2001).

Beyond what has been done at the central level of the Berlusconi party and the opposition coalition, political communication professionalisation has meant that single candidates are forced to find support for their personal campaign because of the new electoral system that focused the voter's choice on single candidates, and the weak condition of the party apparatus that was no longer able to support the large number of local campaigns.

Data, drawn from personal interviews with some of the main 'political consultants' who supported the parties and the candidates during the 2001 campaign, and from a survey conducted with all the elected members of the Italian Parliament[5], shows the existence a low level of political professionalism: 45% of the elected members of Parliament were not supported at all by paid professionals; 46.0% had a very low percentage of support in their campaign activity from paid professionals (less than 25% of their campaign was run with the help of external professionals); 6.2% had more significant support from paid professionals (more than 30% of their campaign was run thanks to the support of external professionals) while only 2.1% of the elected members of Parliament stated that more than 30% of their campaign was run with help from external professionals (Chart 1). Paid professionals gave candidates very poor support in terms of specialised skills, a kind of support that cannot be defined as 'political' or 'strategic'. There is nothing of a strategic quality in taking photographs or giving advice on how to print brochures, as these professionals did. This kind of support does not imply any particular skills in the field of political communication. The same applies with respect to other areas: 74.9% of all the elected members of Parliament stated that they were supported by printers, 44.5% by photographers, and 25.8% by advertisers. These people provide merely technical support. Only 6.7% have used professional pollsters, 4.9%, experts on public relations and 3.2%, professional political consultants. (Chart 2)

Chart n.1. - In what percentage were you supported by paid professionals?

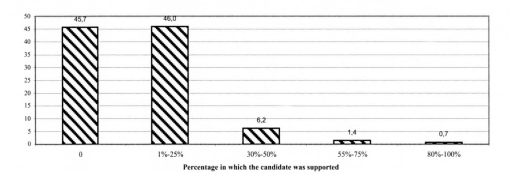

Percentage in which the candidate was supported

Chart n.2. - What kind of paid professionals did you use in 2001 campaign?

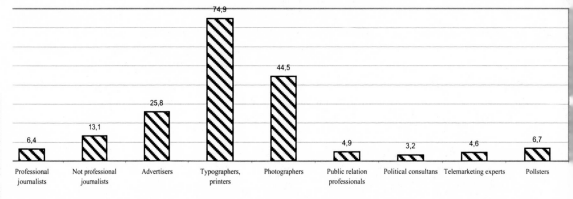

A very large percentage of those who were professionally involved in the campaign came from the same region/town as the candidate, with whom they previously had some sort of relation or familiarity. In contrast, the majority of pollsters came from other regions and they got in touch with the candidates through party structures and colleagues. When specific skills exist beyond the local environment, they need the sort of recognition and reliability that may come essentially through party structures.

As Chart 3 shows, and this also reflects the view of the elected members of Parliament, the role of those who were professionally employed in the 2001 campaign was purely technical. Only 1.8% of the elected members of Parliament stated that their support was more strategic than technical and for 1.4%, this support had a decisive influence on campaign strategy.

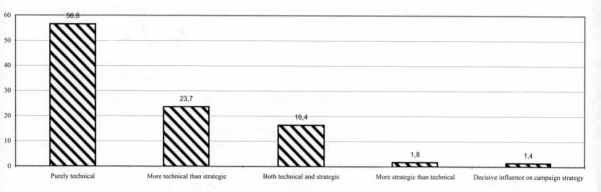

Chart n.3. - What kind of support did you get in 2001 campaign?

Nevertheless, paid professionals were of some importance in making the electoral victory possible: 12.7% of the interviewed (Table 1) state that their election would not have been possible without the support of those people.

Table 1. How would you judge the role of paid professionals in the 2001 campaign?

Without his support I couldn't have campaigned	12.7 %
In some measure he was important for my election	22.4%
He was important in improving some of my campaign	60.0%
He was not important at all	4.9%
	100.0%

It is interesting to see which parties are the most involved in the professionalisation of political communication. From our data, we can see that candidates from Forza Italia (Berlusconi's party) and Alleanza Nazionale (the rightist party) have used external professionals as have candidates from la Margherita (the centre left party of which Rutelli, Berlusconi's opponent in 2001, was the leader). In contrast, candidates from Lega Nord made the least use of external professionals. This data is of some interest: undoubtedly Forza Italia is the party with the leanest and smallest organisation and is, therefore, unable to support local candidates, who need to turn to external professionals from whose field the candidates themselves very often come. At the same time, as we have seen, this is the party that has mostly elaborated 'a culture of marketing', taking strategies and instruments from fields outside politics, mainly from business and corporate culture.

In many ways, Alleanza Nazionale constitutes 'a surprise' in respect of its great use of external professionals: this is a party with a well established and diffused party structure and with its own political culture that privileges the most traditional ways of contact between party and voters (e.g. personal relations, party meetings, etc.). Nevertheless, from our data, candidates of Alleanza Nazionale seem very open to new ways of campaigning. La Margherita is a newly established party with a lean organisation, made up of people coming from different cultural areas.

Of all the parties, Lega Nord is the one which has made least use of external professionals. Lega Nord mainly operates in the northern regions of Italy and is a party that has a very ramified and complex structure of branches, with a widespread network of interpersonal communication able to reach all the voters of that particular area. In many respects, Lega Nord has inherited the old practices of the traditional mass parties linked, in its case, to local environments, and, because of these reasons, does not appear to need to turn to professionals external to the party structure.

IS THERE AN ITALIAN POLITICAL COMMUNICATION PROFESSIONALISM?

The data that has been discussed shows a poor level of professionalism in political communication in Italy. It appears to be so both in terms of its content and in respect of its role within the election campaign. At least this is the image that emerges, looking at the support that elected members of the Parliament have obtained from professionals outside the party structure.

This conclusion, taken together with the earlier discussion in this chapter of what was referred to as the 'Berlusconi professionalism', suggests that what one observes is a high level of professionalisation mainly at the level of party headquarters and a poor level when one observes the local campaigns of single candidates. It seems, therefore, possible to talk of two main elements of professionalism. The first one refers to what can be defined as a 'culture of marketing' approach to politics that is linked to the use of specific practices, such as survey research and centralisation of the campaign, that implies specific professional competencies coming from outside politics. This culture, and the connected use of professionals, mainly concerns the parties' headquarters and government. Berlusconi's experience has been of great importance in introducing this sort of approach to politics, but the other parties have also started to look for the support of pollsters to understand what citizens think and wish. In the meantime they need the support of other professionals (essentially advertisers) to package their message. The use of these professionals is particularly evident during the election period, when the new way of campaigning imposes a high level of centralisation of all decisions. Campaigning implies also a framework of connections with the news media that is evident when parties or candidates reach government positions. This first kind of professionalism exists as the entire party machine, mainly during election campaigns, takes advantage of a more professionalised attitude, focused essentially on centralisation and a marketing approach that is brought about by the involvement of highly specialised personnel coming from business and other fields (e.g. academics) outside the political realm.

A second diffused professionalised practice is the support for single, local candidates given by different professionals in the communication field. Their support is essentially limited to technical duties and does not imply, up to now, specific and specialised competencies in the field of political communication. As we have seen, professionals who are involved in the campaign are printers, graphic designers, photographers. It is hard to define these people as 'political professionals': their skills refer to different fields of communication without any specificity in politics. In part, the low level of professionalism is caused by the little money that candidates have: after *Tangentopoli* a stricter law has been approved that makes it harder for candidates to provide themselves with other money beyond what they can get from the State, once they are elected.[6] More rarely, beyond this technical support, there is also a more elaborated one that touches the strategic decisions of the campaign. In this case pollsters, public relations people and journalists are involved. So far this is not very diffused, even if, as we shall see, in the future this kind of professional involvement may become more important.

The old political professionalism has only partially been substituted by a new political communication professionalism. Beyond the traditional party bureaucrats who still exist, even if in small numbers, there are many people working at a professional level in politics and they come from the mass media field. Up to now they seem to miss some of the major features that Webb and Fisher have stressed as being part of the definition of profession[7] (Webb & Fisher, 2003): in most cases their expertise is essentially technical, doesn't reflect any formal training and it is not particular to the political field. When they have a more developed expertise, they lack the autonomy and the self regulatory capacity that defines the idea of profession.

The distinction we have made so far can be approached in a different way. The 'semi-professional field', as it has been called by some journalists (Cattaneo & Zanetto, 2003), that one can observe in Italy is articulated in three kinds of figures. First of all there is what could be seen as the 'Berlusconi professionalism', a sort of professionalism that seems entirely connected to the national context and that is hardly visible in other countries. This is the professionalism that Berlusconi took from his own firms and transferred into the newly established party structure. It is made up of people skilled in polling and advertising. 'Berlusconi professionalism' also identifies individual political figures who come from the same television and advertising firms that Berlusconi owns and who, therefore, are themselves particularly skilled in communication and are sensitive to the needs coming from this area.

A second kind of political communication professionalism is made up by those Farrel and colleagues call 'marketers' (Farrel, Kolodny & Medvic, 2001): these are professionals who are consulting government and candidates having specific skills in advertising, polling, news management, etc. and who mostly work for clients who are not in the field of politics. Up to now in Italy, the definition of 'marketers' identifies essentially a basic technical support involved in the production of posters, pictures, leaflets, etc. Even if they represent a minority, there are also marketers with more elaborated and specific skills, such as pollsters, advertisers, journalists, who support candidates, party headquarters and government, and who limit their involvement in politics either just to the moment of campaigning or when asked for particular commitments.

On the other hand, there are professionals with a stronger political background. They come from politics, they have passed through some sort of political experience, either within the party organisation (as in the case of D'Alema's assistants) or within less institutionalised political movements. They also have some sort of mass media experience or some sort of connections with this field. Mixing together these two kinds of experience, they start their own private professional activity or establish their own firm in the field of communication: polling, public relations, etc. Generally these are young people with up-to-date skills that do not exist within the traditional party organisation. These people try to give the candidates strategic advice that goes beyond the narrow period of campaigning or of government. Although they overlap with the world of politics, it gives them neither a high level of autonomy nor a capacity for self-regulation. The definition of 'traditional politicos' (Farrel, Kolodny & Medvic, 2001) seems appropriate for this group.

Because of the changes to the electoral system in Italy, and because of the more general process of secularisation that gives the mass media system more important communication functions, we can suggest that in the future both candidates and parties will need more support from external professionals. The weakening of party structures, together with the new technological side of the campaign (essentially the Internet), will push further this requirement, making the political communication professions more developed and complete.

NOTES

1. Source: Istcattaneo.org
2. A dramatic symbolic indicator of the diminished importance of the party apparatus occurred when the Democratici di Sinistra (the new name of the ex-Communist Party) was forced to leave their traditional office, *Botteghe oscure*, as the building was too large and too expensive for the new, lean organisation of the party.
3. It is important to stress that both in 1996 and 2000, Forza Italia obtained 30% of the national vote and therefore a coalition with other parties was needed to form the government.
4. In 2001 he used a different pollster than he had previously: Luigi Crespi, who came from the world of pollsters and whom Berlusconi had already used on previous occasions.
5. A questionnaire has been sent in autumn 2002 to all the elected members of the Italian Parliament (both the Senate and the House of Deputies). 40% of the questionnaires have been returned

6. At the moment each candidate may spend no more than 50,000 euros plus a small amount of money depending on the number of voters of the electoral district.
7. Webb and Fisher states that "a professional may be regarded as a member of the workforce with a relatively high status and strong position in the labour market flowing from a special degree of expertise, commitment, autonomy and capacity for self-regulation which in turn reflects a particular education and formal training" (Webb & Fisher, 2003, p. 11–12)

REFERENCES

Almond, G. & S. Verba (1989) *The Civic Culture*. Newbury Park: Sage.

Bobbio, N., G. Bosetti and G. Vattimo (1994) *La sinistra nell'era del karaoke*. Milan: Reset.

Calise, M. (2000) *Il partito personale*. Bari: Laterza

Caniglia, E (2000) *Berlusconi, Perot e Collor come political outsider*. Soveria Mannelli: Rubbettino.

Cattaneo, A. and P. Zanetto (2003) *Elezioni di successo*. Milan: Etas

Ceccarelli, F. (2003) *Il teatrone della politica*. Milan: Longanesi.

Diamanti, I. (1994) 'La politica come marketing' *Micromega*, 2.

Farrel, D. (1996) Campaign Strategies and Tactics. pp. 160–183 in L. Le Duc, R.G. Niemi & P. Norris (eds) *Comparing Democracies*. Thousands Oaks London: Sage,.

Farrel, D., R. Kolodny & S. Medvic (2001) 'Parties and Campaign Professional in a Digital Age', *The Harvard International Journal of Press/Politics*, 6:4, pp. 11–31.

Gentiloni, P. (2001) 'La campagna di Rutelli' *Comunicazione Politica*, II:5, pp. 226–231.

Holtz-Bacha, C. (2002) 'Professionalization of Political Communication: The Case of the 1998 SPD Campaign, *Journal of Marketing*, 1:4, pp. 23 – 37

Jones, N. (1997) *Campaign 1997. How the General Elections Was Won and Lost*. London: Indigo.

Mastropaolo, A. (1986) *Saggio sul professionismo politico*. Milan: Angeli.

Mazzoleni, G. (1995) 'Towards a Videocracy? Italian Political Communication at a Turning Point', *European Journal of Communication*, 10:3, pp. 291 – 321.

Mazzoleni, G., J. Stewart & B. Horsfeild (2003) *The Media and Neo-Populism*. Westport: Praeger.

Meny, Y. & Y. Surel (2000) *Par le peuple, pour le peuple*. Paris: Fayard.

Murialdi, P. (1986) *Storia del giornalismo italiano*. Turin: Gutenberg.

Panebianco, A. (1988) *Political Parties*. Cambridge: Cambridge University Press.

Peri, Y. (2004) *Telepopulism*. Stanford: Stanford University Press.

Pilati, A. (1987) *Il nuovo sistema dei media*. Milan: Comunità.

Poli, E. (2001) *Forza Italia*. Bologna: Il Mulino

Schudson, M. (1978) *Discovering the News*. New York: Basic Books

Webb, P. & J. Fisher (2003) 'Professionalism and the Millbank Tendency: the Political Sociology of New Labour's Employees', *Politics*, 23;1, pp. 10–20.

8

POLITICAL COMMUNICATION AND PROFESSIONALISATION IN GREECE

Stylianos Papathanassopoulos

This chapter attempts to examine the professionalisation of communication thesis by looking at contemporary Greek politics. It argues that, in the age of modernisation or the Americanisation of politics (Swanson 1992; 1993; 1997; Mancini & Swanson, 1996), the similarities across media and political systems and practices are not, in practice, becoming greater than their differences and that, although there are transnational similarities in the issues involved, each national system still differs in many respects. The same applies to the so-called professionalisation of politics and communication practices, since media and politics reflect the differences between political systems, political philosophies, cultural traits and economic conditions. It argues that in Greece institutions of government and politics show the critical relationship that defines national systems of political communication. The Greek experience shows that the 'spreading' professional model of political communication is too generalised and does not correspond entirely to the practice and theory manifest in other countries like Greece.

THE CHANGING MEDIA AND POLITICS ENVIRONMENT

Greece has been undergoing a series of social transformations, which are creating a new socio-economic framework. These changes are most obvious in the relationship between politics and the mass media, and more particularly in the field of political communication. In the aftermath of the deregulation and privatisation of the television sector, television has become a significant, if not indispensable, medium for political parties and politicians in their efforts to communicate with the public. The 'modernisation' of the Greek media took place in the late 1980s with the deregulation of the broadcasting system and the development of a plethora of private TV channels. Greece has undergone broadcasting commercialisation, adopting a market-led approach, resulting in more channels, more advertising, more programme imports and more politics. And, as in other Mediterranean countries, the publishers and other business-oriented interests have decisively entered the broadcasting landscape (Papathanassopoulos, 1997; 2001a). The result has been an overcrowded landscape comprising 160 private TV channels and 1200 private radio stations. In the 1990s, the Greek newspapers faced the biggest challenge in their history: increasing competition from electronic media and the need to harness the publishing tools offered by new technologies (Leandros, 1992; Psychogios, 1992, pp. 11–35; Zaoussis & Stratos, 1995, pp. 171–187; Papathanasopoulos, 2001b). For newspapers, these challenges required the reconsideration of traditional publishing goals and marketing strategies (Zaharopoulos & Paraschos, 1993, p. 67). However, the political affiliation of newspapers is always manifested in periods of intense political contention,including election periods (Komninou,1996).

During this period, political parties and politicians have faced considerable difficulties in getting their agendas placed before the public. For example, since the mid 1980s, accusations relating to scandals and corruption have become a frequent issue in the public agenda. In the past, political parties, which were based on a system of patronage regardless of whether or not they remained leader-oriented, could not only create news items that were often incorporated into the national agenda, but they could also mobilise strong constituencies ready to support those agendas (Mouzelis, 1986; 1995; Kargiotis, 1992; Tsoukalas, 1986; Charalambis, 1989; Charalambis & Demertzis, 1993; Lyrinztis, 1987).

Political parties are now less able to differentiate themselves one from another on the basis of their political programmes. From about the late 1980s, there has been congruence among the leading political parties (New Democracy and PASOK-Pan-Hellenic Socialist Movement) that has helped to run the country since the restoration of the Parliament in 1974. The entry of Greece into the European Union (EU), the internationalisation of the economy and the changes in the international political order have led the two leading political parties to adopt similar, if not identical, policies (Moschonas, 2001). On the other hand, one could argue that Greece has entered, as Charalambis notes (1996, p. 286), a 'demystifying process', which has allowed real problems to appear in the formation and functioning of the Greek political system and demonstrated the collapse of all sorts of alibis – social and political – available to politicians and political parties.

Hand in hand with these developments is growing disenchantment with traditional politics. Research provided by various pollsters shows that in the last decade Greek citizens have become less supportive of the political parties, less trusting of the political system and more likely to abstain from party membership. This of course increases the

The Professionalisation of Political Communication

scope of political marketing and professionalisation, as political parties and politicians try to find more effective or alternative ways to communicate with the voters. Political parties, on the other hand, despite using and adapting to new media techniques, communication and marketing practices – particularly during the election campaigning period – have remained strong since so-called *'kommatikokratia'* (partytocracy) (Mouzelis, 1996), especially after the restoration of the Parliament, and 'clientelism' has continued strongly in the Greek political system. In the following pages I will try to describe this newly established situation, which I refer to as the 'Greek paradox': political parties have become more professional in the way they manage their public communication, while at the same time this has not much affected their organisation, which remains leader-oriented.

INCREASING USE OF POLITICAL MARKETING
The changes noted above have brought about a new kind of relationship between the media and politics in Greece. In effect, the media have moved centre stage in election campaigning, and they have also gradually assumed a central role in the day-to-day practice of the government and the political parties. There are many features of modern day election campaigning in Greece, and their introduction into the Greek political system shows the growing importance of television as a medium of political communication, and the use of communication professionals, pollsters and advertisers, for Greek political parties. Choreographed precinct walks and nationwide tours have become common campaign routines, whereas crowded partisan gatherings, historically sacred political and media events in Greek campaigns, are now on the wane. Professional advertising, polls and political consulting, scarcely used before, have become indispensable means, not only for campaign strategy, but also in respect of communication by the government and the opposition political parties. Opinion polls, which first emerged in the 1970s, now flood newspapers, television newscasts and current affairs programmes.

Until the end of the 1980s the use of professionals and political advertising was seen as ideological treason: a mediated communication that undermined raw, direct politics. Political communication was considered almost inherently corrupt: a way to cheat people as opposed to serving democracy. In a general anti-American climate, parties using communication professionals were stigmatised. For example, in the 1985 elections, PASOK made a major political issue of the disclosure that Constantine Mitsotakis, then leader of New Democracy, had employed American image-makers to create a profile for him. It was seen as big news, even though at that time PASOK had semi-secret negotiations with Jacques Seguela, the French expert of commercial and political advertising. Their collaboration did not proceed, for reasons that have never been adequately explained. However, American political consultants such as James Carville and Paul Begala collaborated with New Democracy in the election campaign of 1993, again giving PASOK the opportunity to accuse their opponents of using American tactics, mainly negative advertising, while doing exactly the same themselves.

Many observers argue that political advertising and the use of professional image-makers have developed while the model of the charismatic political leader has disappeared. Many refer to the communicative talent of the late Andreas Papandreou, but few know that, apart from his natural talent at communicating with the masses, the PASOK leader had had useful training in the field. In his youth, serving in the American Navy, he studied psychological warfare. Another view debunks the Papandreou myth, seeing him influenced by his wife Margaret, who had already been involved with political marketing in the 1950s on behalf of the American Democrats.

These approaches outline the use of political marketing before the 1990s. Although political communication has always been present in Greece, the methods and intensity have changed. In the past, political campaigning meant home visits, friendly meetings, treats, family connections, cartoons, poems, rhymed libels and patriotic hymns. These were all orchestrated by professionals; in fact from 1981 on, American advisers often visited the Prime Minister's residence at Kastri in Attica, where they mixed business and pleasure over dinner, much to the annoyance of local advisers who resented any encroachment on their territory. Whether or not these experts have had an impact on the strategies of the parties is unclear, though it soon became obvious that politicians grew increasingly comfortable with television routines. As a result, politics saturated television coverage before and during electoral campaigns. Even the pilgrimage of the new PASOK leader George Papandreou to his family ancestral village of Kalenzti during the 2004 elections, which was reminiscent of old-party campaign tactics, provided a sample of the media 'hoopla', with frequent news flashes on each stop to his road to the village.

In the 1990s the use of professionals has increased in the sense that politics is subjected to the rules of television. For example, US and Greek communication experts taught politicians of New Democracy, in a seminar organised by the Institute of Democracy by Constantine Karamanlis in 1998, that body language counts for 55% of the construction of a positive image, 38% for voice tone and only 7% for ideas and arguments (in Serafetinidou, 2002, p. 30). Therefore, while in the past the 'holy triad' of 'political advertising-political marketing-opinion polls' was blamed, since the 1990s, it has been legitimised, and has acquired such mythical status as to raise the question of whether it has replaced real politics.

This does not, however, mean that political parties have displaced 'party strategists' by non-party 'professional' strategists (Scammell, 1999, p. 256). Although professionals – e.g. pollsters, media consultants (mainly journalists, TV producers, advertisers) – from outside the political party have come to play an important role in the conduct of elections, they have not increased their power within the parties. Their role is supplementary to the leader and his group, who control the party. This group, formed by politicians or party strategists, are close affiliates of the leader 'of the day', and this group has responsibility for the party's communication and political strategy. In other words, while there has been a professionalisation of the communication practices, it is hard to argue that outside professionals have any powers. On the contrary, they are expendable. Sometimes, they are the targets of the intra-party opposition for various reasons: they wrongly advised the leader, or, because the intra-party opposition wants to dispute with or criticise the leader, the attack is focused on disputes within the group and with outsiders instead of on him.

Costas Laliotis, ex-Minister of Public Work and the Environment and ex-General Secretary of the party, always played a leading role in PASOK's political communication. He was credited with the inspiration of using the theme from *Carmina Burana* to accompany all PASOK's rallies in the 1980s. Apart from Laliotis, PASOK's official communications team in the 2000 general elections included Nikos Themelis (lawyer, personal adviser to the Prime Minister), Dimitris Reppas (Minister of the Media), Petros Efthimiou (journalist and later Minister of the Education) and Giorgos Pantayias (personal adviser to Prime Minister Simitis). PASOK also employed professionals: Mass Team, a company whose owner has been involved with PASOK for years, and recently, Esftratios Fanaras, pollster and owner of the survey agency Metron Analysis, and Lefteris Kousoulis of consulting company Leyein kai Prattein (Saying and Acting). Kousoulis had the confidence of the prime minister and it is said that he had the idea of focusing the 2000 election campaign more on Costas Simitis, the Prime Minister and Leader of PASOK, and less on PASOK itself. The party's chief slogan in the campaigning of 2000, which appeared on a giant poster picturing the Prime Minister, said: 'We are creating the new Greece, the future has begun.' This communications group had also decided not to repeat the mistake of showing Simitis looking different from how he did in real life. George Papandreou, the new PASOK leader, used his own communication advisors as well as prominent party members (an indication of this is the return of ex-secretary of the PASOK, Laliotis) in the 2004 general elections.

Similarly, the New Democracy leader, Costas Karamanlis, had his own group. During the 2000 elections, the New Democracy communication team was formed by Michalis Liapis (politician, and cousin of Karamanlis), Aris Spiliotopoulos (politician, and at that time responsible of the Press Office of the party), Yiannis Loulis (political analyst), George Flessas (owner of the first political communication and public affairs company Civitas), and advertising agency, Spot Thompson. While PASOK's communications team was focusing their 2000 election campaign on Simitis, New Democracy was responding in kind, contrasting Costas Karamanlis to Simitis. The image of Karamanlis and his wife, singing along to *rembetika* music in a *taverna*, was contrasted with Simitis and practically the entire Cabinet inaugurating the Thessalonica Concert Hall amid much fanfare, as a clear reminder of the slogan, 'Simitis with the vested interests, and Karamanlis with the people'. New Democracy's chief 2000 election slogans, 'A new start,' and 'There is a better Greece and we want it', were mainly directed at the feeling of fatigue that experts claimed Greek society felt after almost 20 years of PASOK rule. The image of Karamanlis as 'young, unspoiled, affable, popular, and comfortable with people' was contrasted with the image of Simitis as 'a cold, inaccessible, rigid and agoraphobic person.' Karamanlis' wife Natasha played a vital part in his public image, and this led the couple, according to some experts, to overdo their joint magazine and television interviews. But in the 2004 elections, as he had to confront the new, young and very people-friendly leader, George Papandreou, Costas Karamanlis was forced to change his style in his public speeches. 'We dare, we proceed, we change,' declared PASOK in the 2004 elections, while ND supplemented this with: 'The country needs political change,' and 'New policy, better Life.'

In both cases, at least in the two leading Greek political parties, the people called 'communication' experts are usually party members and do not come from outside the party or the political system. The difference is that their political marketing techniques are adapted to the new communications environment and media landscape. Their knowledge of professional communication practices is not due to any special political communication training but is rather based on their day-to-day experience with politics. Often, professionals from market and survey research, advertising companies and, mainly political, journalists surround them as a kind of support group. Most of them are politically affiliated to the leader or the group which has the upper hand in the party. Loulis and Flessas, although not party members, are well known affiliates of ND. Fanaras was a close associate of Simitis, while Themelis was a close fried and associate of Simitis since the mid 1980s (Hope, 2003). Only the case of Kousoulis corresponds to the new model of professionalism. He was a communication adviser to the former Mayor of Athens and former leader of New Democracy, Miltiades Evert, in the 1986 municipal elections; to the former leader of New Democracy, Constantine Mitsotakis; and to PASOK leader and Prime Minister Simitis from 1999 (Yannas, 2002, p. 80).

THE ROLE OF TELEVISION IN THE PROFESSIONALISATION OF CAMPAIGNING

The modernisation of Greek political campaigning and marketing has changed as a result of the development and growing dominance of private television. New Democracy's campaign in the 1990 Greek national elections left an indelible mark on the history of Greek campaigning. The incorporation of professional TV advertising, opinion surveys, and television in an election campaign was seen as a critical addition to New Democracy's successful campaign. It is widely believed that its use of modern campaigning practices helped it achieve victory. Since then, the use of new weapons and strategies in campaigning has been slowly legitimised.

In the 1993 general election, 'telepolitics' was introduced and, ever since, political parties have focused their campaigns around television news programming, television political advertising, television debates and appearances by candidates on television talk shows. By 1996, television had moved to centre stage: the 1996 national elections were coined as the first 'TV Elections' and 'the elections on the couch'. The growing importance of TV was confirmed in the coming national elections of 2000 and 2004 and one can trace the growing importance of television in a number of ways.

The first is the replacement of the old campaign styles with new forms of campaigning. In the 1996 general elections, Prime Minister and Socialist Party (PASOK) leader Costas Simitis started his campaign by making a daring public statement: 'We say no to chicken fights, false promises, meaningless rallies … we do not plan a campaign with plastic flags, fake portraits or expensive artificial gatherings'. These practices were to be replaced by a nationwide 'bus-tour' (the 'victory-express'), precinct walks, and televised debates with the main opposition leader, TV interviews and only one major rally in Athens. Simitis further insisted that the 'people must be informed which party has proposals…which party has the necessary solutions to create a modern Greece' and concluded: 'We hope that this campaign will raise the quality of our political life'.

All this was in sharp contrast to the style of the late Andreas Papandreou, PASOK's founder. Papandreou, whom Simitis had succeeded a few months earlier, had based much of his campaign activity on fiery speeches before hundreds of thousands of flag-waving supporters in many Greek cities. This was often seen as the truest form of political communication and a form that did not rely on electronic media. New Democracy's major party gathering in the elections of 2000 moved from the traditional Athens' Sydagma Square to the Olympic Stadium. New Democracy tried to turn its gathering into 'an event which produced important media and policy effects. The congress, as mediated effect, culminated in a spectacle combining image, colour and sound' (Yannas, 2002, p. 83).

The second new feature revealing the growing importance of TV was the introduction of the televised debate. In the past, party workers would mobilise citizens and friends to attend political gatherings and debates. These were used as a kind of poll: observers literally judged which leader had the greatest attendance as an indication of who was likely to win the elections. As campaigning shifted focus towards television, these political gatherings slowly lost their impact. Nowadays journalists look at the TV ratings to see which political leader attracts most viewers during their campaign interviews. PASOK's founder, Papandreou, had refused to participate in televised debates with his, then, opponents, citing personal dislike; although alternative televised debates with lesser politicians did in fact take place. The first televised debate between party leaders – Simitis, for PASOK, and Evert for New Democracy – took place during the 1996 elections. This debate signalled a certain change in election style by a new generation of Greek politicians. The second televised debate was between Simitis and the New Democracy's new leader, Costas Karamanlis. This debate was almost a carbon copy of that of 1996. The same approach was followed in the 2004 debate, but with the difference that the leaders of the five political parties represented in Parliament and the European Parliament participated.

All three debates were broadcast live from the public broadcaster's TV studio, and were simultaneously broadcast on most private channels. Tough bargaining between party representatives over the format of the debates preceded them. Most stations organised post-debate analyses and phone-ins to gauge 'the winner'. In effect, they invited an impressive succession of politicians, entertainers, analysts, media editors and intellectuals to comment on the debates. According to AGB Hellas, the TV ratings research company, of those households that had TV the 1996 debate was seen by 35.8%, the 2000 debate was seen by 41% and the 2004 debate was seen by 44%.

A third new feature was the heavy presence of 'telegenic' politicians, mainly from the two leading parties. In both the 1996 and 2000 national elections, smaller parties complained that there was a 'bi-party' dialogue among the candidates of the main political parties. Private channels preferred these politicians, many times in pairs, so as not to upset their ratings.

The fourth new feature was the growth in negative political advertising. Jay Blumler notes (1990, p. 109) that the modern publicity process may be promoting an increased circulation of negative messages about political actors, events and decisions, a striking example being the heavy use of negative advertising. In Greece, as in other countries that have left public rallies and pamphlet scattering behind, negative political TV advertising has become a key election issue. Since the 1993 election, a major part of the campaign strategy has been based not only on political TV advertisements but also on negative 'polispots' ('black advertisements' or 'black propaganda', as these became known in Greece). These were also in evidence in the 1996 and 2000 elections (Papathanassopoulos, 1997; 2000; 2002) but much less so in the 2004 elections. For example, less than two hours after Prime Minister Costas Simitis called a 'snap election' for September 1996, the main opposition New Democracy party's first campaign commercial aired on television was a compilation of clips of Simitis rejecting the notion of an early election, ending with a voice-over asking: 'Elections on September 22. Can you trust him?' The message echoed the theme pursued by conservative officials in public statements and on talk shows that the Prime Minister and ruling PASOK party had lost credibility by calling the election despite earlier claims that they intended to serve out the four-year term of office. In effect, both parties were accusing each other of being unable to run the country and of not being trustworthy.

The fifth new, but not yet significant, feature is the role of the Internet. A minority of Greeks have access to the Internet, which has meant that, with less than 25% of the population using the web before the 2002 election, the web played little importance in political campaigning. Few candidates had web sites and even fewer used this in any political manner. One has to note also that there are very few media producing news for the web, as most outlets re-publish content that gets published through other outlets (In.gr and flash.gr being the exception). So it is safe to say that the new media did not make their debut in Greek political life until the 2002 election. During 2002, new media and the democratising possibilities of new technologies became the key buzzwords for the Papandreou campaign. New technologies were introduced hand-in-hand with a number of other concepts – slogans such as 'civil society', deliberation ', 'citizens' opinion. Papandreou, who claimed to have a legacy of promoting and discussing 'e-democracy' issues, (proved to an extent by his initiatives during the Greek EU presidency), heavily linked new technologies with his general campaign theme, participatory democracy. The campaign included the publication of a candidate web site (separate from the party web site) that featured many of the items available to citizens in American candidate websites: a web log (with no means to actually discuss entries), curriculum, speeches and information, campaign gatherings and rallies. To complement this web presence, PASOK published two websites featuring on-line polls on political issues, including education, the budget, and immigration policy. New Democracy followed with nd.gr. It is important to mention that both parties failed to really harmonise their web presence with the rest of the campaign, showing once again that campaigning is not wholly slick and professionalised.

The above examples confirm a significant change during the campaigning, and the role of television as the main medium for campaigning. Data on the distribution of funds to television and the other media shows that it has become a major recipient of campaign funds. Television share accounted for around 85% of expenditure during the last four elections. Compared with 1990, television has become the dominant recipient of campaign monies and investments, while newspaper advertising in campaign expenditure has significantly decreased. For example, in the 1990 elections, when private TV had just started, television absorbed 46.4% and 6.7% of the advertising budget of New Democracy and PASOK respectively (Yannas, 2002, p. 77). In fact, the substantial growth of campaign funds allocated to television largely accounts for the significant rise in total electoral expenses during the last decade. Rising television expenditure is perhaps the best symbol of the shift in Greek politics from campaigns traditionally based on efforts made by party organisations and prospective deputies to more professional mass media centred practices.

There is no doubt that, since the 1990s, election campaigning in Greece has become more modern and more professional, and communication practices may have come to play an important role. But it is uncertain to what extent these professional communication practices have come to dominate the development of political parties, or whether they only make sense in the context of the development of the political parties themselves. First of all, the evolution from a party-centred system to a candidate-centred system has not yet materialised in Greece, although the campaigning is indeed focused on the parties' leaders' images. This is because the parties have maintained the dominance over individual MPs, while the party leader personalises the party (Samaras, 2002, p. 167). For example, up to 1996, political talk shows during the election campaign period were more or less unregulated. In the 1996 elections, the main preoccupation of the political parties was the 'quest for the magic formula' that would secure all candidates and political parties equal time and access on TV, including talk shows, without upsetting the ratings of private channels. The discussions between the parties produced a set of guidelines for both state and private television channels, under which all parties would receive 7.5 hours of free airtime on state channels and 5.5 hours on private channels. Clearly, the main issue was to control individual candidates and their personal appearances in a bid to ensure that a handful of popular or 'telegenic' candidates would not get the 'lion's share' of TV coverage.

It is perhaps no coincidence that, in 1996, legislation (law 2429/96) was introduced that set an upper limit of expenditure on parties' and candidates' electoral expenditure. Attempts to enforce this law during the 1996 parliamentary elections proved flawed, but were implemented with some amendments in the elections of 2000. As Yannas notes (2002, p. 79): 'the law does not place severe limits on party political ads but prohibits candidates from advertising on radio and television'.

Furthermore, the analysis of political advertisements has shown, as Samaras (1999, p. 201) notes, that the content of Greek 'polispots' is 'organised around party lines. The leadership appears predominantly in the opponent's spots and in these cases it dovetails with statements on the sponsors' party'. This is because in Greece the new techniques have been integrated within the existing power structure, despite the rise of media (Samaras, 2002, p. 168): a power structure that is based on the centrality of parties rather than on institutions. The major political parties, especially when they come to office, not only drive the operations of most governmental institutions, but also influence the developments in most aspects of the social system; from sports and arts to education and the Church. In Greece, as noted above, this situation is called *kommatikokratia* (partytocracy), and highlights the omnipresence of parties in society. Although this omnipresence does not make them omnipotent, at this stage the political parties have been able to adapt themselves to the new communication environment, having as a main goal the attraction of as many voters they can. This leads us to the next question about the role and effects of opinion polls on the political parties, at least the leading ones.

THE ROLE AND THE EFFECTS OF THE OPINION POLLS

Opinion polls were used in the past and have increased their presence and role in Greek politics, especially since the 1990s. Currently, 'more than 10 Greek polling firms comprise the Greek Association of Public Opinion and Market Research. Among them well known polling companies are MRB, V-PRC, Kappa Research, ALKO and Metron Analysis, to name a few' (Yannas, 2002, p. 77). Political parties and the media use them for their own agendas. Greece is not the only country where political parties use their own polls and their own esoteric interpretations of them, not as a means of getting objective information but rather as just another weapon in the political campaign. Usually the Opposition party, using the evidence of the polls, accuses the government of inefficiency in dealing with the day-to-day problems of the citizens. Politicians also see the polls as a way to monitor their publicity and, where the results are positive, to use them as a tool for their own political purposes.

The mass media, highly politicised as they are, also conduct their own polls – as they do in other countries. This means that, far more than just locating and reporting the 'news' itself, they can then comment on it, often with their own political ends in view. But polls can go wrong, for either technical or political reasons: the sample may be too small, it may be difficult to reach certain people, and so the sample used, even if large enough, may not be truly representative of the population. Other technical difficulties abound. Even in the best circumstances, Greece confronts the pollsters with a nightmarish problem. Normally, upwards of 20% of those interviewed refuse to reveal how they have voted in the past or to give any indication of which party they intend to support in a forthcoming election. In political terms, opinion polls say that Greeks do not trust politicians and political parties, or are not passionate about politics. These attitudes expressed about their political institutions and leaders appear negative, but on the other hand, in a country where politics is omnipresent and citizens are incorporated as both participants and performers, many questions the pollsters typically ask are either out of place or produce highly misleading replies. Greeks are often asked, for example, whether they have problems related to the government (and who does not!). Needless to say, the mass media are an essential part of this scenario. The politicians count on the editorial and journalistic community to provide not just commentary but also interpretation of what is projected by the polls. After a poll, analyses by journalists, analysts and politicians are published in the press and discussed on the electronic media (and *vice versa*). Because in the 2004 national elections it appeared that the electoral race would be a tough one and extremely close right until the finish, there was an unprecedented increase in the number of polls commissioned, at least by the media (about one every three days). It is no coincidence that, during election campaigns, the publication of poll results cannot be publicised 15 days prior to the election in the newspapers, for example, and 30 days for television.

The central role of the media and the pollsters or the use of the opinion poll data are, in my opinion, demonstrated in the case of the creation and demise of a political party, but also in the choice of a political leader.

An example that illustrates the first point is when Dimitris Avramopoulos, in his second term as the Athens Mayor, announced, on 18 December 2000, on TV the creation of a new party which, three months later (on March 6, 2001), he called the 'Movement of Free Citizens' (KEP). Fifteen months later, he announced that his decision to suspend the operations of KEP was due to 'the excessive economic demands...and our refusal to depend on powerful economic interests'. In fact, it was a party based, either in its formation or in its demise, on the results of the pollsters. He received a strong start in the opinion polls, but, despite the heavy promotion of the media, his party never received more than 16% in the polls and in 2001 had slipped below 5%.

The second point is harder to illustrate. Polls seemed to have played a role in the displacement of the old leadership that took place in both PASOK and New Democracy during the last decade. In a country where the leader acts as a personification of his party, in eras of high intensity of political preferences, the pollsters' candidates may give the party ticket to someone acceptable. As Samaras notes:

> On either occasion, the choice of the candidate aims to affect what the party stands for (i.e., the product enhances the brand). Thus, after the death of Papandreou, PASOK elected Simitis as its new leader because the connotations of modernity and effectiveness attached to him would make the party more electable, a choice that was proved wise both in the 1996 and in the 2000 elections... In 1996, N[ew] D[emocracy] elected Kostas Karamanlis because his image of youth could attack connotations of 'new', 'modern' and 'near to the people' and thus helps re-brand ND (2002, p. 171).

The polls for Simitis were showing that PASOK would lose the coming elections under his leadership. Two months before the national elections, Simitis stepped down and was replaced by George Papandreou, a popular politician in the polls. His image as a young, popular and friendly politician was seen as the antidote to PASOK's opponent, Karamanlis. This confirms that, within a party-centred political regime such as the Greek one, the personal qualities of the party leader intertwine with the connotations attached to a party label and the 'use of the issues to formulate the image of the party' (Samaras, 2002, p. 170).

... AND GOVERNMENT NEWS MANAGEMENT

Following the developments in other countries and with the dominance of the media in Greek society, the government, especially since the late 1990s, has tried to adopt and implement a public relations and communication strategy. While in the past there were a few information officers, their number has considerably increased in all ministries, mainly consisting of journalists. In 1994 the Ministry of the Press and the Media was formed, with the Minister to act in most cases as the government's spokesperson, rather than as a minister who tries to form and implement the government's policy on the communication sector.

On the other hand, most government ministries have formed their own press office, again consisting of journalists and, to a much lesser extent, of specialised civil servants, in order to inform the public. Since the late 1990s, and the preparation of the Olympics, and major construction work co-financed by the European Union, the government publicises its achievements directly through commercial adverts. These state adverts are a considerable source of revenue for the media, and it was noted that most of them (and money) were directed towards 'friendly' media. There is also a law (2328 of 1995) that demands that about 40% of state adverts for the press should be directed to the local press media.

THE 'NEW' RELATIONSHIPS BETWEEN POLITICIANS AND THE MEDIA

The media have also assumed a central role in day-to-day politics. Throughout the 1990s, members of the Parliament and other politicians have attached increasing importance to enhancing their visibility by appearing on television. At the same time, the authority of traditional governmental institutions – the Parliament and the Presidency of the Republic – has declined. Research shows that the Greek Parliament, whose sessions at one time used to attract the interest of the nation, has now been downgraded. Images of the empty seats of ministers and deputies emphasise this change. The President of the Republic, Constantine Stephanopoulos, observed that the members of the Parliament preferred TV stations to Parliament. Demertzis and Armenakis (1999), in their research on the Press, Television and the Hellenic Parliament, note that, although the amount of political news coverage increased considerably between 1987 and 1997, since 1987 it has decreased in comparison to other news items and coverage. News coming from Parliament has decreased, even in the political sections of the newspapers and is mostly focused on individuals and tends towards sensationalist treatment. The Parliamentarians have welcomed television, but are wary of its effects. They dislike the way that both private and commercial channels cover Parliament and the political world. Most of them believe that a parliamentary television channel should provide better coverage of parliament (Demertzis & Armenakis, 1999).

These developments clearly point to the fact that politicians in the age of the media are desperately seeking to increase (or stabilise) their visibility through the TV camera. The deputy leader of the New Democracy party, Yannis Varvitsiotis, justified this:

> Previously, a new Member of Parliament used to become known through his work there. Nowadays, no young Member of Parliament bothers. They prefer to become widely known by adopting a heretical point of view on TV. The best proposal in the Parliament sessions can only be read by 300,000 readers [the total sales of Greek newspapers]. A dissident view becomes widely known to the three million viewers of the television channels (*Kathimerini*, 1995, p. 4).

It is probably no coincidence that, since January 2004, Parliament officially has its own TV channel, Vouli, transmitting on the most sought after UFH frequencies.

But can we legitimately interpret these developments as a sign of professionalisation of the political parties and amongst its members? Or are they merely the result of the need politicians have to survive and exist within a more media-saturated social life? Is this a professionalisation process or some unplanned, unstructured effort for media visibility?

The increasing dissidence artificially created by politicians, aimed at attracting media attention, provides important arguments in support of the second interpretation. While in the past politicians had to follow the party line, they nowadays present dissenting views just to attract controversy and appear on 'telly'. In January 1982, less than a year after the Socialist Party PASOK came to office, party leader Andreas Papandreou announced a rule of public behaviour for his deputies. In a ten-page document, he prescribed the rights and the responsibilities of his party's MPs, including the rule not to make statements, send telegrams, write for newspapers or give press interviews without the prior consent of the party directorate (Alivizatos, 1995, p. 173). Fourteen years later (10 September 1995) in a major press interview Papandreou commented:

> The political climate is appalling nowadays. This is due, to a large extent, to television. Television has disorganised us. Every member of the party (not only from PASOK), runs to the screen where he expresses his own positions rather than the position of the party, which we are obliged as members (of PASOK) to communicate to the public. Is it possible for a party with 170 MPs to have 170 positions on an issue? Can we solve this problem by 'expelling' (karatomiseis) party members?

The media have also begun to fight with the politicians over the control of the political agenda and have started to make themselves heard in the process of political communication with a constant stream of criticism of politicians and the actions of the parties (Demertzis & Kafetzis, 1996; Komninou, 1996). The rise of the commercial media may have precipitated this trend and created a situation where today Greek citizens can watch an endless stream of negative stories about political scandals, rivalry, conflict and self-interest. And, as with the media in other liberal democratic countries, the Greek media have tried to create stories about political conflict by giving particular attention to politicians who hold controversial views or who oppose the actions of the government.

What politicians, parties and ministers have tried in response is to develop relationships with the media and journalists. This is achieved in a more traditional way, either by employing journalists in their press office (mainly the ministers) or by developing a close relationship either as a friend, or as a political source, or even by doing them a favour. Such practices, again, could hardly be considered professional. Rather they constitute a more elaborated development of the traditional clientelism that dominated the Greek political system.

GREEK POLITICS IN THE ERA OF PROFESSIONALISATION

There have undoubtedly been new developments in the Greek media environment, and the political system as a whole. More importantly, perhaps, these changes reflect a convergence of developments in both institutions. These changes lend support to many of the statements made by Mancini and Swanson (1996), amongst others, with relation to the growing similarities in election practices across many countries: there are, it would seem, similarities despite great differences in political cultures, histories, and institutions of the countries in which they have occurred (Mancini & Swanson, 1996, pp. 2–3). Such similarities would include: the use of political commercials ('polispots'); candidates being selected in part for the appealing image which they project on television; the employment of technical experts to advise on strategies; the professionalisation of campaign communication and the like. These, and the increased expenditure on strategies aimed at the medium of television, show just how far the media have moved to the centre of the election process, even in Greece.

But the Greek case illustrates some, not all, of the elements that have been identified as comprising 'modernised' or 'media-centred democracy' (Blumler, 1990 & 1997; Mancini, 1991; Swanson, 1993; Mancini & Swanson, 1996; Negrine, 1996; Scammell, 1995; Mazzoleni, 1987; 1995). Despite this, there has not been a professionalisation of political communication as commonly understood (Scammell, 1999). As we have seen, there has been an increased use of media professionals; an increased – and more professional – use of television and media practices; a personalisation of politics; a detachment of parties from citizens; more political spectacle; and the media becoming more autonomous or central to the conduct of politics. As already noted, in adopting television-centred campaigning, the parties have moved away from the traditional emphases on public rallies and personal contacts with party workers, so lessening the opportunities for citizens to participate directly in campaigns and further distancing the parties from voters. In the past, public rallies in major cities were significant events but today it is the television debate, where 'telegenic' politicians debate all the issues on the TV channels. Little wonder, then, that *Avriani*, a populist newspaper sympathetic to PASOK, declared on its front page 'You can't win elections on the couch' and pleaded that 'All PASOK officials should take to the streets and deal with the people's problems first hand' (*Avriani*, 1996, p.1).

In other words, political parties have remained important, and the centralisation of communication has always been in the hands of the group that has the upper hand in the party. Furthermore, campaigns follow the traditional model: they are party-centred and labour intensive; receive free television time for the public political broadcasts; leaders front the main TV interviews and main political gatherings; they are publicly funded; and most importantly are managed by party staff. What may have changed are mainly the techniques the parties use for their political communication purposes. Media and communication professionals are employed within this context and, in most cases, only during the campaign period. In the case of Greece, it could be argued that the new communication environment has not so much eliminated the traditional particularistic political pressures associated with 'clientelism' or the party organisation, as changed the form of communication. The problem with politicians and political parties is that an election campaign and day-to-day politics that confuses politics with consumer marketing practices quickly become less credible.

REFERENCES

AGB Hellas (1996) *TV Yearbook 96/95*, Athens, (in Greek).

Alivizatos, N.K. (1995) 'Brackets and other centres of power', *Economicos Tachydromos*, June, 22, pp. 171–176 (in Greek).

Avriani (1996) 'You can't win elections on the couch!', 28 September, p.1 (in Greek).

Blumler, J.G. (1997) 'The origins of the crisis of communication for citizenship', *Political Communication*, 14:4, pp. 395–404.

Blumler, J.G. (1990) 'Elections, the Media and the Modern Publicity Process' in Marjorie Ferguson (ed) *Public Communication: The New Imperatives*. London: Sage.

Charalambis, D. & N. Demertzis (1993) 'Politics and Citizenship in Greece: Cultural and Structural Facets', *Journal of Modern Greek Studies*, 11, pp. 219–240.

Charalambis, D. (1996) 'Irrational contents of a formal rational system', pp. 289–311 in Ch. Lyrintzis, E. Nicolacopoulos, & D. Sotiropoulos (eds) *Society and Politics: Facets of the Third Hellenic Democracy, 1974–1994*. Athens: Themelio, (in Greek).

Charalambis, D. (1989) *Clientistic Relations and Populism*. Athens: Exantas.(in Greek)

Demertzis, N. & A. Armenacis (1999) *The Parliament in the Press and on Television*. Athens, University Research Institute of Applied Communication/ Department of Communication & Mass Media, University of Athens, (in Greek).

Demertzis, N. & P. Kafetzis (1996) 'Political Cynicism, Political Alienation and Mass Media: The Case of the Third Hellenic Republic', pp. 174–218 in Ch. Lyrintzis, E. Nicolacopoulos, & E. Sotiropoulos (eds) *Society and Politics: Facets of the Third Hellenic Democracy 1974–1994*. Athens: Themelio, (in Greek).

Demertzis, N. (ed) (2002) *Political Communication in Greece*. Athens: Papazisis, (in Greek)

Hope, K (2003) 'Power behind the Throne', *Financial Time/Magazine*, 28 June, pp. 10–11.

Kargiotis, Th.C. (ed.) (1992) *The Greek Socialist Experiment: Papandreou's Greece 1981–1989*. New York: Pella Publishing Company Inc.

Kathimerini, (1995) 'The media promote heretic views', 9 April, p. 4 (in Greek).

Komninou, M. (1996) 'The Role of the Media in the Third Hellenic Republic', pp. 219–246 in Ch. Lyrintzis, E. Nicolacopoulos, & E. Sotiropoulos (eds) *Society and Politics: Facets of the Third Hellenic Democracy 1974–1994*. Athens: Themelio.

Leandros, N. (1992) *Mass Printed Press in Greece*. Athens: Delfini, (in Greek).

Lyrintzis, Ch., E. Nicolacopoulos, & E. Sotiropoulos (eds) (1996) *Society and Politics: Facets of the Third Hellenic Democracy 1974–1994*. Athens: Themelio, (in Greek).

Lyrintzis, Ch. (1987) 'The Power of Populism: The Greek Case', *European Journal of Political Research*, 15, pp. 667–686.

Mancini, P. (1991) 'The Public Sphere and the use of news in a "coalition" government', pp. 137–154 in P. Dahlgren & C. Sparks (eds) *Communication and Citizenship; journalism and the public sphere*. London: Routledge.

Mancini, P. (2000) 'Political Complexity and Alternative Models of Journalism: The Italian Case', pp. 264–278 in J. Curran & M.J. Park (eds) *De-Westernizing Media Studies*. London, Routledge.

Mancini, P. & D.L Swanson (1996) 'Politics, Media and Modern Democracy: Introduction', pp. 1–26 in D.L. Swanson & P. Mancini (eds) *Politics, Media and Modern Democracy: An International Study of Innovations in Electoral Campaign and their Consequences*. New York: Praeger.

Mazzoleni, G. (1987) 'Media Logic and Party Logic in Campaign Coverage: The Italian General Election in 1983', *European Journal of Communication*, 2:1, pp. 81–103.

Mazzoleni, G. (1995) 'Towards a "Videocracy", Italian Political Communication at a Turning Point', *European Journal of Communication*, 10:3, pp. 291–319.

Moschonas, G. (2001) 'The path of modernisation: PASOK and European Integration', *Journal of Southern Europe and the Balkans*, 3:1, pp. 11–24.

Mouzelis, N. (1995) 'Greece in the Twenty-first Century: Institutions and Political Culture', pp. 17–34 in D. Constas, & Th.G. Stavrou (eds) *Greece Prepares for the Twenty-first Century*. Baltimore and London: The John Hopkins University Press.

Mouzelis, N. (1986) *Politics in the Semi-Periphery: Early Parliamentarism and Late Industrialism in the Balkans and Latin America*. London: Macmillan.

The Professionalisation of Political Communication

Negrine, R. & S. Papathanassopoulos (1996) 'The "Americanization" of Political Communication: A Critique', *Press/Politics*, 1:2, pp. 45–62.

Negrine, R. (1996) *The Communication of Politics*. London: Sage.

Papathanassopoulos, S. (1997) *The Power of Television*. Athens, Kastaniotis, (in Greek).

Papathanassopoulos, S. (1999) 'The Effects of Media Commercialization on Journalism and Politics in Greece', *The Communication Review*, 3:4, pp. 379–402.

Papathanassopoulos, S. (2000) 'Election campaigning in the television age: The case of contemporary Greece, *Political Communication*, 17:1, pp. 47–60.

Papathanassopoulos, S. (2001a) 'Media Commercialization and Journalism in Greece', *European Journal of Communication*, 16:4, pp. 505–521.

Papathanassopoulos, S. (2001b) 'The Decline of Newspapers: the case of the Greek press', *Journalism Studies*, 2:1, pp. 109–121.

Papathanassopoulos, S. (2002) 'Television and Elections in Greece in the 1990s' pp. 39–94 in N. Demertzis (ed) *Political Communication in Greece*. Athens: Papazisis, (in Greek)

Psychogios, D.K. (1992) *The Uncertain Future of the Athenian Press*. Athens: Diaulos, (in Greek).

Samaras, A.N. (2002) 'Political Marketing, Partytocracy and the Transformations of the Political Communication System', *Journal of Business and Society*, 15:1 & 2, pp. 158–174.

Samaras, A.N. (1999) 'Party-Centered Campaigning and the rise of Political Advertising in Greece', pp. 187–205 in L. Kaid, (ed) *Television and Politics in Evolving European Democracies*. Commack, New York: Nova Science Inc.

Scammell, M. (1999) 'Political Marketing: Lessons for Political Science', *Political Studies*, XLVIII, pp. 718–739.

Scammell, M. (1995) *Designer Politics. How Elections are Won*. Basingstoke: Macmillan.

Serafetinidou, M. (2002) *Political Sociology*. Athens: Gutenberg, (in Greek).

Swanson, D.L. (1997) 'The Political-Media Complex at 50. Putting the 1996 Presidential Campaign in Context', *American Behavioral Scientist*, 40, pp. 1264–1282.

Swanson, D.L. (1993) 'Political Institutions in media centred democracy'. (Paper presented at the course on Parliament and Public Opinion sponsored by the Universitad Complutense de Madrid, El Escorial, Spain, 2–6 August).

Swanson, D.L. (1992) 'The political-media complex', *Communication Monographs*, 59, pp. 397–400.

Tsoukalas, K. (1986) *State, Society, Labour*. Athens: Themelio, (in Greek).

V-PRC (Project Research Consulting Institute) (1998) *The Profile of Greek Journalism*. Athens, (in Greek).

Yannas, P. (2002) 'The Role of Image-Makers in the Greek Political Scene', *Journal of Political Marketing*, 1:1, pp. 67–89.

Zaharopoulos, T. & E.M. Paraschos (1993) *Mass Media in Greece, Power Politics and Privatization*. Westport, Connecticut: Praeger.

Zaoussis, A. & K. Stratos (1995) *The Newspapers 1974–1992*. Athens: Themelio, (in Greek).

9

The Evolution of French Political Communication: Reaching the Limits of Professionalisation?

Philippe J. Maarek

Today, professionalisation of French political communication seems like a *fait accompli*. Whether during electoral campaigns or while carrying out day-to-day government or local government public relations, modern French political communication seems to be as sophisticated as it is in most democratic countries. All the main French politicians are now expected to possess a high degree of awareness and mastery of political communication skills, and even the Mayor of the smallest French town has now changed its logo, hired a Public Relations Officer and is keen on publishing a monthly or quarterly magazine.

Roughly thirty years ago the average citizen first took notice of this phenomenon when Valery Giscard d'Estaing, a rather bourgeois liberal politician, successfully ran the 1974 presidential race by posing with his two daughters on his campaign posters, and by playing the ever-so traditional accordion in front of the television cameras. Just seven years later no French citizen could ignore the fact that political communication advisor Jacques Séguéla had conceived a winning slogan 'La force tranquille' (the quiet strength), which ignited François Mitterrand's 1981 presidential winning streak and had been plastered on most of the huge double advertising billboards placed all along French roads and highways.

We will establish here that the presence on the front page of professionalised political communication did not happen in a day; it has subtly and thoroughly penetrated the

French public sphere. But we will then try and assess if the cycle has not now come to an end: some legal measures have been enforced in order to contain the excesses of modern communication, while, in some cases, political communication might be seen as one of the causes of the defeat of some politicians.

We will also notice that professionalised political communication has not limited its effects to elections only, but has had an influence on the whole French democratic system, and on its balance of power.

PROFESSIONALISATION OF POLITICAL COMMUNICATION SINCE THE SIXTIES: FIGHTING FOR THE BEST POLITICAL MARKETING CONSULTANT...

From 'Mister X' to Valery Giscard d'Estaing: the increasing presence of professionalised political communication

Some have forgotten the first true appearance of modern 'professionalised' political marketing techniques in France: in September 1963, journalist Jean Ferniot started a teasing campaign in the weekly magazine *L'Express* intended to put in orbit socialist politician Gaston Deferre for the presidential election to come two years later. Titled 'Monsieur X... contre De Gaulle' (Mister X... against de Gaulle), the paper started to elaborate on which qualities a politician should possess to be the best candidate against General de Gaulle, the then incumbent President of the French Republic. From week to week the news magazine deliberately kept composing the portrait of an 'ideal' political leader, who was in the end disclosed as being Gaston Deferre, Mayor of Marseilles.

Ultimately Deferre did not run in 1965, leaving room for François Mitterrand, and, probably because there was no concrete presidential candidacy outcome from this 'teasing', the introduction of modern political marketing techniques has become more often associated with the good results obtained by Jean Lecanuet, a then unknown centrist politician. He had hired, as his main advisor, a promising marketing consultant, Michel Bongrand, who had spent several months in Joe Napolitano's staff in the United States learning the new rules of the game. For the first time in modern history, French voters were presented with the image of a 'smiling' politician on political posters, with such a Hollywood-like grin that Jean Lecanuet was immediately nicknamed 'dents blanches' (white teeth) by journalists and opponents alike!

At the time, since French radio and television were still a State monopoly, it had been ruled that politicians competing for an election could not buy advertising spots, or any other kind of televised show, but would be granted free airtime on an equal basis within 'official campaign programmes'. Again advised by Bongrand to strongly differentiate himself from De Gaulle, Lecanuet kept building the same kind of image with his first statement in these programmes. His opening words were 'I am Jean Lecanuet, I am an ordinary French citizen, not a hero', and so on, in a familiar tone never before employed by French politicians.

Of course Lecanuet did not make it, and De Gaulle was re-elected. But most politicians and journalists have credited his dynamic and professionalised campaign with the fact that De Gaulle was not immediately re-elected and had to endure a second round of voting.

Two years later, the final recognition of this thunderous arrival in France of professionals in political marketing and communication came from the Gaullists themselves, campaigning for the 1967 parliamentary elections. They hired none other than…the same Michel Bongrand! He successfully fulfilled his task and dutifully helped their party, the UNR, to win, notably against his former centrist customers. His most clever accomplishment was to get the endorsement, so to speak, of the image of the *Sower* which had been present on one side of French coins for decades: he included its drawing on the visuals of most of the campaign material.

The same appraisal of Jean Lecanuet's ability to surround himself with the best possible political communication professionals was made some years later. Denis Beaudoin, the communications specialist he had appointed at the head of his party's first communications cell, was later lured away and hired by Jacques Chirac to become the Head of Communications at the Paris town hall when the latter was elected Mayor of the French capital.

Public opinion polls also burst noisily on the French scene, thanks to the 1965 presidential election. While most of politicians and journalists had been assuming that De Gaulle would easily be re-elected in just one round of voting, the main pollsters bravely advocated that their figures, against all odds, were predicting a second round. When the real outcome came to match the polls, their credibility was established. This probably explains why French politicians have been so blindly trusting of pollsters ever since, as we'll see later.

Valery Giscard d'Estaing, winning the 1974 presidential campaign, contributed further to establishing professionalised political marketing as the core element of victory. Giscard d'Estaing knew that he was hindered by his well-established image of a rather bourgeois Finance Minister – the one who collects taxes in the eyes of the average voter. So he tried to soften this impression by introducing personal details about his life in his campaign. In one of the main campaign posters, he was for instance presented as a charismatic father alongside his daughter, with his name only mentioned at the side and with no political slogan: quite a 'first' for a French politician. For the first ever televised 'decisive debate' in France, on May 10th, Giscard d'Estaing's media training had been so intensive that he was able to deliver effortlessly many superb quotes, which are still fresh in the memory of the viewers and admired by politicians[1]. Twenty five million viewers witnessed the ease of the president-to-be in contrast to his obviously ill-prepared opponent: François Mitterrand looked as if he was seeking shelter behind the piles of notes he kept consulting to support his answers.

François Mitterrand's era: triumph of political communication techniques
After the first attempts by Jean Lecanuet, Valery Giscard d'Estaing was one of the first prominent French politicians to systematically organise his campaigns and his communication according to modern professionalised political marketing. For instance, when he became President, he was the first to establish a polling cell within the presidential administration, located in the Palais de l'Elysée itself, the residence of the French presidents. The cell was in charge of regularly supervising the image of the President in French media and of ordering surveys from the pollsters whenever necessary.

In the 1981 presidential election, when François Mitterrand was again running against Valery Giscard d'Estaing, he had learned his lesson and he did not make the same mistake of underestimating professionalised political communication. He hired one of the best political marketing consultants at the time, Jacques Séguéla, a founder of one of the most well-known advertising agencies, RSCG. He trusted him so much that he agreed to dental surgery in order to erase the tip of his canines, which allegedly gave him the look of a vampire when he opened his mouth too widely…

No campaign ever followed more closely the rules of professionalised political communication than Mitterrand's 1981 victory. His main slogan, 'La Force Tranquille' (The quiet strength), had been devised by Séguéla who had astutely taken into account sociological research led by polling institute Cofremca: their thesis was that the 'wild' generation that had thrown pavement stones at policemen in 1968 had now transformed into established bourgeois spouses with kids, enriched, furthermore, by twenty years of money inflation which had considerably alleviated their bank debts. This astute positioning proved right. It was supported by hundreds of posters all around France: billboards showing Mitterrand in front of a 'typical' French village, where the local church bell tower was prominently displayed, in order to symbolically summon traditional French values to the aid of the socialist leader.

Similarly, this time, the 1981 'decisive' debate was much better prepared for by Mitterrand. Weeks ahead, he had sent his communication advisors, including veteran television director Serge Moatti, to meet Giscard d'Estaing's team in order to agree on an easier format, which would prevent any form of mutual interruption while the politicians were speaking. The cameras were also constrained into scrupulously shooting only the candidate who was speaking, without any insert of the face of his opponent. The show's director was not even allowed to change the live camera angle without the authorisation of the two candidates' own directors, who were sitting next to him in the control room! The two moderators, journalists Michèle Cotta and Jean Boissonnat, had also been chosen after agreement between the two teams. Comforted by these precautions, Mitterrand, for the first time, fared much better than Giscard, and the 'decisive' debate was one of the cornerstones of his presidential victory.

During the fourteen years of François Mitterrand's era, professionalisation of electoral campaigning was not an isolated phenomenon. As ruling President, he extensively used all the range of professionalised political communication, not only to help enforce his policy, but also, in a deliberate and systematic way, to build and sustain his image. In 1984, he was the first French President to permanently employ a political communication consultant, Jacques Pilhan, who guided even his most insignificant public appearance. In particular, within a year of being hired, Pilhan conceived for Mitterrand a memorable image-building televised show 'Ca nous interesse monsieur le Président' ('It's of interest to us, Mister President') where he had Mitterrand capitalising on the popularity of Yves Mourousi, one of the most popular television journalists and host at the time, in order to start rebuilding his image after the socialist party defeat in the 1986 parliamentary election. Here, Mitterrand was presented as knowing how youngsters really talk and what interested them, as a first step of a long-run image-building strategy intended to help his re-election in 1988 and to obliterate the fact that, by then, he would be much older than most of his probable opponents.

This professionalisation of the Presidential public relations and communication went down to every level of his administration. The 'official' communication office of the Government was also reorganised as a strong taskforce by communication theorist and professional Jean-Louis Missika, who considerably strengthened the status of the Service d'Information et de Diffusion du Premier Ministre (Information and Diffusion Office of the Prime Minister), now known as the Service d'information du Gouvernement (Government Information Service). Similarly, directors of communications started to become high-ranking officers within the Ministers' staff.

The final stroke of the professionalisation of political communication during Mitterrand's era paradoxically happened right after it had ended. Such was Jacques Pilhan's ability in advising Mitterrand that as soon as his long time adversary Jacques Chirac had been elected President, in 1995, Pilhan was surprisingly asked to join Chirac's staff. This caused turmoil, notably among the socialists, who felt betrayed by Pilhan, though in truth the latter had never been a socialist activist. Surprisingly, this unexpected combination worked very well, and Jacques Pilhan got along quite nicely with Chirac's main political communication advisor, his daughter, Claude. Pilhan effortlessly advised Chirac in the same way as he had Mitterrand, for instance placing him on television in December 1996 in front of journalists who did not normally cover politics in order to sustain his popularity. So, in a way, Jacques Chirac has followed the lead of his former old-time adversary with regard to his use of the whole range of the routines of professionalised political communication. This collaboration was only broken by the premature death of Jacques Pilhan in June 1998.

Such was the grip of political communication consultants during Mitterrand's era that, in a bold move, Jacques Séguéla started right after the 1981 campaign to boast in television interviews about his 'part' in the victory, and somehow presented himself as winner of the campaign as much as Mitterrand himself. This public 'backstage' exposure of the political campaigns has been constant since that period, and the fact that François Mitterrand never uttered any reproach to Séguéla (at least publicly) and, on the contrary, hired him again for this re-election campaign in 1988, somehow tacitly granted the consultant a special status among his peers, and also in the eyes of the average citizen.

An indirect, but not negligible consequence of this public exposure of political marketing techniques was an increasing awareness of the consultants' methods and their influence on politicians, a phenomenon which probably caused some disillusionment among the average citizen by making them look like manipulated puppets on a string, so to speak.

At the beginning of the 1988 presidential run, this public exposure had become so common that the same Séguéla was repeatedly invited onto the main televised evening newscasts in order to explain what kind of campaign he had prepared for the re-election of the incumbent President. He was even asked by journalists to comment publicly on how he had devised his new gimmick, the slogan 'Génération Mitterrand' (Mitterrand's generation), in order to defuse any attack on Mitterrand based on his old age, in comparison with the other politicians running.

For the first time, the limitation on candidates' use of free airtime on the public service television channels was also relaxed. This allowed Mitterrand to introduce into official television campaign programmes short spots presenting in a few seconds the most well-known events in French History, thus making him appear as heir of the Nation's past.

THE PAST DECADE: REACHING THE LIMITS OF PROFESSIONALISATION?
The failure of legal limitations: the paradoxical influence of the 1990 law
The rise of professionalised political marketing pushed electoral advertising expenses to an extremely high level during the 1988 campaign[2]. Moreover, the funding of most of the campaigns was not really transparent, to say the least. So journalists and judges alike started to take an interest in the sources and methods of this funding, which soon provoked a media campaign denouncing the excesses. Consequently, politicians devised the first law to regulate campaign expenditures in 1988, which was not very thorough, and, in short, was intended rather to protect them from jail, since it also introduced an automatic amnesty for any past offences committed by the politicians. Hence soon after, on January 15th 1990, there was a new, stricter law, which still rules French electoral campaigns. It extended the former prohibition of buying advertising spots on radio and television to all kinds of paid advertising and similar ways of communication during the three months before any important election. Only the fact that the Internet did not exist in France in 1990 prevented it from following the same fate: its French forerunner, Minitel, was no longer allowed.

This means that not only television or radio commercials, but also billboard advertising, adverts in newspapers and magazines, and direct marketing (mailing, phone marketing, etc.) are now strictly prohibited to politicians at the peak of electoral campaigns, forcing them to be content with 'old fashion' media, like meetings, leaflets, canvassing and so on.

The only direct access to audiovisual media left is the very short airtime given free to candidates or political parties on Public broadcast channels, and of course, to the final 'decisive debates'. Naturally, politicians' campaigns are also reported, under strict equal access rules during newscasts or political programmes according to the newsrooms' electoral coverage decisions, but journalists being, in France like elsewhere, inclined to follow the 'horse race' story line, this coverage is quite deficient, both on issues and contents, and on the 'smaller' candidates' campaigns. The situation even worsened recently for the 2004 regional and European elections, when the French Audiovisual Supervising Board, the Conseil Supérieur de l'Audiovisuel (CSA) took the unprecedented step of ruling out any appearance of politicians during the same three month period on any kind of programme except the newscasts or specific political programmes dedicated to the campaign. No Arsenio Hall anymore, so to speak, or his French counterpart, Michel Drucker, the ever pleasant talk-show host, for French politicians during the three months before election day…

Political marketing consultants and specialists immediately complained, and are still complaining, alleging limitations to freedom of speech caused by the new law. Fifteen years later, they are still trying to get rid of some of the limitations of this law, with some partial results coming from their persistent lobbying, but without changes to the main rules. For instance in 2004, they have managed to get a decision from the CSA granting some leeway in the preparation of the free time allocated on official television campaign programmes: for the first time, during that year's European parliamentary elections, the French audiovisual regulatory board allowed political parties to shoot any kind of spots they wanted for the free airtime given on the Public broadcast channels, where they were previously forced to limit themselves to the restricted technical means put at their disposal by the CSA.

But political marketing consultants did not really obtain any major change in the 1990 Law for a simple reason: while it has indeed influenced the operating ways of the campaigns, it has in fact increased the need for professionalisation of the campaigns, and therefore the need for their help. While limiting the range of media that political campaigns can now use, the application of the 1990 Law has led to more thorough and organised campaigns. It has even increased the level of professionalisation by forcing politicians to redesign their campaigns more thoroughly, in order to comply with the new Law.

In 1995 and 2002, two presidential campaigns have indeed unrolled with no real technical hassle (not counting a plethora of campaigns for parliamentary or local government seats, for the European parliament, etc.). The only real hindrance has been to put a heavier load on the candidates themselves on a purely physical level. Instead of making a few limited appearances in a reduced number of mass meetings and getting a lot of television coverage, including talk-shows, they now have to canvass in their constituencies much more extensively than before: the only way now, to reach citizens directly, or indirectly through the newscasts that report these contacts. Of course, this means running around the whole of France for Presidential elections, a lesson Edouard Baladur, then incumbent Prime Minister, learned the hard way when his 1995 campaign sank in disarray because of the lack of meetings and canvassing.

Conversely, crowd pleasers like Jacques Chirac, who personally enjoys canvassing and shaking hands, have clearly benefited from the new law. But this leads to a much tighter campaign organisation: having the main politicians crossing France and speaking in two or three different towns a day means having a stronger than ever campaign manager or field coordinator. Speeches have to be written on time and to be punctually in the politicians' hands (or on their prompters) two or three times a day, with variations according to the time and place, or according to the kind of crowds expected. Previously, an appearance on a popular talk show demanded only a few specialists for some days of media training.

Another side effect of the new prohibitions coming from the 1990 law has been the increase of pressure on media and journalists by politicians and their press agents in order to obtain access to the regular newscasts, since here the law only requires an equal access under the supervision of the CSA. So public relations events, orchestrated by the candidate's campaign organisation in order to get media attention, have been purposely escalating in order to compete for the journalists' attention – another breakthrough for increased professionalisation in the candidates' public relations.

To give one example from the 2002 Presidential race: Lionel Jospin's campaign management, understanding at some point that he seemed to be lacking popular support, organised a huge meeting in Lille, a town in the North of France, inhabited for historical reasons by many socialist activists and sympathisers (it is the capital of a former mining region). Jospin's entrance into the meeting room was very carefully planned. Instead of going directly to the stage, he was shown in at the very far end of the meeting room, thus needing quite a lot of time to cross the floor. Those attending were very happy to be able to reach the socialist leader so easily and to shake his hand; so it took him nearly one hour to get to the stage through the crowd. The scene was effectively televised in the evening news by most of the journalists, duped by the so-called 'popularity' of the politician so evidently exposed… Here, a not so subtle trick of day to day political marketing fared well, not unlike what happened two years later in the United States when, to boost his popularity, John Kerry's campaign management begged him to drop his jacket during his meetings.

Another interesting consequence of the 1990 law was an increased need to recruit new party militants and activists on a more regular basis. Before its enforcement, direct marketing had rather loosened the link between parties and political activists and militants: the 'direct communication' between campaigning politicians and the citizen apparently established by modern media had by-passed them and had been discouraging them by making them somehow redundant. In contrast, the 1990 law, by forcing politicians to organise more meetings across their constituencies, has amplified the need to get the support of strong local networks of local militants able to greet campaigners, to bring sympathisers to the meetings, to help organise them and also to give clues of local specificities so that the politicians' speeches appear to address the needs of each particular audience. This has remotivated political activism and strengthened parties or politicians to try to benefit from a dense network of local supporters.

These attempts to revitalise the militant structures were even more obvious at the beginning of 2005 when three of the main political parties, the Socialist Party, the UDF (Union pour la Démocratie Française) and the UMP (Union pour un Mouvement Populaire) started a campaign to recruit a new kind of 'temporary' militant[3]. For the Socialist Party, the 'projects members' should be allowed to enroll without any previous screening by established militants cells, and even to do so online on the Socialist Party Website. They would just need to pay a symbolic flat fee instead of the high fee in proportion to income paid by the 'regular' party activists. But they will only be able to take part in the elaboration of the Socialist Party's new electoral programme, and won't be able to vote for the choice of the Socialist Party candidates in the future elections, for instance, unless they decide to become 'full' militants and are accepted as such. In the same way, the UMP plans to establish a new category of 'partner militants', exempt from dues, and only able to take part in the debates on issues and programmes. Finally, the UDF plans to stabilise some of its non-affiliated 'companions' by enrolling them, in a similar pattern, as 'associated militants'.

By increasing the number of public meetings, the 1990 Law has also forced politicians to return to a stricter application of the old method of the 'Unique Selling Proposition or Point' (USP) transposed from the marketing techniques: when all is said and done, the USP is the best way of maintaining a clear and strong image. Jacques Chirac's 1995 campaign, led by his daughter, Claude Chirac, has clearly demonstrated this. She devised a clever targeting of the left with a political programme mainly intended to reduce the so-called 'fracture sociale', (social breach) between rich and poor. It worked by being incessantly repeated to the crowds, as perfectly as Bill Clinton had done for his two campaigns' USP on economics.

Lionel Jospin's unexpected 2002 debacle: too much professionalisation?
While the Law had not really managed to constrain political communication, even if it was without any doubt influencing its ways, professionalisation probably came to find

its own limits in 2002. That year, the presidential race led to a surprise as great as the unexpected difficulties of re-election met by De Gaulle in 1965. The first round of voting eliminated the incumbent Socialist Prime Minister, Lionel Jospin, competing again, though he was thought to possess all the necessary skills and weapons to push incumbent opponent President Jacques Chirac into early retirement. What came as a shock was not only that Lionel Jospin could not make it to the second round of voting, but that in failing to do so he gave way to the far-right extremist leader, Jean-Marie Le Pen.

Lionel Jospin had put up a very sophisticated and professionalised campaign, even taking the time to think twice about the nickname of his campaign headquarters: instead of calling it the 'Headquarters', or any similar banal name, he had it baptised 'L'atelier de campagne' (The campaign workshop), a subtle effort to try and distance himself from the professional political marketing techniques he was paradoxically obeying in doing so.

More importantly, as soon as his campaign started, in his first interview during one of the main evening television newscasts, Jospin exposed an extremely bold target, which most probably put off more than one of his potential supporters on voting day. He made an unexpected statement: 'Le projet que je propose au pays n'est pas un projet socialiste' ('The project I am advocating for the country is not a socialist one'). In the following days of his campaign, he consequently outlined campaign issues that were quite far from what was expected of a socialist candidate: for instance, he insisted on the question of the personal security of the citizen, in the streets, in their home, or for their children at school, thus choosing to expose himself by trying to take his adversaries' field, but proving ill at ease with that choice[4].

It seems that this targeting strategy had been mainly conceived by his main political campaigning advisor, the ever present Jacques Séguéla, with the help of his younger protégé, Stéphane Fouks, a new star in the political marketing business and at the helm of one of Séguéla's company subsidiaries, Euro-RSCG Public. They were thinking that Jospin, like Mitterrand in 1981, could only win the race if he could attract citizens inclined to vote for the centre or even for the right. This choice proved wrong: the targeted new social category of *Bourgeois Bohêmes* (Bohemian Bourgeois), now inhabiting the main towns, and notably the French capital (leading to the arrival of a socialist mayor at its helm for the first time), was clearly not in a majority in France. Also, this targeting might have fared better for the second round of the race, but was not suitable for an initial round, when citizens mainly cast their vote for the politician they most favour, before deciding in the second round which one is less distant from them, so to speak.

A confirmation of this mistake came two years later, with the local government and European parliamentary election results, which saw the Socialist Party regain its usual results by a plain repositioning on the left side of the political chessboard. While the two far-left competitors of Jospin in 2002, Arlette Laguiller from Lutte Ouvrière (LO) and unknown newcomer Olivier Besancenot, from the Ligue Communiste Révolutionnaire (LCR), had managed to attract about 10% of the voters, an unusually high figure, and double their 'normal' result, they returned to the norm in 2004, leading once more to a socialist party in full power, even when still bereft of the former leader.

So the 2002 Jospin campaign, which was meant as a 'conquest campaign' as demonstrated in political marketing books, clearly misfired – probably because of mistaken field analysis. Not only did Jospin not convince his own to vote for him by denying his socialist past, but he had also failed to convince his new target. By not even defending his left wing mandate achievements at the start of the campaign, somehow Jospin appeared insincere – quite an image problem for someone whose posters were claiming that he would be 'a better President'.

These campaigning mistakes were obvious to the average citizen because a new phenomenon had appeared and clearly impeded Jospin. French media coverage is now more and more focused on the campaign itself. Somehow, the accomplishment of the professionalisation of the political communication process in France has been that campaigning and campaigning techniques by themselves have become news items, and, in particular, have benefited from a strong agenda effect during the 2002 campaign, thus immediately exposing the slightest mistake of the competing politicians – and here Jospin was a first-rate target because his targeting choice had put him on a wrong foot. This came as a logical consequence of the 'coming out' of political marketing consultants. Led by Jacques Séguéla's bold media exposure in the past two decades, it had been followed by most of his main competitors, who wrote numerous books based on the past campaigns, insisting on their 'part' in the election of the politicians they had been working for, and therefore increasing the public awareness of campaigning techniques.

In a way, Lionel Jospin had gone over the line by over-excessively professionalising his campaign: following too exclusively the precepts of well-organised political marketing techniques, he had lost his authenticity in the eyes of his potential voters, and therefore their support

An excessive trust for the pollsters: professionals also make mistakes…
A final factor that can be noticed about French political communication is the enormous confidence politicians and media alike are still giving to public opinion polls in spite of several severe mishaps. At least twice in recent years front runners have been severely beaten because of an ill-placed trust in public opinion polls, and this on-going blindness raises questions about their ability to work without a safety net.

The first case of an excessive trust in the public opinion polls occurred in 1997, when President Jacques Chirac decided with his then Prime Minister, Alain Juppé, to call a parliamentary election for an anticipated date. His opponents from the socialist party easily led a winning coalition, which forced him to endure five years of near-passivity in front of his new oppositional Prime Minister, Lionel Jospin. As it happens, the February (1997) polls results had been so favourable towards Jacques Chirac that he assumed that this support would remain constant for the next three months and thus was prepared to wait for the anticipated election date. This deadly mistake cost the job of the polling company director, Jerôme Jaffré. This appears extremely over-confident, especially since it is now a well-known fact that undecided voters are making their decisions later and later, sometimes even at the last moment as they enter the polling stations.

Another recurrent problem of French pollsters is the constant underestimation of the results of far-right politicians, and notably those of the notorious leader of the Front National, Jean-Marie Le Pen. Compared to countries where only two or three main parties exist, and thus encompass the majority of the votes, France has always had a variety of smaller parties, and also of parties representing the whole range of the political spectrum, from the communists and the Trotskyites to the far-right. As a consequence, many French citizens, and notably those who are close to the 'extremes', do not publicise their political beliefs, and even deliberately lie, even when questioned by pollsters guaranteeing anonymity. Two decades ago, when the National Front and other extreme parties were hardly getting any votes, this phenomenon did not matter. But since the mid-eighties, Jean-Marie Le Pen and his party have been regularly getting between 12% to 15% of the votes, even 17% in 2002[5]. This means that, during the past twenty years, pollsters have been forced to 'manually' modify their own results in trying to assess how many 'wrong' answers during the surveys had been given by people who would then vote for the far right. Even with these empirical corrections, the number of untruthful answers is still usually underestimated, probably because pollsters do not dare to over correct the figures they obtain.

In spite of this knowledge, in 2002, Lionel Jospin and his team trusted the poll results as much as Jacques Chirac had wrongly done in 1997. Since the polls' results had been similar for many months before the start of the campaign, clearly showing himself and Jacques Chirac holding the two top positions for the first round, Jospin and his team never thought that it could be otherwise, and thus never really took proper notice of their 'minor' first round opponents, nor their two competing far-left neighbours, Arlette Laguillet and Olivier Besancenot, nor the National Front leader, Jean-Marie Le Pen. This made a pathway for Le Pen, as we now know. It must be noted here that the danger had been correctly spotted by a few people in the final weeks of the campaign, notably by Jospin's main public opinion polls specialist, advisor Gérard le Gall, who was discourteously dismissed by the candidate himself and by his team[6]. If Jospin's campaigning team had listened to these warnings and not given preference to the pollsters, they may have realised the urgent need for a strong communication 'blitz' in the closing weeks of the first round in order to change its outcome. Most of the 'professional' communicators advising Jospin had made a lethal mistake, 'wishful thinking' so to speak, in believing the polls that satisfied them.

CONCLUSION: DIRECT AND INDIRECT EFFECTS OF PROFESSIONALISATION OF POLITICAL COMMUNICATION

Some say that when General de Gaulle was extensively using BBC airwaves during the Second World War to enunciate that the Free French would once more proudly brandish the French flag on French soil, he was already and spontaneously the utmost political communicator. To come back to a less heroic use of media by politicians, we can clearly conclude that French Political Communication has without any doubt taken its toll on French Politics since the mid-sixties – as in many similar democracies – following more or less willingly the American role model of the use of modern media.

The French variation has probably been owed to the lesser amount of technical freedom allowed by law to political communication professionals. But these regulations have, paradoxically, even increased the role of the political communication advisors, whose help is even more needed by campaigning politicians. The 1990 law, which was trying to limit the excesses of modern media use by banning paid advertising during the three last months of the campaigns, pushed professionalisation in the same way, since the campaigns had then to be led more rigorously than ever.

But the danger of putting too much trust in professionalised political communication ways and means is two-fold and has been clearly seen in the recent years in France.

First, since modern 'marketed' campaigns have been trying to reach the undecided or non 'politicised' voters, or their opponents 'fragile' supporters, political campaigning advisors have asked candidates to 'depoliticise' their communication in order to reach them. The resulting insistence on personality instead of issue positioning, for instance evidenced by appearance on non-political television shows, or by a public exposure of mundane family activities and private life, has led to a significant loss of symbolic strength for political life which can be linked to the decrease of participation. Here, one cannot help thinking about the wrong example given by Adlai Stevenson unnecessarily exposing himself in a 1956 advertising television spot – he was shown coming back from a shopping mall with huge paper shopping bags and trying to keep his composure...

Secondly, professionalism can also fail, especially in France where public opinion polls are less and less dependable – due to the extreme versatility of French voters, tempted by the presence of a wider range of political parties than in many other democracies. Campaigns are more often lost than won: 'Beware of helping professionals', perhaps.

Lionel Jospin was then a double victim of professionalisation failures in 2002, while Jacques Chirac, a victim in the 1997 parliamentary elections, won two consecutive

Presidential elections, in 1995 and 2002, thanks to very thorough campaigns led by the best possible professional one could get: a daughter, able to carve the utmost personally-designed campaign thanks to her extensive knowledge of her father-politician and by her easy access to him.

As a final remark, we should note that these changes in political communication and campaigning have had effects other than their direct consequences on election results. They have indirectly considerably influenced the whole French political system and modified the balance of power towards a considerable increase, in many respects, of the President's role.

Already the keystone of the French democratic system, the presidential election has given a greater influence to the elected presidents. By inducing a stronger and stronger personalisation of politics in the election process, the professionalisation of political communication has considerably strengthened them, not only in regards to their losing opponents, but also in relation to their own fellow party members. Political parties have been considerably weakened; they are now in some way 'anonymous' in the media to the eyes of the voters since they have no tangible existence in regards to the faces and words of the politicians who dominate and represent them. Therefore, they have quite clearly lost a lot of their ideological input value and are more and more used only as tools to achieve better election results.

The clear proof of this first effect is the way that the past two French presidents have been able to build their parties into very efficient electoral machines without much opposition. The socialist party was never as well disciplined as during the Mitterrand's era, and the RPR was very clearly assembled since its foundation in 1976 by Jacques Chirac to help him achieve his goal of becoming president. More recently, in taking control of the UMP, the party which succeeded the RPR, former economy and finance Minister Nicolas Sarcozy is following the same path.

This personal ascent of politicians who can endorse the ways and means of modern professionalised political communication has not been limited to a power struggle between those politicians and their parties. It has given an unheard of prominence in policy making to the elected Presidents, whose constitutional powers had already been strengthened by the 1958 Constitution of the 5th Republic. Ironically, this phenomenon has never been as obvious as during François Mitterrand's era. The same politician who had rejected the Constitution of the 5th Republic and called it a 'Coup d'Etat permanent' (A permanent Coup) in his famous book published right before the 1965 presidential election, has moulded himself quite easily in the seat of a quasi royal figure, changing Prime Ministers as he wished, and imposing most of his whims, without any opposition, thanks to the aura given to him by his two presidential victories. The loss of the 1986 parliamentary elections was not even enough to stop him playing a prominent role in French politics during the so-called 'cohabitation'. Similarly, Prime

Minister Jean-Pierre Raffarin's rather long stay at the helm of the French Government, despite an extremely low popularity rating in the polls, has clearly shown that only the will of President Jacques Chirac kept him in the job, another proof of the very strong grip on the whole political system given to French Presidents by the professionalisation of political communication.

In a way, when De Gaulle had devised the Constitution of the 5th Republic to strengthen the President, he had probably not imagined that the professionalisation of political communication was later going to give a much more definite support to his ideas. It does not only single out the President in regards to political parties, which was De Gaulle's plan, but also allows him to enforce his policies with little opposition... unless, of course, his supporters lose the parliamentary elections. But the recent constitutional change that links parliamentary and presidential mandates makes this option now less likely.

NOTES

1. His 'Monsieur Mitterrand, vous n'avez pas le monopole du Coeur' (Mister Mitterrand, you do not have a monopoly on the heart) is still vivid for that generation of French voters
2. Mitterrand's 'official' spending came to 99 million francs, and Jacques Chirac 95 million, but experts estimate both their campaigns to have cost about five times more if the hidden costs are included – whether by choice of hiding some expenses or just in adding the militants' work costs, invisible 'gifts to the cause', and so on.
3. in *Le Monde* , January 23–24, 2005
4. He even admitted once during an interview that he had not properly dealt with personal security issues while at the helm of Government, and probably had been too 'naïve' in thinking that solving the unemployment problem would also improve the citizen's personal security...
5. This latter relative rise in percentage was mainly caused by the rise of abstentions for the first round of the 2002 presidential election: Le Pen had only convinced about 233.000 more voters than for the 1995 election, but the participation decrease made him climb from 15% to 16.86% of the expressed votes.
6. A television crew was allowed to follow the Jospin campaign from within, so everyone has been able to see Gérard Le Gall brutally – and wrongly!– reprimanded in one of the campaign's management meetings by the Socialist Party Parliamentary Group Leader, Jean-Marc Ayrault (Maarek, 2004a).

REFERENCES

Ansolabehere, Stephen & Shanto Iyengar (1994) 'Of Horseshoes and Horse Races: Experimental Studies of the Impact of Poll Results on Electoral Behaviour', *Political Communication*, 11: 4, Oct–Dec 1994.

Ansolabehere, Stephen & Shanto Iyengar (1995) *Going negative, (How Political Advertisements Shrink and Polarize the Electorate)*. New York: The Free Press.

Bongrand, Michel (1986) 'Le marketing politique' Presses Universitaires de France, coll.. *'Que sais-je?'* N° 1698.

Davis, Richard (1999) *The Web of Politics', the Internet's impact on the American political system*. New York, Oxford: Oxford University Press.

Davis, Richard & Diana Owen (1998) *New media and American Politics*. New York, Oxford: Oxford University Press.

Diamond, E & S. Bates (1992 [1984]) *The Spot (The Rise of Political Advertising on Television)*. Cambridge, Mass.: MIT Press.

Heinrich, Francis (2002) 'Monsieur X à Bordeaux', in Les Français et la politique dans les années soixante (II), *Bulletin de l'Institut d'Histoire du temps prese*nt, October 2002 (also online at http://www.ihtp.cnrs.fr/).

Holtz-Bacha, Christina (2002) 'Professionalization of Political Communication: The Case of the 1998 SPD Campaign', *Journal of Political Marketing*, 1:4, pp. 23–37.

Jaffre, Jerôme (2003) 'La crise de la politique française un an après', *Le Monde*, April 23rd, 2003.

Godwin, R. Kenneth (1988) *One billion dollars of influence (The direct marketing of politics)*. Chatham, New Jersey: Chatham House Publishers, Inc.

Maarek, Philippe J. and Gadi Wolsfeld (2003) *Political Communication in a New Era*. Routledge, London and New York.

Maarek, Philippe J. (1995) *Communication and Political marketing*, London: John Libbey.

Maarek, Philippe J. (2001) 'Communication et Marketing de l'homme politique', 2e edition, LITEC, collection Carré Droit.

Maarek, Philippe J. (2002) 'Les mauvais choix de communication de Lionel Jospin', *'Quaderni'*, 48, pp. 5–12.

Maarek, Philippe J. (2003) 'Political Communication influence in the unexpected 2002 French Presidential Elections', *Journal of Political Marketing*, 2:4.

Maarek, Philippe J. (2004a) ' La Communication politique française après le tournant de 2002, September 2004, éditions L'Harmattan, coll. *Communication et civilisation*. Paris.

Maarek, Philippe J. (2004b) 'Professionalisation of Political Communication: A necessity or a Danger ?', in Juliana Raupp and Joachim Klewes, *Quo Vadis Public Relations?* Wiesbaden: Vs Verlag für Sozialwissenschaften.

Melder, Keith (1992) *Hail to the Candidate (Presidential Campaigns from Banners to Broadcasts)*. Washington and London: Smithsonian Institution Press.

Negrine, Ralph (1996) *The communication of politics*, London: Sage.

Negrine, Ralph (1996) 'The 'Americanization' of political communication', *The Harvard International Journal of Press and Politics*, 1:96.

Scammell, Margaret (1995) *Designer politics, how elections are won*. London: Saint Martin's Press.

West, Darrell M. (1991) *Air Wars: Television advertising in Election Campaigns, 1952–1992*. Washington: Congressional Quarterly Press.

10

POLITICAL TRANSITION AND THE PROFESSIONALISATION OF POLITICAL COMMUNICATION

Ildiko Kováts

INTRODUCTION: POLITICAL COMMUNICATION – BEFORE AND FOLLOWING THE POLITICAL REGIME CHANGE

The issue of the professionalisation of political communication in Hungary is inseparable from the process of political and social transformation that took place during the 1980s and 1990s, as politics itself was also professionalised. Political communication is an organic part of politics in that it is closely tied to the objectives of the key political players, their definitions of their tasks, their concepts of their roles, and the visions of society that they wish to communicate. Although there are widely and seemingly universally applicable methods of effective political communication, their analysis cannot be separated from the actual contexts of their usage.

Hungary's political transition is generally said to have begun in 1990 when the first free elections took place. In reality the transformation began earlier, but the first multi-party parliamentary elections ushered in a new type of democratic politics. Even though change was incremental, and although the former state party or party state utilised certain techniques associated with so-called professional political communication, 1990 can be considered the beginning of the process of the professionalisation of political communication because of the principal change of politics: the transformation to a pluralistic democracy.

During the last period of the socialist one-party system inner pluralism developed within the party leadership, and the party's reform wing stepped up its fight within the party against those who insisted on the old methods of control and governance. The reform wing's fight strengthened the activity of certain opposition groups outside the party. These evolved from the alternative civil and intellectual sub-cultural movements that had coalesced in the 1970s and 1980s around such issues as human rights, religious tolerance, environmental conservation, national culture, and the rights of Hungarian minorities in neighbouring countries.

These groups had emerged as substitutes for opposition parties that were not allowed to exist during the one-party system. They were later to form parties in parallel with the traditional renascent parties that had been suppressed 40 years earlier. A number of things linked these embryonic parties, including their nature as movements, their 'elite' character, their lack of embeddedness in society at large, and either small membership or a lack of formal membership.

In the second half of 1989, the rules and the circumstances for the first free elections were agreed at discussions between the former and emerging political powers at the so-called 'Round Table Negotiations'. Following this, these political groups had only a few months to organise themselves as parties and to persuade potential voters that only they were capable of solving the nation's problems and worthy of election in the first free elections in 40 years. Potential voters, on the whole, were discontented with the situation – desiring change but politically inarticulate and badly in need of adequate information on which to base their choice.

Given the fact that the overwhelming majority of the new players in the public sphere were newcomers, it goes without saying that they had no experience in how to run a multiparty election campaign, how to attract attention and how to compete against one another. They were, in other words, political amateurs and dilettantes. The label of political amateurism, however, referred much more to the new players in the public sphere than to the 'successors' of the incumbent socialist party who were also competing. The latter, however, also found themselves in a new situation and without their former mass party membership (before the transition the socialists had about 800 thousand members, on the eve of the transition this dropped to 30–40 thousand). They were thus deprived of the possibility of mobilising at the work place, which had previously been their home ground.

On the surface, the circumstances of campaigning were similar to those observed in established democracies where the society was individualised: mass parties no longer had central bases, confidence of voters in political parties had been shaken, and party loyalty was weak. As a result, high levels of voter uncertainty and volatility were common. Although the causes that led to this situation were totally different, the result was similar. It is understandable though that, when the Hungarian parties were forced to develop effective methods to win voters, they tried to copy or adopt the methods which had proved to be successful in the most advanced democracies. This tendency was reinforced by western parties' willingness to support Hungarian parties of the same ideological bent, mainly with advice, campaigning know-how and communication training. Nevertheless, the parties tried to keep secret the support and the lessons they had learned because, for Hungarian voters who were unfamiliar with political plurality or competition, this would have indicated their desire to win, or suggest a forced pursuit of popularity which would be seen to be equivalent to manipulation and would have therefore had a very negative connotation. In addition there were fears (especially on the nationalist side) that the political changes would be influenced or biased by foreign power players (especially in favour of the liberals and socialists).

CHANGING POLITICS – CHANGING MEDIA

At the dawn of the political transition, the Hungarian parties in the process of formation depended greatly on the printed and electronic media and were particularly sensitive to the idiosyncrasies of the media system (Kováts & Whiting, 1995). There were at least three reasons for this sensitivity. First, the new embryonic parties did not have a far-reaching, nationwide infrastructure to spread their ideas and garner support for their campaign for the elections. Second, it was assumed that there was a great difference in the journalists' attitude toward the various parties. Most of the parties (including the former socialist party) assumed a bias by the journalists towards the liberals; others assumed a bias towards the socialists. This was based on the fact that the change in the political system had not resulted in any significant changes in the personnel of the various media. Third, there were major inequalities in the communication competence of the various parties' leaders. The great majority were unfamiliar with the principles of how the media operated, because previously they had no access to it.

The new political players – outsiders in the former political system – differed greatly in their media competence, i.e. in the degree to which they were able to create news events capable of capturing media attention. This ability, or lack thereof, resulted in significant competitive differences amongst the new parties. On the one hand they were (reluctantly) open to new methods for reaching voters and to the employment of new campaign tactics, while, on the other hand, they jealously watched each other and wanted to control the media in order to reduce to the smallest degree possible the competitive advantage *vis-à-vis* the media.

The journalists' role and, consequently, the relationship of politicians to journalists during the political transition were ambiguous and complicated. The politicians greatly needed the help of journalists to disseminate their ideas but at the same time they accused journalists of confusing their role, of playing active political roles. In truth, the various new political players expected from journalists not objectivity but support. Indeed, the majority of journalists played active (and facilitating) roles in the political transition and symbolically prepared the peaceful transfer of political power. The political transition undoubtedly necessitated a reliable presentation of the various alternative perspectives in the media, and the personal engagement of the journalists seemed to be the most trustworthy.

In parallel with the political changes, the media landscape was also transformed when the press was privatised in 1990. Attempts to transform the state radio and broadcast system into a public service system proved troublesome and, in one way or another, the independence of public service broadcasting has not been realised, nor have the standards of professionalism in public service broadcasting been developed.

In 1996 commercial radio and television services were introduced. The privatisation contributed to creating a more 'Western style' professional journalism and it gave rise to a printed press – and later a commercial electronic media – that was much more independent of politics and politicians. The criteria of newsworthiness in the commercial media were certainly different from those of the state owned or public service media. Nevertheless, not a single attempt was made to share radio and television channels between the different political parties (first the state, later the so-called public service). Between 1998 and 2002 the right-wing government actively contributed to the development and establishment of newspapers and journals with right-wing orientation. In 2002, the right-wing political forces founded the first private news television cable channel. As a consequence, there is today (2005) a range of viable media outlets with a right-wing bias that act as a 'balance' to the other media outlets that continue to be accused, by the right-wing, liberal and socialist bias.

In summary, the tense relationships between the different media and politics were rather the consequence of the circumstances of the political transition and of the national and international developments of the media system itself and it was not a system copied from the outside. Certain special elements of the mediatisation of politics used all over the world seem to have spread with the media technology and the internationalisation of the media. In this process, successful techniques of political communication and campaigning in western democracies received more attention and were more likely to be adopted in Hungary. This is discussed below.

PROFESSIONALISATION OF COMMUNICATION – THE ROLE OF THE PUBLIC OPINION POLL, POLLSTERS AND ADVISORS

Certain forms of political public opinion research began in Hungary in the early 1970s as part of the activity of the Mass Communication Research Centre. Surveys provided the party with feedback about the public's perceptions and reaction to important political events and decisions, e.g. concerning price rises, or current international events such as the Israeli-Palestine conflict. The party did not influence the methodology or the assessment of the results of the research, but the results were not widely published, which was a significant advantage to those in power. The methodology used was copied directly, or adopted from – primarily Western – textbooks. In fact, many of the pollsters had studied in the U.S. in the 1970s and 80s.

In 1988, a number of pollsters from the Hungarian Public Opinion Research Institute (the former Mass Communication Research Centre) formed private polling firms and began to publish their results. At the beginning of 1990, major multinational firms – for example the US Gallup, the French Szonda Ipsos, and the German GFK – established subsidiaries in Hungary (Gallup Hungary, Szonda Ipsos, Gfk Hungary) and employed these experienced local pollsters. (Their professionalism is demonstrated by the fact that, in spite of the extraordinarily complicated Hungarian electoral system, they predicted very accurately the composition of the first Hungarian parliament.)

Public opinion polling undoubtedly strengthened the legitimacy of the newly emerging political forces. The results of the polls informed the public of the existence of the new political players and parties. Not surprisingly, the first polls showed that voters were unfamiliar with the various parties and that a large proportion was confused. Moreover, a large proportion rejected the multi-party system, an attitude that diminished only slowly. Over time, the polls recorded shifts in opinion in favour of the new political actors. The regular polls – conducted by independent companies – gave an illusion of order in an often-chaotic political system.

But polls were often rejected amidst accusations of party bias. Each political group was convinced that it alone represented the people and shared their goals. If this was not reflected in the polls, the results were false. However, as the polls revealed, the party programmes had nothing in common with the needs of society and of the public at large. Instead, they defined the tasks, goals, and ideals of the individual intellectual groups that had founded the parties. One other reason why polls were rejected lay in the attitude of certain parties – especially the conservative and/or nationalist ones – to polling. Public opinion polls were believed to be inappropriate in more traditional societies, characterised by the kinds of close-knit bonds that conservative political factions wished to strengthen in Hungary.

Nonetheless, over the last 15 years, the role of the public opinion research firms has changed considerably – although their importance has not diminished – and most can now be clearly distinguished by their political affiliations. The major parties, especially those that had been ruling parties at some point, were able to build stable relationships with certain public opinion research companies through governmental commissions. Overall these relationships remained even when the parties were no longer in government as ruling parties. Szonda Ipsos, for example, is linked to the Socialist Party, Gallup Hungary and Tarki to the right-wing coalition led by the Young Democrats, Median to the (liberal) Alliance of Free Democrats. These relationships are confidential and the companies receive political market research commissions on which strategic decisions of the parties can be based. The political affiliation of other public or market research companies can be determined by identifying the politics of the newspaper or magazine in which their results are published. More generally, the leading directors and public opinion researchers belong to the formal or informal circles of communication advisors of the party leaders or members of the government. While adhering to the professional requirements of public opinion research, the independence of these companies seems to be a myth in the polarised and over-politicised public life of the country. By providing regular surveys of the changing political mood and opinion of the public, the polling companies can be considered as background institutions to the decision-making processes of the main parties and, in some ways, not unlike the advisory groups that surrounded every party and government in the past (Pesti, 2000). Before the mid 1990s few advisers specialising explicitly (or exclusively) in communication were in evidence and, although their numbers subsequently increased, they were often selected on the basis of their political contacts and relationships with the media rather than for their abilities to influence public opinion, i.e. their professionalism.

PROFESSIONALISATION OF COMMUNICATION – PARTY ORGANISATION AND COMMUNICATION

At the time of the political transition it was feared that voters would be split amongst too many parties, and that too many parties entering Parliament might endanger its operation. Accordingly, the Hungarian electoral system was developed in a way that is advantageous to the larger parties, and thus the concentration of the political party system was literally encoded into the electoral and party legislation. During the initial period of the political transition more than 70 parties competed for votes but only 6 were elected to the first free Parliament. Over a period of 15 years not only did the number of parties go down from 6 to 4, but by 2004 one could speak of Hungary as a quasi two-party system: on one side the 'successor' Hungarian Socialist Party on the other side the national-Christian-conservatives dominated by the Young Democrats.[1]

As a rule, the elections were not won by the opposition forces alone. The incumbent governmental coalitions, which either used only extremely negative campaign methods (in 1994) or did not campaign at all in the beginning of the campaign period (in 1998 or 2002), also helped their opponents to victory. Often the challengers helped their cause by using new methods of campaigning techniques. Examples include, in 1998, the use of automated telephone calls combined with an automatic answering programme and with an audible message delivered by the challengers Fidesz party's leader, or the Direct Mail, e-mail and SMS messages used by the Socialists in 2002.

The peculiarity of the Hungarian election campaign system, with its two cycles, intensifies the competition between the first and second cycle, especially when the results are in the balance and there is cut-throat competition. In this short two-week period, aggressive and dramatic campaign methods are used, and only the short-term aim of winning is important. One of the results of such a tense situation was the introduction of debates between the candidates for prime ministerial candidates in 1994, or the huge mass meeting with more than a hundred thousand participants in 2002, and extreme negative campaigns at every election campaign.

Negative campaigning has been a feature of Hungarian election campaigns from the very beginning of the change of the regime. The labels the parties used in these negative campaigns (murderers, communists, fascist, dictators, former state secret service agents, Jews, anti-nationalist, cosmopolitans, etc.) had far-reaching consequences beyond the contest amongst the parties, and resulted in deep trauma within the public, whose members otherwise would not be emotionally involved in the political process. The negative and emotionally-charged campaign created a short circuit between the parties and their potential supporters, which was to make a simple difference between 'us' and 'them' and create an identity (mainly as a form of 'hating them'), and an emotional involvement that was a substitute for the social embeddedness and party loyalty that was lacking. The question remains as to whether this type of hate speech, supported by modern marketing principles of symbolical and emotional approach, will be limited to the period of party building and party identification, or whether it will remain a permanent feature of Hungarian party politics.

The use of so-called professional communication methods undoubtedly exacerbated the intense competition between the parties. Competition over a period of ten years was reduced to a hard fight between the two large parties. The result, and the secret to the success of the dominant Hungarian parties, is that, in using professional marketing and PR tools, they brought to the surface and intensified the latent dividing lines that had long characterised Hungarian society: traditional, historical religions versus atheism and new small churches; nationalism versus cosmopolitanism; urban versus rural; anti-communism versus socialism and liberalism.

The last election in 2002 was less a competitive struggle and more akin to a civil war that produced almost equal electoral results for the two camps.[2] The two parties were different both in their values and in their campaigning styles.

THE COMMUNICATION STYLE OF THE TWO MAJOR PARTIES: THE TWO DIFFERENT MODELS OF PROFESSIONALISATION OF POLITICAL COMMUNICATION
The Alliance of Young Democrats ('Fidesz') (1988) – 'Fidesz' – Hungarian Civic Party (1995) – 'Fidesz' – Hungarian Civic Alliance (2003)
Of all the Hungarian parties, the Alliance of Young Democrats was the first to recognise the role of political marketing – and even more importantly, the use of political market research methods – in forming and articulating its policies to the public. Accordingly, it exploited professional political marketing and PR communication tools in both its triumphant 1998 campaign and also while in government from 1998 to 2002.[3] Based on results of social and political research they analysed carefully the causes of the failings of the first right-wing government (Stumpf, 1998). The party ordered political

market research to investigate the preferences of the public, and when in power, they put at the centre of their politics communication and popular measures. Recognising the importance of the media and public sphere, they strove to totally eradicate the opposition parties from the Hungarian public sphere.

The Alliance of Young Democrats was the product of the political transition, not comparable in their origin, in their social contacts, in their organisation, or in their aims or forms of activity to the other parties in Hungary (Fritz, 2000). It was dubbed the 'answering machine' or 'media party' early in its development, terms that referred not only to its communication abilities, but also to its party organisation. The Young Democrats were able to turn a seeming disadvantage, their small membership, into an advantage. A small organisation can be held together by different kinds of links than those of an impersonal, larger party.

The introduction of a new type of professional campaigning can be associated with the leader of the Young Democrats, Viktor Orbán.[4] He was a young charismatic leader, a representative of the new generation of politicians, and untouched by the previous regime's compromises. He was backed by a small team of reliable friends, former college-mates, a carefully selected and loyal professional apparatus, and with the aid of modern campaign and PR methods, successfully led to victory the then collapsing right-wing forces. He introduced a totally new style of political communication: first a very simplified but pragmatic political speech with metaphors and emotional elements, which later included more and more ceremonial and historical elements. He turned directly to the people and their families, disregarding the role of the different interest mediating institutions – even that of the parties.

At the heart of the party was a small 'hard core' of 6 or 7 people, who had formed a close alliance since their years at university in the beginning of the 1980s. The *eminence grise* at the side of the party leader, Viktor Orbán (prime minister, 1998–2002) was his personal communications adviser, a Hungarian consultant, András Wermer. Wermer was not formally employed by the party[5] and only joined the party leader at its nadir (1994–96) and at the point when the party leader, Orban, put together his larger advisory team, and succeeded in creating a loose alliance of the fragments of the right-wing parties.

Beside him there were the young businesslike Hungarian professionals who were occupied with practical tasks of the party's political communication – they had just left university, Hungarian and foreign, and acted according to the marketing textbooks. There were even rumours, largely unconfirmed, about foreign experts helping the Young Democrats – for example, in 2002 allegedly sent from Italy, from Berlusconi.

Close personal connections and modern principles of effective organisation were supplemented by the party's own think-tank and political educational organisation

The Professionalisation of Political Communication

Századvég ('End of the Century'), which, for example, educated the new political elite and developed the party's 1996 platform which was based on its analysis of the first conservative government's experiences in 1990–94, and the socialist government's radical loss of popularity because of their unpopular economic decisions. The lesson the party leaders learned was to consider the political communication implications of the political decision-making process from the outset, to avoid unpopular decisions while offering popular options, and to recognise the role of the media. The strategic aim of the party was to establish a strong and socially embedded conservative political right, and at the same time to destroy totally the social and economic network supporting the left and liberal sides, so aiming to complete the 'regime change' begun in 1990 by the first right-wing government.

The 'novelty' brought by the Young Democrats into political communication between 1998 and 2002 was the intertwining of the state and party communication processes into a common PR strategy. The basis of this was to reject the idea of a neutral, 'value free' state: the government's task was to realise the aims and values of the winning party. The final consequence of this angle was the intertwining of the state 'success propaganda' (aiming at touting its own achievements), and the Young Democrats' election campaign.

Following their failure at the first round of the 2002 parliamentary elections, the Young Democrats introduced other types of innovation into Hungarian political communication. They mobilised huge masses, called them to the streets where mass meetings were organised to encourage the losers and to terrify the winners of the first round of the elections. Morally highly questionable methods – for the majority of the Hungarian public – were used: extremely negative propaganda and scare tactics such as alarming rumours about their opponents' future intentions if elected. The smear campaign was spread by word of mouth, e-mail, SMS text messages, hand-written flyers and, even, by church leaders who counselled their congregations on where to stand and whom to support.

The Young Democrats also expropriated national symbols as means of identification, labelling the other side as non-Hungarian. In schools, workplaces and on the street, people looked to see whether one wore the tricolour rosette, the symbol of the 1848 Revolution. This cooption of patriotism was underscored by one of the Young Democrats' leaders when he said that those who do not support the national-conservative value system had better hang themselves. However, this message had a boomerang effect, generating fear of extreme nationalism, a fear that was amplified by the opposition.

Having gone into opposition, the party has been able to introduce a politically galvanising formation outside of Parliament, new to Hungary and perhaps best compared to Forza Italia 'Hajrá Magyarok!' or 'Go Hungarians!'. The Young Democrats have formed a distinct network of civil organisations around the party and in general declared the party system inadequate for their objectives and called for something different, such as a broader umbrella group based not on ideology but on values. Their negative campaign against the other side became permanent and total, far beyond of the normal government-opposition relationship. They questioned everything, from the very legitimacy of the new government to the results of the elections. The 2006 campaign started on the first day of the new government cycle.

The Hungarian Socialist Party – a conflict of the old and new type of professionalisation of politics and political communication
The Socialists and their leaders had sought to transform their party into a Western European-style social democratic party, an essentially modern party aimed at the efficient management of society. But they had inherited an organisational structure and a communication culture that arose in response to fundamentally different needs: those of a mass party in one-party conditions. They also inherited a belief in the separation of the state and party communication processes, the emphasis of special expertise in both fields, and the differentiation of internal and external party communication. The coalition with the liberal party, the Alliance of Free Democrats, further emphasised the rejection of propaganda, PR techniques, emotional and symbolical styles of communication.

Their partly unexpected triumph in the second elections in 1994 was more the result of the voters' dissatisfaction with the first free government, and of the government's exceptionally negative media campaign against the Socialists, than of their own campaigning. During the 1994–1998 Socialist-Liberal government, they announced their plan for the crisis management of the economy and introduced a policy of economic stringency. This action was approved of by well-known economic experts and such institutions as the World Bank. Unfortunately, these policies were not appreciated by potential voters, who cared more for their own actual welfare than for the financial state of the country. The Socialists and Liberals hoped that the fruits of these policies would succeed just in time for the elections, but this was not the case.

Their loss of power in 1998 was the result of the unpopular economic policies and the ruling parties' exaggerated self-confidence in attempting to manage the country by experts without taking care to inform and persuade the public of the benefits of the policies. Undoubtedly, their loss of power was also connected to the use of new effective campaign methods by their opposition, the Young Democrats. The only innovation introduced or accepted by them between the two rounds of the election campaign was the prime minister's television debate with the young good-looking and energetic Fidesz party leader in opposition, Viktor Orbán. This did not help the Socialists, and many experts felt that it contributed to the victory of the latter.

In fact, the Socialists conducted their first real campaign for the 2002 elections. Frustrated by the humiliating political activities of the ruling right-wing between 1998 and 2002, and fearing that the right-wing was preparing for a long-term political reign, the Socialists succeeding in rallying the party and challenging the incumbent government. This time they had carefully prepared their programme, involving many intellectuals from the left and liberal side. The perceived crisis situation helped them to overcome the objections to using so-called professional campaign tools and methods.

The Socialists were ambivalent about using so-called professional communication methods and had for a long time been reluctant to employ them, arguing that they have negative effects on the democratic process. Politics based on symbolism and emotion is foreign to their modernist philosophy of politics, based on rational dialogue, discussion, and deliberation. (This philosophy received strong support from their coalition partner, the liberal Free Democrats.) Equally foreign were the push-button techniques of advertising, and the military discipline of promoting the message. The belief in internal pluralism and of internal party democracy contradicted the principles of effective advertising and PR, and could result in difficulties in communication to the outside world. Another obstacle for the Socialist party in communicating with the public was the fact that it was accustomed to institutional, impersonal, legal, or bureaucratic regulation and coordination, and their communication style reflected this legacy.

The Socialists (and their allies, the liberal Free Democrats), who pointed out the risk to democracy of using professional political communications tools[6], nonetheless could not afford to ignore these tools as long as the opposition used them. It was interesting to observe, for example, that the Socialist Party used political communicational tools and methods similar to those of the Young Democrats in the 2002 campaign, at the same time exploiting the advantages of their traditional, relatively extensive party organisation. The use of scandal and negative campaigning and targeted communication were also characteristic of the Socialists. The campaign was organised by a well-known expert from Israel, Ron Weber. (Incidentally, this provided an opportunity for the right-wing press to point out the Socialist Party's connection with Israel, thereby conflating the unsavoury character of 'manipulative' political market methods with explicit or implicit anti-Semitism.)

The Socialists' campaign in 2002 was strictly planned, organised, and coordinated with special emphasis on internal party information and cooperation. The novelty of the 2002 campaign was the 'dual campaign': the campaigns of the Socialist's prime ministerial candidate and the party were conducted separately, but in concert. The intention was that they would complement each other, and so expand the circle of potential voters in the middle. Peter Medgyessy, the prime ministerial candidate of the Socialist Party, stressed his relative independence from the party (he wasn't a party member at the time), and wanted to be judged on his own merit, and hoped to enlarge the circle of voters of the left. He and his campaign team ran an American-style, personalised, road show campaign. According to its result, the campaign was successful: the Socialists won, and Peter Medgyessy became their first prime minister.

The disciplined cohesive communication of the Socialists, however, lasted only for the period of the campaign. Following the elections the Socialists wanted to return to the 'campaign-free' 'normal way of life', emphasising the need to bring together the two opposing halves of the society. But this was not possible because of the permanent campaign activity of the opposition, started from the first day of the new governmental period.

Moreover, the plurality of the Socialist party hampered coordinated and effective political communication. Internal party discussion – extensively published by the media – was seen as a sign of weakness and not a sign of democracy in action. Furthermore, the overwhelming majority of the Socialist party leaders were unable to adapt to the new requirements of modern mass democracy and mediated politics. They had long believed that intra-party performance was much more important than public opinion. It was clear, however, that a permanent and total campaign used by the opposition would either consume the Socialist party or force it to make the kinds of structural or organisational changes needed by mass democracy and mediated politics. The results of the public opinion polls forecast a failure at the next elections in 2006 if there were not to be considerable changes. In the summer of 2004 certain changes in the leadership, organisational form and style of communication were started, but whether these will be enough to win in 2006 remains to be seen.

1998–2002: A PUBLIC RELATIONS GOVERNMENT?

The political communication system created by the Young Democrats' government between 1998–2002 merits special attention because it can be seen as a perfect example of a public relations government, or 'mediatised populist democracy' (Körösényi, 2002). This could be characterised by the following elements: PR and political communication aims in the centre of politics; concentration of public policy; a presentation to the public of an over-simplified politics with an emphasis on slogans and symbols; constant and all-encompassing campaigning; and the emphasises of prime minister's personality as symbolically unifying the nation and 'without any party bias'. Finally, seeking to unite society as a union of 'natural communities' (that is Hungarians and their families) and not as a society with 'functional groups' (Navracsics, 2000).

To realise their far-reaching aims, the governing parties limited the opposition's ability to appear before the public via the media by reducing parliamentary sessions from once a week to once every three weeks. More dangerously, this procedural shift reduced the opposition's opportunities to debate and critique the government's proposals and actions. Furthermore, to reduce the effects of the opposition's critiques,

The Professionalisation of Political Communication

the time limit for the prime minister's obligatory response was extended from three to nine weeks. In contrast to the erosion of parliamentary power, the government's functions were strengthened and expanded, particularly in the realm of publicity. Thus, the most important public statements regarding the nation's fate were issued not by Parliament but by the prime minister's office or the governing party's headquarters.

The prime minister's cabinet played a vital role in coordinating the work of ministries and in preparing the decisions of the prime minister, who exploited to the full the possibilities offered to him by Hungary's chancellery type of government (Nagyhazi, 2003). The post of Minister of the Chancellery was given to the director of the think-tank that had prepared the government's programme and which trained future politicians. 22 political and communication advisors worked in the prime minister's cabinet, with 80 more serving in the various ministries. Much more important, however, was the prime minister's informal advisory network. Comprising members of the 'independent intelligentsia', the nucleus of this group was the founders of the Young Democrats.

The prime minister's personal PR and communication advisor, András Wermer, played a central role in defining and realising the government's rhetorical strategies. A large apparatus within the cabinet carried out pragmatic tasks of governmental communication on a day-to-day basis. The organising principle of the government's communication strategy – as if taken directly from a communication handbook – was the articulation of a limited number of clear, simple messages. These messages were selected with great care, and their pronouncement was highly unified and coordinated. As in an advertising campaign, they were repeated as many times as possible. The communication strategy was an integral part of the government's work schedule, influencing concrete decisions, their timing and their contexts. The central aim was to constantly bombard citizens with positive messages to assure them that the government was working on their behalf at all times.

One of the most striking characteristics of the government was its capacity to create events of news value and to package its information in such a way that it was attractive even for commercial media. Different methods were used for achieving these aims, such as organising governmental meetings in visually pleasing environments. The Young Democrats had the good fortune to be in office when the nation celebrated its millennial anniversary in 2000. This occasion provided vivid and dramatic opportunities for the government to celebrate its continuity with 'historical' Hungary.

In addition to using public relations techniques and creating pseudo-events, the prime minister used opportunities provided by the so-called public service broadcasting. Hungarian Radio and Television had now been purged of the 'hidden network' of socialist-liberal journalists and other employees, and the prime minister was ready to accept the invitation from the news director of Hungarian Radio to participate weekly in an interview segment of its morning news and public affairs programme. Orbán also appeared in major interview series on state radio and television.

Another important characteristic of this period was the personalisation of the political power of government (Stumpf, 2002). The prime minister embodied the government and its diverse activities. The government's programme was thus represented by a sympathetic, strong-minded but smiling young man with a good sense of humour who spoke eloquently but in a simple, uncomplicated manner. He was tough with the enemies of the government, because the government represented the Hungarian citizens. According to the portrait that projected his personality, he was a church-going Christian, a family man with an attractive wife and four children.[7]

WHAT THE SOCIALISTS HAVE AND HAVE NOT LEARNED

There had long been a belief in Hungary that the Socialists and their governments perform well but are unable to communicate their successes (Ágh 1999). During their campaign and following their victory in 2002, the Socialist party and the government wanted to resolve the problem by employing foreign consultants – both the party and its government employed consultants, but two different ones: the party used Ron Weber, and the prime minister, Medgyessy a US consultant, Stanley Greenberg, one of the leaders of the Greenberg Quinlan Rosner Research Inc. It was hoped that the employment of foreign communication advisors would bring about direct and immediate results in improving their political communication, and to accelerate the process of adaptation to the new requirements. Ron Weber, the Israeli advisor, led the Socialist party to victory in 2002 and directed the Socialists' EU parliamentary election campaign. This later resulted in an unfavourable outcome for the party. His negative campaign style was attacked by journalists and the opposition.

Medgyessy, the prime minister, who had performed well during the campaign, and had a good reputation among economic and financial experts, however proved weak in public communication and in the media when in government. He made strong and visible efforts to respond to this challenge, but without much success

In 2002, the new Socialist government had inherited the Young Democrats' governmental system and political communication machinery. As a first reaction, they changed everything and dismissed those at high level appointed by the previous government. Given the fact that the state and party politics and communications in principle and practice were intertwined, the organisational and personnel changes were considerable. The new Socialist prime minister, Medgyessy, quickly discovered, however, the advantages of the organisational forms of governmental communication introduced by his predecessor and he developed it further. But this meant more a quantitative development rather than a qualitative one. The main criterion for the selection of the staff was their confidence and not their professionalism.

Stanley B. Greenberg and his consultant firm from the US were charged with developing communication strategies for the government, as well as with assisting the prime minister with his personal communication. The methods and tools do not appear to have been successful. One of the examples of this 'failure' occurred when the Hungarian prime minister finished one of his important speeches in the same manner as American presidents, but in a manner totally alien to Hungarian political culture: 'So help me God'. Although the American consultants had Hungarian advisors to help them to understand Hungarian culture and social psychology, it seems that they were either not persuasive, or the American advisors were overconfident of their expertise. Of course this does not mean that the failure of the Socialist Party at the EU elections, and of Prime Minister Peter Medgyessy at the end of the summer of 2004, was a direct result of the deficiencies of their political communication, but certainly it had a considerable effect.

At the end of the summer 2004 the ruling parties – the Socialist and the liberal Free Democrats – withdrew their support from the prime minister, Medgyessy. The new prime minister, Ferenc Gyurcsany, emerged out of nowhere in a quasi-putsch. The opposition was surprised by the new socialist political personality and his confrontational and informal style of communication. The new prime minister was characterised by the specialists of a leading political consulting company, Vision Consulting, as follows: he is the first politician on the left, who acts according to the terms of a democratic, competitive political system; he definitely knows that he has to respond to the expectations of the voters; he has excellent communication capabilities; political charisma; and a good political background supporting him. All this can be considered as a significant step on the way to professionalisation of the politics on the left. Behind this the new Socialist prime minister has clear political aims that can compete with, and are opposed to, the symbolic aims of the nationalist opposition: to support the poor and to take from the rich, combined with a liberal angle. The Gyurcsány and Orbán rhetorical styles are similar in many respects, primarily due to a generally confident and clear manner of speaking, but also to a common populist element. Related to this there are two possible dangers which need to be mentioned: the emergence of a leftist populism (as opposed to the nationalist populism of the right) and that his confrontational style of communication could sharpen the division of the nation. In any case, the Hungarian political scene has become more symmetric, both sides having professional politicians and professionalised political communications.

SUMMARY
The experiences concerning the development of Hungarian political communication during the last 15 years can be summarised as follows:

The main features of this development of political communication were the results of the specific circumstances of the Hungarian political regime change, combined with the development of the general tendencies of media systems discernible throughout the world, but mainly originating in the United States. The Western – especially American – media and 'democracy' advisors contributed significantly to this development, but often the results were different from those expected because of the different political cultural environment. The effects of so-called professional political communication were much stronger in a society where the tools of political marketing and persuasion were less common, and the society was rather vulnerable. The differences in the competence in utilising the new tools and methods affected significantly the fate of the different political forces, the political power relations, and therefore the political articulation of the country and the character of the new democracy. The role of personality of the political leaders seems to have been a determining factor in the fate of a political party due to the personalisation of the political competition. The use of so-called professional communication methods undoubtedly exacerbated the intense competition between the parties and, at the same time, the use of professional marketing and PR tools brought to the surface and intensified the latent dividing lines that had long characterised Hungarian society.

It can be added that, following the change of regime, the efficiency of professional communication tools was considerable influenced by the interplay of the professionalism of the politicians, the professionalism of journalists, characteristics of the media and the over-politicised Hungarian society, which was partly the result and partly the condition of using these tools.

As a conclusion, it seems that, with the tools and methods of political communication developed first in the United States, certain specificities of the populist democracy were imported as well. The question as to whether this is good or bad remains to be answered.

Notes

1. In 1995 the Young Democrats changed their name to the Young Democrats – Hungarian Civic Party, in 2003 absorbing the overwhelming majority of the right wing forces they established the Young Democrats Hungarian Civic Alliance but they are still generally referred to, as this chapter does, as the Young Democrats.

2. The situation is similar to the one described in Stanley B. Greenberg (2004) *The Two Americas* (New York, St. Martin's Press 2004.) Greenberg, it should also be noted, was one of the communication consultants used by the Socialist government and prime minister in 2004. Although there are also two smaller parties, they are relatively insignificant.

3. Their defeat in the 2002 elections was partly due to the result of the over-confidence of the Young Democrats' government, and also to the fact that they prepared to forget about the other half of the country, which they had treated as an enemy.

4. The Young Democrats run an interesting course in the political arena. As one of the first parties in opposition, they dedicated themselves to the fight against the former one-party system, ideologically against communism, first identifying themselves as liberals, later, reacting to the changes in the Hungarian political arena, concerned about the results of the political transition, by the return of the socialists, placed themselves at the lead of the conservatives. In building their team, they asked the members of their future professional

apparatus to join them during the party's oppositional period, to pre-empt the offer of careerists. The professionals or sympathising intellectuals were actively involved in the development of the party programme, so they could feel that they are participants in an intellectual experiment to build a better society.

5. Communication tasks may be outsourced and purchased in part by kind of 'IOU' to be 'cashed in' during the governing period. As a consequence, for instance, the PR and communication advisor to the president of the Young Democrats received the lion's share of government publication commissions when the Young Democrats came into power. The conditions for the task could be precisely defined, beforehand, in private contracts.

6. Orbán, the personification of the conservative-Christian-national politician guided by communicative considerations, is compared by the parties on the left to Berlusconi or Putin.

7. Orbán was the first prime minister to post his family's photographs on his website. The private lives of politicians are not of public concern in Hungary's political culture. It seems that the vulgarisation of the press results in the vulgarisation of political life as well.

REFERENCES

Ágh, A (1999) 'A szociálliberális koalíció öröksége', pp. 29–40 in Kurtán S., P. Sándor & L. Vass (eds) *Magyarország Politikai Evkönyve, 1998-ról*. Budapest, Demokrácia Kutatások Magyar Központja Közhasznú Alapítvány.

Fritz, T. (2000) 'Európa és a magyar pártrendszer', pp. 60–69 in S. Kurtán, P. Sándor & L. Vass (eds) *Magyarország Politikai Evkönyve, 1999-rŒl*. Budapest: Demokrácia Kutatások Magyar Központja Közhasznú Alapítvány 2000.

Greenberg, Stanley B. (2004*) The Two Americas*. New York: St. Martin's Press.

Kováts, I. & G. Whiting (1995) 'Hungary', pp. 97–127 in D.L. Paletz, K. Jakubowicz, & P. Novosel (eds) *Glasnost and after. Media and Change in Central and Eastern Europe*. Cresskill, NJ: Hampton Press.

Körösényi, A. (2002) 'Az Orbán-kormány és a kormányzati hatalom szerkezete 2001-ben', pp. 17–36 in S. Kurtán, P. Sándor & L. Vass (eds) *Magyarország politikai évkönyve 2001-rŒl*. Budapest: Demokrácia Kutatások Magyar Központja Közhasznú Alapítvány.

Nagyházi, G. (2003) *?The One-Armed Giant? Government Communicational Policies and Organisations in Hungary*. Country assessment report. United Nations Development ProgrammeUNDP RBEC sub-regional project RER/01/003/A08/13. Improving Communications from Governments to Societies in Central Europe & the Baltic States. http://rbec.undp.org/files/uploads/PAR_AC_Communications/CommHungEdited.doc

Navracsics, T. (2000) 'A kormányzati kommunikáció másfél éve', pp. 78–87 in S. Kurtán, P. Sándor & L. Vass (eds) *Magyarország politikai évkönyve 2000-rŒl*. Budapest: Demokrácia Kutatások Magyarországi Központja Közhasznú Alapítvány.

Navracsics, T. (2002) 'Vázlat a kormányzati kommunikációról', pp. 96–106 in S. Kurtán, P. Sándor & L. Vass (eds) *Magyarország politikai évkönyve 2001-rŒl*. Budapest: Demokrácia Kutatások Magyarországi Központja Közhasznú Alapítvány.

Pesti, S. (2000) 'A kormányzati döntéshozatal mechanizmusai' Magyarországon', *Jogelméleti szemle*, No. 4. http://jesz.ajk.elte.hu/pesti4.html

Stumpf, I.(1999) *?Kormányváltás 1998-ban'*, pp. 324–355 in S. Kurtán, P. Sándor, & L. Vass (eds) *Magyarország politikai évkönyve 1998-ról*. Budapest, Demokrácia Kutatások Magyarországi Központja Közhasznú Alapítvány,.

Stumpf, I. (2002) 'A XXI század kihivása: a „jó kormányzás', pp. 90–95 in S. Kurtán, P.Sándor & L. Vass (eds) *Magyarország politikai évkönyve 2001-rŒl*. Budapest: Demokrácia Kutatások Magyarországi Központja Közhasznú Alapítvány.

11

THE PROFESSIONALISATION OF POLITICAL COMMUNICATION: DEMOCRACY AT STAKE?

Cees Hamelink

As the preceding chapters demonstrate, communicative functions of political systems have become increasingly the domain brief of professionals: the perception managers, the spin-doctors, the pollsters, the consultants, the media trainers, the PR experts, and the marketeers.

The key question for this chapter is what happens to the political process when these functions are professionalised? And more in particular, what are the consequences of these professionalisation processes for the democratic quality of the polity?

THE COMMUNICATIVE FUNCTIONS OF POLITICS

As Fared Zakaria writes: 'We live in a democratic age' (2004, p.13). Across the world the democratic arrangement is seen as the single most legitimate form of managing society's affairs. Communicative action is essential to the sustainable functioning of this arrangement. As this communicative action becomes increasingly professionalised, the inevitable question is whether this process improves the democratic quality of the polity.

There are different stakeholders in democratic political systems. These may be the elected political representatives of the citizenry, the unelected holders of key administrative offices, the lobbyists for special interests and the citizens at large. For all of them communication may fulfil different functions:

■ For the elected politicians the key functions of communication are to persuade
  electorates to accept political decisions as legitimate; to persuade people to support

the political party and to vote for its representatives; to profile political leaders; to manage the political party image; to manage the daily political news flow in the media and to collect information about people's opinions.

■ For the unelected officials there is the peculiar need to rather steer away from the exposure to the pressures of public communication and to guard the confidentiality of their decision making processes.

■ For the special interest lobbyists essential communicative activities are the finding and using of direct channels to access decision makers and the provision of selected pieces of information to politicians and citizens.

■ For the citizens at large, communication serves their participation in deliberative processes; their demand for the public accountability of political officeholders and their search for information from political institutions and office holders.

In all the communicative activities of these stakeholders, professionals today play an essential role. Yet, there is at present no empirical evidence to conclusively suggest that professionalisation has definite effects on the democratic quality of modern societies. Even so, there is sufficient reason for the kind of concern that constitutes the basis of the current chapter.

THE PROFESSIONALISATION PROCESS

In a great number of European countries professionalisation refers to a process that is linked to societal changes in the political process, in the performance of the mass media, and in the mediatisation of politics. These changes are themselves linked with the current modernisation processes as they develop in European societies.

As the preceding chapters describe, we find in most countries rather similar developments such as the decline in membership of political parties and the diminishing of party loyalties, the decreasing interest in voting, the centralisation of communication activities in both government and political parties, and the growth of cynicism among citizens. In this climate, professionalisation comes of age with 'the rise of direct-marketing methods, the proliferation of electronic channels, and the advent of new opinion-assessment technologies' (Blumler & Kavanaugh in Bennett & Entman, 2001, p.16).

The Dutch electronics firm Philips used for many years as its marketing slogan: 'Let's make things better'. This seems to sum up what the earlier chapters say about professionalisation: it is an effort to make things better. Better tends to be understood as more rational, more effective, and more persuasive. The things that should be made better are the mobilisation of voters, the targeting of electoral groups, the polling of public opinion, the media presence of politicians, the efforts to get political messages across through overt or covert methods, the coping with media logics, the restoration of public trust in the political system, and the management of daily news.

The Professionalisation of Political Communication

A particularly acute ground for 'making things better' is the dysfunctional state of the political system across Europe. There is a low level of civil respect for politics, and a low level of civil participation in party politics and even in voting. At the same time there is a range of urgent issues that need to be addressed, such as migration, terrorism, and organised crime. This demands an awesome volume of professional persuasive communication. The dilemma is, however, that all the professional campaigning and lobbying risks increasing even further the citizens' disregard for politics.

If the professionalisation of political communication would indeed make things better, what issues does this raise in the context of the question about democratic quality?

Are all the stakeholders equally well served by the professionalisation of communicative functions?

Professional communicators obviously serve the special interest lobbies. The examples abound around such global trade negotiations as take place at the World Trade Organisation. The pharmaceutical industry, for example, lobbied through professionals very effectively during the preparations for the Agreement on Trade-Related Intellectual Property Rights in the early 1992. Equally, the unelected office holders – such as Central Bankers or EU Commissioners – use professional spokespersons, external relations managers, and news analysts.

In this chapter the focus is on the communicative actions that take place between the elected politicians and the citizens.

Since democracy in whatever theoretical model does imply relations – cooperative or combative – between citizens and politicians, an evident issue is which side in the political system benefits most from the professionalisation process.

Professionalisation seems to focus almost exclusively upon the politicians' side of the communicative functions of the political system. This may begin to change with the professionalisation of communications by social movements. Or, at any rate, with the improved capability of many civil groups to reach out to audiences (among others through a great variety of websites) and their growing effectiveness in media news management. But for citizen movements certainly there are resources available comparable to those the political parties have for their professional communication advisors.

Politicians in most countries are, by and large, more assisted by professional helpers in their communications with citizens than citizens are professionally advised in their communications with the politicians. Current processes of professionalisation emphasise the democracy of representatives, not the democracy of citizens. There is a tendency among elected political officials to claim that their decisions are the people's decisions. Since, in their view, citizens do not always understand that the political choice is in fact made by the people and for the people, the professional intermediary is essential to explain that what was decided without direct consultation with the citizens is still in their best interest.

The tentative conclusion may be that the current professionalisation of political communication further widens the inequality between politicians and citizens in terms of the capacity to manipulate political messages, perceptions and opinions.

Is a better informed citizenry and more inclusive citizenship developed so that the citizen's influence on public choice may be more significant?

Key to the democratic process is the notion that if citizens cannot directly take decisions about public matters, their influence upon public choice should at least be maximised. A prerequisite for this is obviously the need for citizens to be properly informed about matters of public interest. In principle one might then expect that professionalisation serves primarily the maximisation of information flows to citizens. However, for electoral and party political reasons, the professionals tend to narrow down information flows to those selected audience segments that they consider useful in the electoral sense. By implication they do not contribute to the broadening of information flows so that a well-informed citizenry may emerge. Because of their limited assignment, they do not see it as their task to promote processes of well-informed deliberation among all citizens. As a result, specially targeted audiences may be relatively well informed but always – selectively – on those issues that matter to the politicians. This segmentation and selective targeting of the public sphere (Gandy, 2001, p. 104) conflicts with the normative standard – as among others proposed in the writings of Habermas – that the process of political deliberation should be inclusive. When – as is common procedure in commercial advertising and marketing – people become targets for electoral campaigns, and they are divided into useful and excluded segments, they become political consumers. Much professional political information caters for groups that face specific problems that they want to see addressed, and that they perceive as more urgent than the interests of the overall society. This isolates people from each other; it undermines a general social commitment and a shared notion of the common good. The selective targeting of political information to segmented audiences erodes a common knowledge and understanding of public issues and thus the common engagement of people with political issues. This approach to political communication also tends to reinforce incidental and short-term populist politics rather than serve long-term politics for sustainable societies in which citizenship implies that people search for solutions to common problems. Political consumership replaces citizenship.

The tentative conclusion may be that the professional political communicators contribute to the development of 'democracy without citizens'.

The issue of leadership

The professionalisation of political communication expands the capacity of political elites to manipulate the democratic system to the advantage of their interests. One of the essential tasks of the professionals is the building and sustaining of the image of the political leader.

In the common, liberal, representative democracy one finds great emphasis on the public presentation of the 'Capo'! Frequently the media present photo opportunities with political leaders. Heads of state, prime ministers and diplomats are seen to shake hands, embrace, pat shoulders, while keenly looking at the cameras. These sessions demonstrate that the key actors indulge without inhibition in the *Roi Soleil* feeling. They seem to say 'we have the power, you may look at us and then we withdraw to our secretive meetings where we decide what is good for you'. There is an unquestioned assumption in these rituals that expects no contestation from the onlookers. It would be a wholesome day for democratic politics if one day the press photographers stayed at home.

Democracy has a troubled relationship with political leadership. There is often a strong public demand for visionary and powerful leaders, and yet the charismatic 'Capo' may pose a grave threat to democracy. Strong 'capoship' fits perfectly within the representative, liberal form of democracy that characterises the political systems of most European countries. It fits badly in the notion of a strong, participatory democracy. In this system the citizens guide the way towards the future, and the politicians carry out the citizen's orders. In a weak democracy politicians lead citizens, in a strong democracy it is the other way around. As soon as politicians entertain capo ambitions they refuse to listen to their citizens and they employ the professional persuaders to lead us into the morasses of Kosovo, Afghanistan or Iraq. A society that demands strong political leadership has given up on democratic aspirations.

The tentative conclusion may be that the emphasis of professionalised political communication on creating images of strong political leadership strengthens totalitarian tendencies in political systems rather than contributing to the development of open, participatory and deliberative societies.

The issue of trust

A core problem in contemporary politics is undoubtedly the growing cynicism of citizens *vis-à-vis* the political system. The crucial question this poses is whether the professionalisation of political communication provides an adequate approach to the restoration of public trust. It is ironic to note that in many countries there is a remarkable parallel development of professionalisation of political communication and a growing electoral cynicism. The spin doctors advise the politicians to say 'Trust Me' and the credibility of politicians comes tumbling down.

The often-cited European democratic deficit finds today a concrete expression in the low level of participation in elections for the European Parliament. In the most recent elections this was less than 25% of the citizens in the participating countries. This should surprise no one as long as European politics operates at a great distance from the citizens in European countries. There is hardly any democratic decision-making process on such essential matters as the control over vital resources or public services. The emerging Europe has a neo-liberal signature yet is steered by market fundamentalism, in the politics of which the management of essential services (such as energy and water) is outsourced to private interests, and welfare-type social services are rapidly thrown away as too burdensome. The real test case for Europe's political communication will be the referenda that several European countries organise in the course of 2005 in relation to the proposed European Constitution. Strong political interests are at stake in this case, as the EU-governments have already committed themselves to the Constitution. Apart from those citizens that support the Constitution, it is clear that a large number of Europeans are ignorant about the matter, are not interested, are non-committal or, for a variety of reasons, against the project. All the tools of the professional kit are needed to first inform European audiences about a difficult document that is ill-understood even by many experts and then to persuade them to support its adoption. The critical issue with the Constitution is that the text provides no solution for the European democratic deficit. Not even its most loyal supporters would claim that the Constitution deals with Europe's lack of democracy in a satisfactory manner. The dilemma now is that the more effectively the professionals engage in a sales campaign to persuade citizens of the European ideal, the more the political system will be confronted with distrust and cynicism when all the 'spinning' provides no role for citizens in the shaping of their own futures. The trouble is that the more professionally political ideals are promoted, the more manifest the political hypocrisy that is put on the public agenda. This is likely to alienate people even further from political life.

The tentative conclusion may be that more professional political communication is likely to enlarge the current democratic deficit.

The issue of power

In the final analysis, democracy is about the distribution and execution of power in society. In the development of representative democracy, power became increasingly the prerogative of the elected governments. This left the power of election in the hands of the people, but the significance of this power turned out to be far less than the power the election process bestowed upon the elected. Since the elected representatives claim to represent the people, they also tend to claim to be the people themselves and could thus accumulate power without questions asked. The more this is contested, the greater the need for professionals in persuasion techniques. In representative democracy people have 'outsourced' their power to make decisions. This constitutes an awkward modality of governance that would probably be far more contested if it were not for the slick professionals who manage to persuade people that this is what they want.

The tentative conclusion may be that professional political communication tends to obscure the distribution and execution of real power in society.

CONCLUSION

The preceding national analyses of professionalisation of political communication show that this is a process that – at least in Europe – is rather different from other similar processes in disciplines such as law, medicine or journalism. Professionalisation is usually a social process in which groups of people who are engaged in specific activities that demand a level of expertise become a professional group when they begin to demand a level of legal protection for the independent execution of those activities, and a measure of societal respect for their expert status. Part of the process of becoming recognised 'professionals' is that associations of experts are established that adopt codes of conduct for their members. These professional codes serve the distinction between genuine professional and con-artists and they offer a platform for public accountability. In the US one finds the American Association of Political Consultants that has a code of professional ethics (www.theaapc.org/ethics), but there is no European equivalent. The professional political communicator in Europe remains a somewhat haphazardly operating expert without clear ethical rules and without a clearly defined public accountability.

However, the professionals are prominently present in today's European political arena and our question remains what they do to 'the democratic quality of the polity'. This can only be answered if we make a normative choice about the operational definition of democratic quality. It could be argued that this is a choice between the prevailing model of liberal, representative democracy ('thin democracy' as Barber (1984) calls it) and a robust participatory democracy ('strong democracy' according to Barber).

Taking together the tentative conclusions above, there is sufficient evidence to argue that the current process of professionalisation of political communication reinforces across European countries an elitist, representative liberal conception of democracy ('thin democracy'), whereas this process does little to assist the development of strong, participatory, deliberative democracy.

In terms of 'making things better' the professionalisation of political communication can reasonably be expected to contribute to the democratic quality of the polity, but within the framework of the limited democracy model. Professionalisation would seem to provide an important contribution to the functioning and the legitimation of liberal representative democracy with the proviso that it does not seem to be competent to cope with some basic troubles that haunt this democratic model: little or no civic confidence, and little or no civic engagement. But then, to some extent, this is not a real problem since the thin democracy is 'democracy without citizens'. The professionals provide important services to party elites and particularly to political leaders. An important service is also provided by the use of professional persuasive communication to make people believe the inevitability of developments against which public opinion is overwhelmingly negative, such as the Iraqi invasion or the EU expansion. The need of this kind of professional service will grow stronger as politics becomes more the management of elite interests. This makes it necessary, in very skilful ways, to persuade common people that the decisions taken for them, without them and often against their interests, are, in some miraculous way, good for them. In a democracy without citizens professional political communication serves 'the control of information by policy elites' as Dahl argues in Bennett & Entman (2001, p. 469).

The professionalisation of political communication fits perfectly well in the liberal theory of democracy. Professionalisation reinforces the role of people not as active participants but as passive supporters of those who represent them.

The focus of the professionals is very much upon the operation of democratic institutions. This maintains the suggestion that the efficient operation of these institutions equals democracy and that these institutions offer citizens real choices and participation in real choice making.

If one would take a different normative choice and opt for 'strong democracy', the services of the political communication professionals look rather more questionable. They are not directed at the facilitation of the active engagement of citizens with the political management of the state. They do not contribute to the creation of a broad well-informed polity. They protect the elected against the interference of those who elect them.

The current modality of professionalisation renders politics the expert arena where professionals do what they do, while citizens elect them to do so. And Barber writes, 'Strong democracy is the politics of amateurs, where every man is compelled to encounter every other man without the intermediary of expertise' (2003, p. 152). In a participatory democracy the citizens are in fact the professionals who communicate with other citizens.

In the 'strong democracy' model, democracy is – beyond an institutional and legal framework – primarily a way of thinking. It is a modality of thought about the distribution and execution of power that acknowledges the sovereignty of people. The democratic way of life requires knowledge, attitudes and skills that are not necessarily part of the human genetic constitution. The conditions for democratic quality need to be learned and the learning process should start very early. The training on how to become a democratic citizen should, at the latest, begin when children reach school age, but preferably already earlier in families. Since it may be expected that many parents will have no clue as to how to do this, formal and informal (through the media) teaching options should be on offer at accessible times, locations and costs. It would be a great contribution to the democratisation of Europe if all the presently available professional talent in political communication could be re-directed towards the development of a robust democratic perspective for Europe.

Professional political communications fulfils clear functions within 'thin' democracies. If, however, societies decide for a strong model of democracy, they will need all the professionalism they can muster to engage in the grand-scale teaching of democratic minds. The fact that this type of professionalism is today not considered the absolute top political priority in European countries does not augur well for the future of European democracies.

REFERENCES
Barber, B.R. (2003[1984]) *Strong Democracy*. Berkeley: University of California Press.
Bennett, W.L. & R. Entman, (eds) (2001) *Mediated Politics*. Cambridge: Cambridge University Press.
Gandy, O.H. (2001) 'Dividing Practices: Segmentation and Targeting in the Emerging Public Sphere', pp. 141–159 in W.L. Bennett & R. Entman (eds). *Mediated Politics*. Cambridge: Cambridge University Press.
Zakaria, F. (2004) *The Future of Freedom* New York: W.W. Norton.

ADDITIONAL MATERIAL OF RELEVANCE
Bennett, W.L. & J.B. Manheim (2001) 'The Big Spin: Strategic Communication and the Transformation of Pluralist Democracy', pp. 279–298 in W.L. Bennett & R. Entman (eds). *Mediated Politics*. Cambridge, Cambridge University Press.
Blumler, J.G. & M. Gurevitch (2001) '"Americanization" Reconsidered: U.K.-U.S. Campaign Communication Comparisons Across Time', pp. 380–403 in W.L. Bennett, & R. Entman (eds). *Mediated Politics*. Cambridge: Cambridge University Press.
Entman, R.M. & W.L. Bennett (2001) 'Communication in the Future of Democracy: A Conclusion', pp. 468–480 in W.L. Bennett & R. Entman (eds) *Mediated Politics*. Cambridge: Cambridge University Press.
Gans, H. (2003) *Democracy and News*. Oxford: Oxford University Press.
Gould, C.G. (1988) *Rethinking Democracy*. Cambridge: Cambridge University Press.
Hamelink, C.J. (1995) 'The democratic ideal and its enemies', pp. 15–37 in Philip Lee (ed.). *The Democratization of ommunication*. Cardiff: University of Wales Press.
Ober, J. (1989) *Man and Elite in Democratic Athens*. Princeton: Princeton University Press.

Index

The Professionalisation of Political Communication